The Rough Guide Book of Brain Training

Gareth Moore & Tom Stafford

www.roughguides.com

Credits

The Rough Guide Book of Brain Training

Editors: Matthew Milton, Ruth Tidball
Design: Ruth Tidball
Proofreading: Susannah Wight
Production: Rebecca Short

Rough Guides Reference

Director: Andrew Lockett
Editors: Kate Berens, Peter Buckley,
Tracy Hopkins, Matthew Milton,
Joe Staines, Ruth Tidball

Acknowledgements

Gareth Moore: Thank you to my family for years of puzzle checking without complaint, and special thanks to my brother for the competition which helps keep me on my toes! Thanks also to everyone at Rough Guides who have helped make this book what it is. Last but not least, thank you to Kellie, who helps in more ways than I can ever describe.

Tom Stafford: Thanks to Peter Tallack, Ruth Tidball and Matt Milton at Rough Guides, Ade Deane-Pratt (who read a draft of the full text) and the researchers, friends and colleagues who were generous with their time, expertise and ideas: Cathryn Bardsley, Vaughan Bell, Dan Carroll, Christian Jarrett, Cigir Kalfaoglu, James Moore, Rod Nicolson, Matt Walker, Tom Walton and Stuart Wilson. I would like to dedicate this book to my grandmother, Moira Mount.

Publishing information

. This first edition published January 2010 by
Rough Guides Ltd, 80 Strand, London, WC2R 0RL
Email: mail@roughguides.com

Distributed by the Penguin Group:
Penguin Books Ltd, 80 Strand, London, WC2R 0RL
Penguin Group (USA), 375 Hudson Street, NY 10014, USA
Penguin Group (Australia), 250 Camberwell Road, Camberwell, Victoria 3124, Australia
Penguin Group (Canada), 90 Eglinton Avenue East, Suite 700, Toronto, Ontario, Canada M4P 2Y3
Penguin Group (New Zealand), Cnr Rosedale and Airborne Roads, Albany, Auckland, New Zealand

Printed and bound in Singapore by Toppan Security Printing Pte. Ltd.

288 pages

A catalogue record for this book is available from the British Library.

ISBN 13: 978-1-84836-518-6

1 3 5 7 9 8 6 4 2

Introduction

Research in the science of the brain has led to an amazing discovery: our brain changes continuously throughout our lives, and it changes according to what we do with it. This discovery, called "plasticity" by scientists, leads naturally to the idea of trying to improve our mental faculties: brain training. If our environment and experiences affect the development of our brain, surely it must be possible to train our brains. With the right combination of activities we should be able to make ourselves smarter, faster and more creative.

It isn't magic, and it can be hard work, but it is beyond doubt that practice of the right kind can make us smarter, faster and more creative. This book will set you some challenges that will allow you to get first-hand experience of some simple brain training exercises, and get a feel for some of the things that you are good at and some that you might want to work on.

The idea of brain training seems so simple, why is it that we aren't all doing brain exercises before breakfast, treating them like a course of heart pills? Well, we aren't because it isn't actually quite that simple. Although we are sure that our brains can be trained and improved, we aren't sure how exactly, and we aren't sure how to measure the benefits of any particular method. With any claim about brain training there are two fundamental uncertainties.

Firstly, how general are the benefits? Practising almost anything will make you better at it: if you do sudoku puzzles you'll certainly get better at sudoku. But the holy grail of the brain training researcher is identifying the practices that unlock "far transfer" – improvements that have widespread and general benefits for other tasks. Finding brain training tasks with far transfer has been difficult, although research reports are now beginning to appear that suggest it is possible. The practical implication is that if you are interested in keeping an active brain you should do a range of tasks and puzzles. This book is a good place to start. Try to do puzzles of each type, not just the ones you like.

The second uncertainty about any brain training method is exactly why it works. Even if you could prove that some activity, such as crosswords, makes people smarter, you might still want to know why exactly that is. Is it crosswords specifically, or is it just important that you do a puzzle with words? Or a puzzle you find difficult? Or a puzzle that is convenient to carry and which doesn't require batteries? Perhaps the gain in intelligence is because people tend to do crosswords with other people and it's this interaction that makes you more lively? Any or all of these could be possible, and teasing them apart is difficult. For now, it is safe to say that we don't know of any magic bullets for brain training – there is no single kind of task or set of tasks which will improve brain fitness. And anyone who claims otherwise is probably trying to sell you something.

What is certain is that puzzles are one of life's greatest innocent pleasures. As well as being one way of keeping happy and productive, staying mentally active has been proved to increase your chances of a healthy mind in later life (see feature box "The ageing brain" following Day 45). If you're thinking of taking a course of brain training, then almost any set of challenging activities will do to start with, along with exercise, company and a healthy diet (see "Feeding your brain" following Day 25). The important thing is that you need to find a programme that will keep you engaged, because the studies suggest that the benefits of any activity require that you keep it up, and it is hard to keep up something you don't enjoy.

So, why not grab this book and take it for a walk around the park. Find a sunny spot (or a café for a cup of tea if it is raining), invite a friend, and try a few of the puzzles together.

How this book works

This book contains 100 double-page workouts, each providing a day's worth of brain training. There are also tests at regular intervals to break up the workouts and help you track your progress, plus feature articles giving detailed information on a whole range of brain-related matters. Solutions are at the back of the book, followed by a Resources section which will point you in the direction of other brain-related books, games and more.

The daily workouts

Do the daily workouts as regularly as you can. Start at the beginning of the book, rather than dipping in randomly, because the workouts get significantly tougher as you progress.

Every daily workout contains five different puzzles. Three of these vary from day to day, and the instructions for these are always given. But each day also has a word ladder and a brain chain. To solve the **word ladder** (at the bottom of the left-hand page), change one letter per step to move from the first word to the last word, using only regular English words. You won't ever require any obscure words to do this (although you could use them if you really wanted to). There are several possible solutions, one of which is given in the solutions section at the back of the book. To solve the **brain chain** (at the bottom of the right-hand page), you must start at the initial number and follow the chain of mathematical operations in your head – without making any written notes – writing the final number reached in the blank space at the end.

If you find you've reached a brick wall in an exercise, don't worry. Never be afraid to check the answers at the back to work out what to do. It all counts as brain-training. Some puzzles will take you longer than others, but make sure you try them all, even if you eventually decide to move on.

The test workouts

Every ten days there's a test. These always feature the same four types of puzzle, each covering a different skill area. By testing yourself with these, you'll be able to track your progress, noting how your speed and accuracy improve. Unlike the daily workouts, these are all at a similar level of difficulty. Here is a brief explanation of what you'll find in them.

At the start of each test is a **Hanjie logic puzzle**. You'll know if you have solved one of these correctly because they reveal a picture when complete. Simply follow the instructions alongside every puzzle, shading certain squares while also marking an "x" in squares you are sure are empty. Beneath this you will find a **verbal challenge**. With these, you must find as many words as you can from the letters in the word wheel. You form each word by making an anagram of the centre letter and any other set of letters from the wheel. But you must not use any letter more than once in a word. Next up is a set of **mental arithmetic** questions. These feature some basic maths, some elapsed-time questions – where you must work out how much time has passed between each pair of times – and some money calculations. Finally, at the bottom-right of every test is a **memory task**. Simply study the pattern of shapes on the left for as long as you wish, then cover it over and repeat it as accurately as possible in the empty grid to the right. Every arrangement has some underlying patterns – if you spot these you may find it easier to recall the shapes.

Keeping track of your progress

Give yourself fifteen minutes on the first test, and then stop once time is up, whether finished or not. If you finish early, give yourself a more challenging time such as ten or twelve minutes for later tests, and then stick to that time throughout the book. If you feel you need a lot more time to tackle the four tests, make your time limit 20 minutes or more in future. You ought to be pushed for time, but not so much that you can't have a good go at all four tasks. Remember: it doesn't matter how fast or slow you are to start with – the important thing is to set a benchmark against which you can chart your progress.

Once your time is up, check against the test solutions at the back of the book (following the main solutions section). Score 1 point for every mental arithmetic question you've got right, 1 point for every valid word you've found, and 1 point for every Hanjie grid cell you've filled in correctly – either shaded in or marked as blank with an "x". Give yourself 2 points for each shape you recalled accurately, plus 1 point for each shape you judge that you *nearly* recalled correctly (the right shape but the wrong orientation, for instance). Record your scores in the table opposite as an overview of how you're getting on.

Test	Hanjie	Verbal	Maths	Memory	Total
1					
2					
3					
4					
5					
6					
7					
8					
9					
10					

One other tip – if you get stuck or confused on the Hanjie the first time you do it, return to it after your test is over and work out how to solve it completely before you attempt the next test.

Remember: your brain wants to be challenged!

1

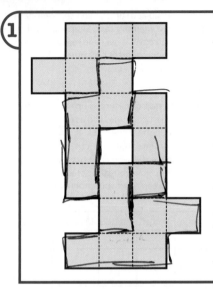

Fact: A healthy mind in a healthy body is not just an old cliché. The evidence that physical exercise can help prevent brain deterioration is stronger than the evidence that mental exercise can help prevent it.

Can you draw along the dashed lines in this figure in order to divide it into four identical shapes, with no pieces left over?

The shapes may be rotated versions of one another, but cannot be flipped over.

2

This 6x6 Jigsaw Sudoku puzzle works in a very similar way to a regular Sudoku puzzle, except that:

» Instead of being 9x9, it is 6x6. Therefore you must place the numbers 1 to 6 into each row, column and bold-lined region.

» The bold-lined regions are irregular jigsaw shapes, rather than rectangles.

3	5	4	1	6	2
1	4	5	3	2	6
4	1	2	6	5	3
5	3	6	2	4	1
2	6	3	4	1	5
6	2	1	5	3	4

3 DIAL 〉 DILL 〉 TILL 〉 TILE 〉 TONE 〉 TONE

4

Four friends have been out shopping for gifts. Can you work out who bought which item, and how much it cost?

» Matthew bought neither the cheapest nor the most expensive gift.

» The fondue set cost twice as much as the aftershave.

» Cat's champagne was not the most expensive item, but it still cost twice as much as Daniel's DVD.

Person	Spent	Gift
CAT	30	Champagne
Daniel	15	DVD
Matt	25	Aftershave
Kellie	50	fondue

People:
Daniel, Matthew, Kellie, Cat

Gifts:
Aftershave, Champagne, DVD, Fondue set

Amounts spent:
£15, £25, £30, £50

You might find the chart on the right helpful when completing this puzzle – place ticks and crosses to indicate what you have deduced.

		£15	£25	£30	£50	Aftershave	Champagne	DVD	Fondue set
Person	Daniel	●	X	X	X	X	X	●	X
	Matthew	X	●	X	X	●	X	✓	X
	Kellie	X	✓	✓	●	X	X	X	●
	Cat	X	✓	●	X	X	●	X	X
Gift	Aftershave	X	●	X	X				
	Champagne	X	X	●	X				
	DVD	●	X	X	X				
	Fondue set	X	✓	X	●				

17 → Multiply by three → +15 → 1/2 of this → ÷11 → +39 → ÷6 → ×8 → 1/4 of this → **RESULT** 14 **5**

2
17
×3
51

51+15 = 66   33÷11 = 3 +39 = 42÷6   7×8 = 56÷4 = 14

1

For both of the following sets of five letters, can you rearrange them to form four different English words? Each word must use all five letters.

For bonus points, can you find a fifth, slightly more obscure, word in each case?

ACDER
AEKST

RACED raced steak
arced takes
cared teaks
cadre skate
STEAK
SKATE TAKES

Imagination is a powerful thing

The Lerner Research Institute has shown that just *imagining* using a muscle can increase the strength of that muscle. Volunteers imagined using muscles in their arms and hands for 15 minutes a day for 12 weeks.

At the end of this training, their muscle power had improved 35%, even though the volunteers hadn't been tensing the muscles that grew stronger.

The effect works by increasing the strength of the signal that people are able to send from their brain to their muscles.

2

By choosing exactly one number from each ring of this dartboard, can you find three segments whose values add up to a total of 75?

For example, to reach a total of 100 you would take 24 from the outer ring, 36 from the middle ring and 40 from the inner ring.

For bonus points, if you were to pick one number from each ring at random, what total is the most likely result?

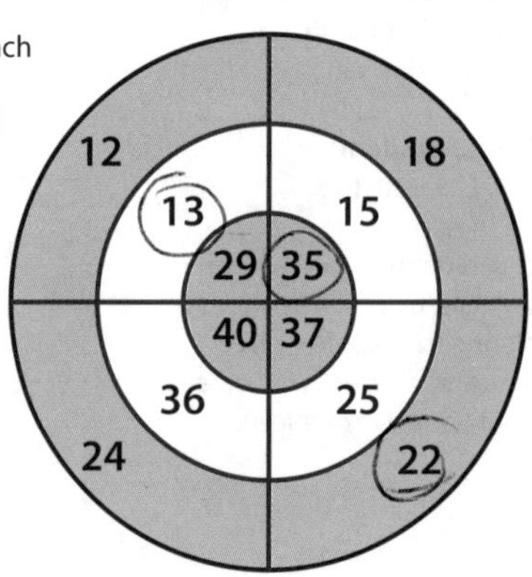

3

PLAY > > > > > TENT

9/4   8/5   7/6   15: 9/6 8/7   14: 9/5   8/6

9/7

4

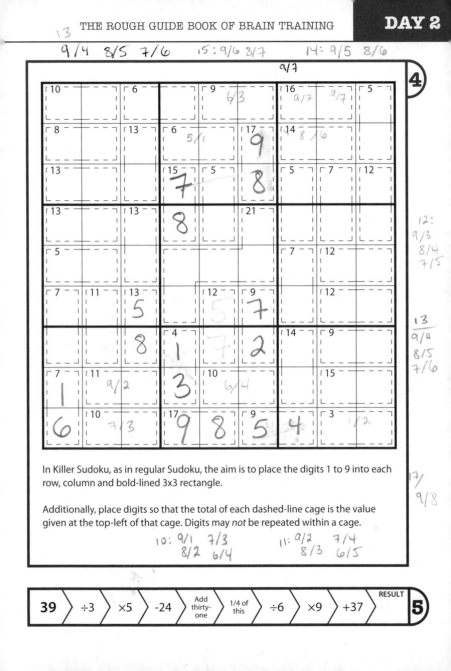

12:
9/3
8/4
7/5

13
9/4
8/5
7/6

In Killer Sudoku, as in regular Sudoku, the aim is to place the digits 1 to 9 into each row, column and bold-lined 3x3 rectangle.

Additionally, place digits so that the total of each dashed-line cage is the value given at the top-left of that cage. Digits may *not* be repeated within a cage.

17/
9/8

10: 9/1   7/3   11: 9/2   7/4
    8/2   6/4   8/3   6/5

| 39 | ÷3 | ×5 | -24 | Add thirty-one | 1/4 of this | ÷6 | ×9 | +37 | RESULT |

5

1

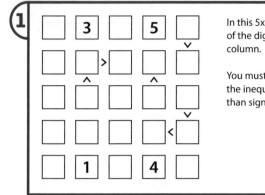

In this 5x5 Futoshiki puzzle, place all of the digits 1 to 5 into each row and column.

You must place these digits such that the inequality less-than and greater-than signs ("<" and ">") are obeyed.

Fact: Your brain uses around 20% of the total of your body's energy, which is about 400 calories per day, or a rate of 15 watts – the same as a dim light bulb.

2

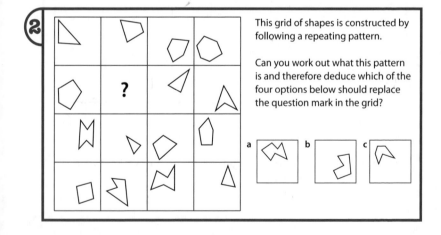

This grid of shapes is constructed by following a repeating pattern.

Can you work out what this pattern is and therefore deduce which of the four options below should replace the question mark in the grid?

3 TIME 〉 〉 〉 〉 BANK

4

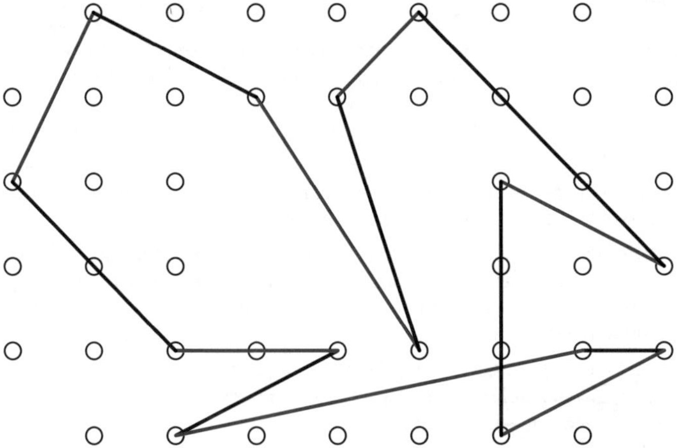

Study the above figure for no more than two minutes, then cover it up and try to redraw all of the black lines from memory on the partial copy below.

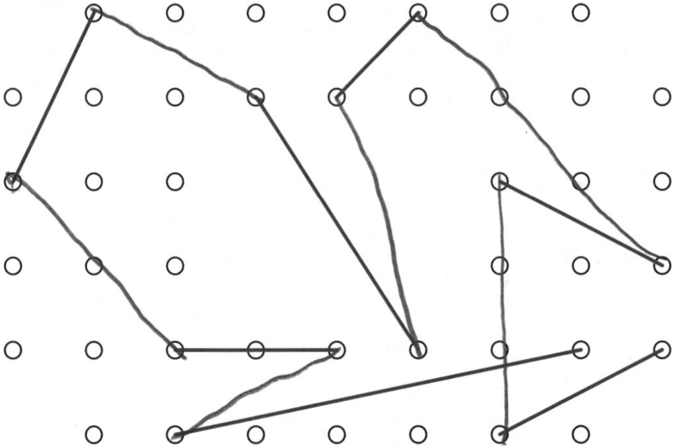

32	÷4	1/2 of this	+24	Twenty-five percent of this	×5	-19	÷8	Multiply by three	RESULT

5

How to remember

Your memory isn't like a filing cabinet or a computer hard disk. You can't rely on things coming out the same as when they went in. In many ways, though, our memories are far more powerful and flexible. The trick to successful memorizing is to recognize the differences that your memory has from a computer and exploit them.

» Your memory can be strengthened by practice at retrieval. Don't assume that just because you've learnt something once it is in there.

» Your memories are stored in associative networks, meaning that richer connections make things easier to remember. When you are trying to retrieve something, don't just focus on one or two important facts about it: bringing to mind any and all associations may force the memory into the light.

» Context is important. Often our recall is tied to the situation where we learnt information. If you get really stuck with trying to remember something, try going back to exactly the circumstances where you learnt it.

1

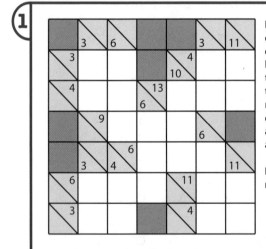

In this Kakuro puzzle, fill in each white square with a digit from 1 to 9, so that each horizontal run of consecutive blank squares adds up to the total to the left of that run, and each vertical run of consecutive white squares adds up to the total directly above that run.

No number can be used more than once in any run.

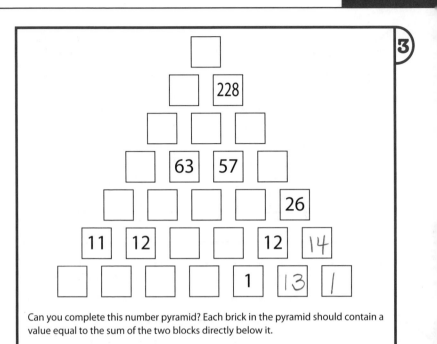

Can you complete this number pyramid? Each brick in the pyramid should contain a value equal to the sum of the two blocks directly below it.

Try decoding this quotation by replacing each letter with another one a fixed number of places forwards/backwards in the alphabet. (Wrap around from Z to A or from A to Z when counting.)

E gaal iu ezawho, xaywqoa ej olepa kb aranupdejc, E opehh xaheara pdwp laklha wna nawhhu ckkz wp dawnp.

Wjja Bnwjg

1 Study this arrangement of the numbers 1 to 6 for no more than two minutes. When the time is up, cover it up and try to redraw it on the blank grid. Look out for patterns that may help you remember.

6	16	7	3
10	1	11	13
14	12	2	8
4	15	9	5

Fact: The UK's Ben Pridmore holds the world record for the quickest time taken to memorize the order of an entire pack of newly shuffled playing cards: 26.28 seconds.

2 Imagine overlaying these two images – how many black lines are there?

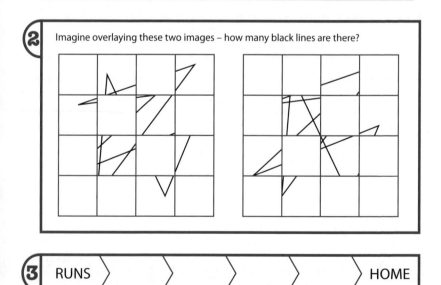

3 RUNS 〉 〉 〉 〉 HOME

④

1	2	5	0	5	2	0	0
6	6	3	6	5	4	1	5
2	0	4	6	4	4	4	0
6	0	3	5	1	2	5	0
3	2	6	2	2	4	3	6
1	4	4	1	6	5	3	1
5	3	3	1	2	0	3	1

Can you place a full set of dominoes into the above grid, where "0" represents a blank? Each domino will occur exactly once in the finished puzzle.

You can use the chart on the right to keep track of which dominoes you have already placed.

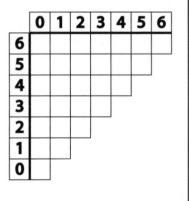

16 〉 -6 〉 ÷2 〉 +47 〉 1/4 of this 〉 +25 〉 50% of this 〉 ×4 〉 -22 〉 **RESULT** 5

Introducing your brain

Reader, let's introduce you to your brain. It weighs about the same as half a house brick and has the consistency of warm butter. If you could hold it in your hands it might sag a bit between your fingers, but it wouldn't fall through.

Your brain, its mysterious topography, labyrinthine wiring and incessant electrochemical activity is the site of every thought you've ever had, every emotion you've ever experienced and all your hopes and fears.

Your brain is responsible for the funniest joke you ever told, the funkiest dance move you ever made and the tastiest meal you've ever eaten. No wonder that everyone – scientists and laypeople alike – is fascinated by their brain and the brains of everyone else. Here we will tell you about different parts of the brain and introduce a few names that people use when discussing the function and structure of this organ.

However, if you hate learning names and technical terms, don't worry. Knowing a little bit of brain jargon can help you to avoid being confused when people use it, though it's hardly essential when talking about brain training. If someone tells you that their new tennis teaching technique works because it activates a part of the brain called the striatum, you don't need to know about the striatum to decide whether you want to take their lessons or not – you need to know if their technique makes you a better tennis player. But knowing some of the names will help you feel at home with your brain, and is the beginning of a fascinating journey into understanding its workings. Here are the basics.

The brain cells, that send and receive information around your brain, are called **neurons**. The amazing thing each neuron does is fire tiny pulses of electricity, called "action potentials" or spikes, which are carried along their long wires to other neurons. Each neuron is listening to the pulses sent by other neurons and, based on what it hears, decides when to fire itself. It is the pattern of this activity that creates your thoughts. A bundle of well-connected neurons is called a **nucleus**.

The place where the wires from two neurons connect is called a **synapse**. It's here that chemicals called **neurotransmitters** affect the firing of the neurons. Neurotranmitters come in different flavours, as it were, and some of them are famous because their quantities are affected by drugs. Caffeine, for example, affects a neurotransmitter called dopamine; Prozac affects a neuro-transmitter called serotonin.

You can't see all this microstructure with your naked eye; you need the specialist equipment of the neuroscientist's lab. What you could see with the naked eye (if you folded back the skin and opened the skull) is the gross physical shape, the folds and layers.

The surface of the human brain is corrugated like a walnut, and is divided into a left and right half. Like the rest of the body, most bits of the brain come in pairs, one in each half. In the brain these two halves are called **hemispheres**. The surface of the brain, and the part that is largest in humans, is called the **cortex**. Underneath the folded surface of the cortex is the **subcortex**. This is the most evolutionarily ancient part of the brain, and the part that sometimes gets called the "reptilian brain".

The subcortex looks after the really fundamental stuff of life: body regulation, emotions and feelings of hunger, thirst and lust. The behaviour that we think of as particularly human – art, language, understanding other minds and empathy – all require the cortex.

You'd need a whole book to detail all the important areas of the brain, so for now we'll just introduce the four main divisions of the cortex: the **lobes**. These are the main landmarks of the cortex. At the front are the **frontal lobes** (one on each side, of course); at the back are the **occipital lobes**; between these two and on top are the **parietal lobes**; and coming forward and behind your ears are the **temporal lobes**. The different lobes seem to have different responsibilities. For example, the occipital lobes process visual information and the temporal lobes are important for our memories.

Finally, tucked underneath and at the back of the brain lies the **cerebellum**. A mysterious structure, the cerebellum contains about half the total number of neurons in the brain. It seems to be important for controlling movements, but is also involved in many other mental functions.

So now you know your subcortex from your temporal lobe. As you read and work through the rest of the book, electricity will be zinging around all these areas, producing the experience you are having and the thoughts you think.

1 Study these pictures of different weather conditions for up to two minutes, then cover them over and try to redraw them on the blank clouds to the right as precisely as possible.

Tools for thinking: probability and statistics

Everyone finds probability and statistics confusing. Psychologist Gerd Gigerenzer, director of the Max Planck Institute for Human Development in Berlin, came up with recipes for avoiding confusion when using statistics. He drew on decades of research into how people use and understand probabilities to make the following recommendations:

» Replace conditional probabilities with frequencies. For example, rather than saying "if you have swine flu, the swine flu test will be positive 96% of the time" you would say "if you tested 100 people who had swine flu, 96 of them would test positive".

» Try to translate probabilities into what they actually refer to. What "the probability of rain on sports day is 6%" actually means is that "it has rained on 6 of the past 100 sports days" or "it has rained on 6 of the last 100 June the 6ths".

» Use absolute percentages rather than relative percentages. Relative percentages are very hard to interpret. For example, an increase of 20% could mean the difference between five in a million and six in a million – from very very small to marginally less small – or equally between five in ten and six in ten – the much more significant change from a 50-50 chance to a "more likely than not".

2 BEAN 〉 〉 〉 SOUP

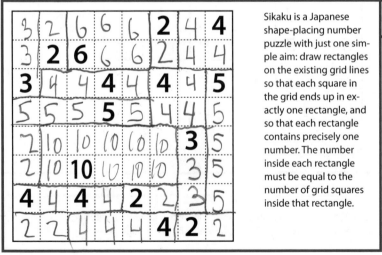

3

These three boxes follow a visual progression. Which of the three lettered options should come fourth in this sequence?

a

b

c

4

Sikaku is a Japanese shape-placing number puzzle with just one simple aim: draw rectangles on the existing grid lines so that each square in the grid ends up in exactly one rectangle, and so that each rectangle contains precisely one number. The number inside each rectangle must be equal to the number of grid squares inside that rectangle.

| 39 | 1/3 of this | Subtract four | Add nineteen | ÷7 | Fifty percent of this | Multiply by nine | -1 | +26 | **RESULT** 43 | **5** |

1 What number should come next in each of these three separate mathematical progressions?

5	18	31	44	57	70
65	56	47	38	29	20
3	6	12	24	48	96

2

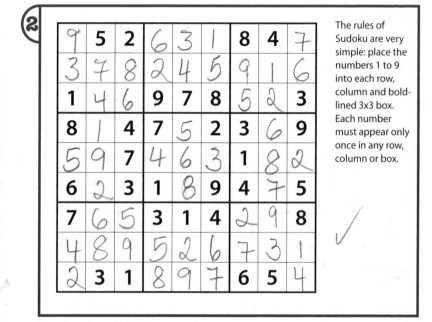

The rules of Sudoku are very simple: place the numbers 1 to 9 into each row, column and bold-lined 3x3 box. Each number must appear only once in any row, column or box.

Fact: Your brain has about 100,000,000,000 brain cells, called neurons. If each neuron was a grain of sand, the sand would fill the average two-storey house.

3 DAYS 〉 〉 〉 〉 AIRY

By cracking the code, can you complete this crossword grid? Each of the 26 letters of the alphabet has a different numerical value, which you can write down in the box at the bottom once you've worked it out. Start by examining the "L", "D" and "I". As you allocate each letter to a number, cross the letter off the list running down the sides of the grid.

4

45 > +29 > 50% of this > +7 > ÷11 > √ > ×12 > 1/4 of this > +50% > **RESULT** **5**

1 The aim of Masyu is to draw a single loop that passes through the centre of every circle. At shaded circles the loop must turn through a right angle and then continue straight for at least one square each side. At white circles the loop must pass straight through without turning but then must turn through a right angle on either one or both of the adjacent squares. The loop cannot enter any square more than once, and it may only consist of horizontal and vertical lines.

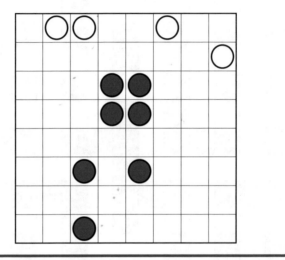

2 How good are you at remembering related words? Study this set of words for no more than two minutes, then cover it over and see how many you can recall correctly.

Cardigan	Trousers	Sweatshirt	Trainers	Belt
Scarf	Skirt	Blazer	Boots	Gown

CARDIGARL
SKIRT, SCARF, SWEASHIRT, BLAZER, GOWN, *BOOTS BELT*
TROUSERS
TRAINERS

3 LAST 〉 〉 〉 〉 ROAD

Can you draw three straight lines in order to divide this box into five separate regions, each containing one of each type of shape?

4

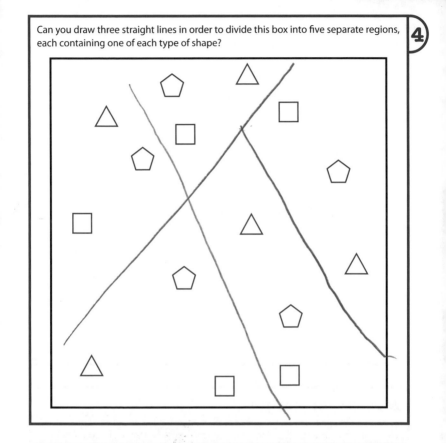

Fact: It's often said that taking a step back can help solve tricky problems. But it seems there's a truth behind this axiom. One experiment showed that people were better at solving problematic conundrums if they were told the problems had been developed in a lab a long way away.

23 ⟩ ×2 ⟩ +23 ⟩ Subtract twenty-four ⟩ ÷5 ⟩ √ ⟩ Add nine ⟩ 1/3 of this ⟩ ÷2 ⟩ **RESULT** 2 **5**

1 Can you reflect all of the lines in this grid in the dashed-line "mirror" that runs down the middle? You should end up with a picture.

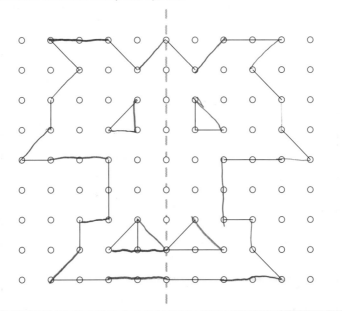

Mix up your practice

Practising skills in blocks makes them easier to learn, but harder to remember. When we're learning a skill like shooting hoops in basketball, handwriting or even surgical techniques, the temptation is to practise in blocks of each type of motion. For instance, in learning to write, we'd do 100 perfect As, then 100 perfect Bs, etc. Unfortunately, although research has shown that practising like this helps us get better quicker, the effect is short-lived – it leads to worse retention than if we practise in mixed blocks.

2 RANK 〉 〉 〉 〉 SORT

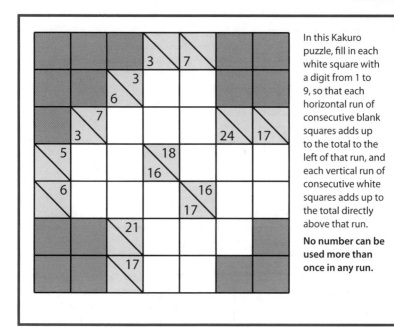

3

In this Kakuro puzzle, fill in each white square with a digit from 1 to 9, so that each horizontal run of consecutive blank squares adds up to the total to the left of that run, and each vertical run of consecutive white squares adds up to the total directly above that run.

No number can be used more than once in any run.

4

All of the vowels have been eliminated from each of the following four words. Can you work out what the original set of words was?

strtsphr   STRATOSPHERE

cmlnmbs   CUMULONIMBIS

trnscndntl   TRANSCENDENTAL

dlttnt   DILUTTANT

5

| 13 | ×2 | +10 | 50% of this | +16 | One half of this | Subtract one | Seventy-five percent of this | ÷2 | RESULT 2 |

1

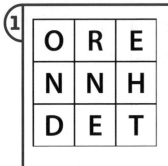

O	R	E
N	N	H
D	E	T

How many English words can you find in this word square? For each word, start on any square and move only to adjacent squares – including diagonals – but without visiting any square more than once.

There are at least 28 words to be found, including a nine-letter one.

THE   HER
ORE   THEN
DEN
TEN
TENOR

2

9	8	9	4		4		5	2
3	4						8	9
			8	9	8	4		
8	9	3	38	4	07	9		
		4	5	1 7	9	8		
8	9	3	16 7	2	38	9	4	
4	2	9	6	7	6			8
1	3	78	9				6	4
5	6	78	4		4		9	

Sudoku-X adds one extra rule to a traditional Sudoku puzzle: you must not only place the numbers 1 to 9 into each row, column and bold-lined 3x3 box, but also into each of the two main diagonals (shaded on the puzzle).

3 QUIT 〉 〉 〉 〉 PLAY

Cover up the set of words on the right (in blue). Then spend no more than two minutes looking at the list of word-pairs on the left. Once the time is up, cover the word pairs instead. See if you can recall each pair when given just one of the two words.

Doughnut	Jam	Decorative
Floral	Decorative	Display
Peanut	Spread	Tree
Acorn	Tree	Radio
Time	Clock	Peanut
Indecision	Confusion	Jam
Radio	Transmitter	Indecision
Screen	Display	Time

The number-rhyme peg memory system

This is a simple way to remember ten things and a good example of how mnemonic systems work in general. The first component is a set of "mental pegs" on which you can hang the things you need to remember. You have to learn these by heart, but once you've learnt them you can use them as a powerful way of remembering arbitrary lists of items. To make these pegs easy to learn, they rhyme with the numbers one to ten:

One is gun; two is shoe; three is tree; four is door; five is hive; six is sticks; seven is heaven; eight is gate; nine is wine; ten is hen

Now, to remember a list of items you need to create a vivid mental image of each item with a peg item. So, for example, if your first two items were chilli sauce and cinema tickets, you might imagine a chilli sauce *gun* for use in restaurants (taking time to visualize the exact shape of it, the bottle of sauce you fit to the top as ammunition etc) and then a clown in ridiculous clown *shoes* running down the street, having stolen your cinema tickets. The more outlandish and surprising the scene you imagine, the easier it will be to remember.

To remember the list you count from one to ten and use the rhyming peg word to bring to mind the vivid image you've created for each item. You have to try it to get a good idea of just how effective this kind of system is. The basic principle of structure and imagery can be extended to help remember hundreds or even thousands of items. To find out how, consult a book on memory techniques. Ron Hale-Evans' *Mind Performance Hacks*, for instance, contains this technique and many others.

| 32 | 1/2 of this | ×4 | Subtract nineteen | 1/3 of this | ÷5 | Add thirty-one | -50% | +4 | RESULT 5 |

1

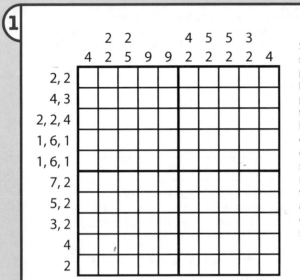

Shade in the correct squares to reveal a picture. The numbers are clues that provide – in order, from the left/top – a list of the length of every sequence of consecutive shaded squares in each row/column respectively. Sequences are separated by one or more empty squares.

2 How many words of three or more letters can you find in this word wheel? Each word must contain the centre letter, plus any selection of the other letters no more than once each.

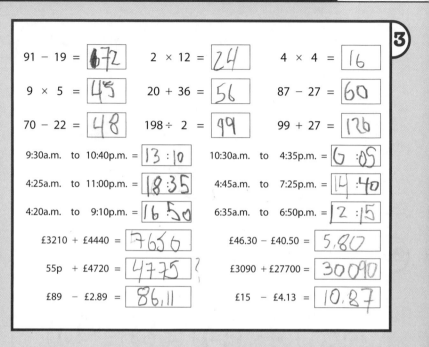

3

91 − 19 = 672   2 × 12 = 24   4 × 4 = 16

9 × 5 = 45   20 + 36 = 56   87 − 27 = 60

70 − 22 = 48   198 ÷ 2 = 99   99 + 27 = 126

9:30a.m. to 10:40p.m. = 13:10   10:30a.m. to 4:35p.m. = 6:05

4:25a.m. to 11:00p.m. = 18:35   4:45a.m. to 7:25p.m. = 14:40

4:20a.m. to 9:10p.m. = 16:50   6:35a.m. to 6:50p.m. = 2:15

£3210 + £4440 = 7650   £46.30 − £40.50 = 5.80

55p + £4720 = 4775   £3090 + £27700 = 30090

£89 − £2.89 = 86.11   £15 − £4.13 = 10.87

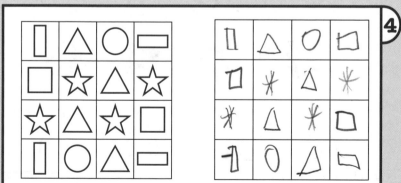

4

Spend no more than two minutes studying this grid of shapes, then cover it and redraw it as accurately as you can in the empty grid to the right.

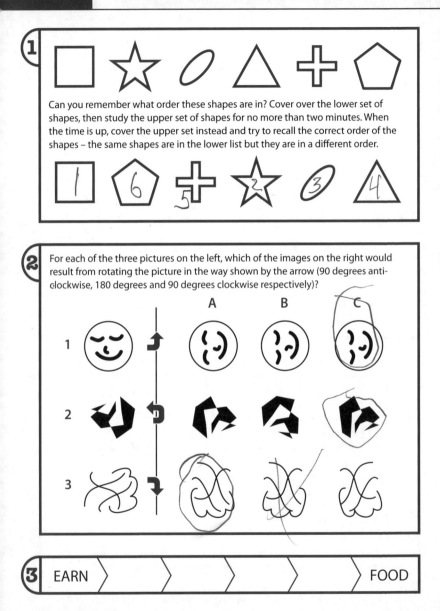

1 Can you remember what order these shapes are in? Cover over the lower set of shapes, then study the upper set of shapes for no more than two minutes. When the time is up, cover the upper set instead and try to recall the correct order of the shapes – the same shapes are in the lower list but they are in a different order.

2 For each of the three pictures on the left, which of the images on the right would result from rotating the picture in the way shown by the arrow (90 degrees anti-clockwise, 180 degrees and 90 degrees clockwise respectively)?

A   B   C

1

2

3

3 EARN > > > > FOOD

Light Up is a type of Japanese logic puzzle. The aim is to place "light bulbs" in white squares so that all of the white squares in the puzzle either contain a bulb or are "lit up" by at least one bulb. A light bulb illuminates all squares in its row and column, but only up to the first shaded square encountered in each direction. **No light bulb is allowed to illuminate any other light bulb**, even though empty squares may be lit by more than one bulb.

Some shaded squares also contain numbers – these numbers indicate how many light bulbs must be placed in the neighbouring squares immediately above, below, to the right or left of these shaded squares. Not all light bulbs are necessarily next to numbered squares, however, and you will need to deduce the presence of these from noting which squares are not otherwise illuminated.

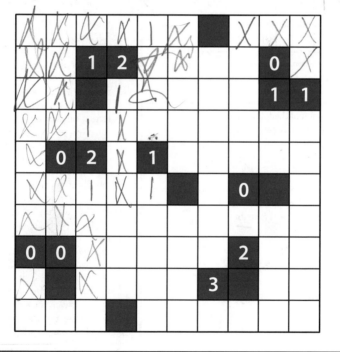

1

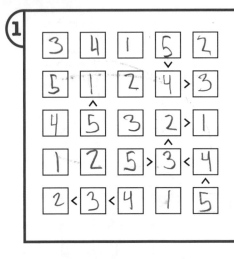

In this Futoshiki puzzle, place all of the digits 1 to 5 into each row and column. You must place them so that the less-than and greater-than signs ("<" and ">") are obeyed. Although no numbers have been given for this one, you can still get going by following the "<" and ">" signs carefully.

2

Using each of the following numbers and signs once each, can you reach a total of 43?

1	2	3	5	7
+	-	×	×	

You can use as many brackets as you like. For example, given 1, 2, 2, 3, + and ×, you could have (2+2) × (1+3) for a total of 16.

Size isn't everything

Several cases have been known of people who have only half the brain tissue of a normal adult, or even less, but who have normal intellectual functions. Any of us could be like this, and no one would know unless we had a brain scan. Usually illness or an accident has caused the loss of brain tissue. The reason these people appear normal is that they suffered this loss in early life, and the amazing reorganization capacities of the brain have compensated for the missing brain matter. However, if you lose brain tissue that you've grown up with, the effects on your thought and behaviour are a lot more serious.

3   BUSY 〉 〉 〉 〉 CAFE

4

Three of the following shape nets fold up into identical cubes, while the fourth is slightly different. Which shape net is the odd one out?

Tools for thought: speed reading

The trick to speed reading is to have different reading "gears" for different material. Skimming the title, introduction or back of a book can tell you if you need or want to read it, of course, and browsing the beginning of chapters or the contents page can tell you what it is about. But for real understanding you'll have to read the content word by word, re-engaging your skimming or browsing gears for information you already know or aren't interested in.

Claims that you can read up to 10,000 words a minute are exaggerated; this simply isn't possible while retaining the level of comprehension that you get with a normal reading speed of 200–500 words a minute.

14	One half of this	Multiply by six	50% of this	+28	-43	×9	Add seven	Subtract six	RESULT

5

To solve this game of Battleships, locate the hidden ships listed on the right in the grid. Each ship can be placed horizontally or vertically only, and cannot touch another ship in any direction. Numbers next to each row and column indicate the number of shaded ship segments in that row or column.

Find the following ships:

1 x Aircraft carrier
1 x Battleship
2 x Cruiser
2 x Destroyer
3 x Submarine

Ships cannot touch (including diagonally)

POLL 〉 〉 〉 〉 CARD

3

4					
	1	3			
		2			
1	4			3	
			2		3
	1				

To solve this Nurikabe, shade in certain squares so that every given number in the puzzle remains as part of a continuous unshaded area of the stated number of squares. There can be only one number per unshaded area. Shaded squares cannot form any solid 2x2 (or larger) areas, and together all the shaded squares must form one single continuous area. White areas cannot touch each other in either a horizontal or vertical direction.

4

Cover over the bottom three rows and then spend no more than two minutes looking at these first three sets of words. When your time is up, reveal the lower rows and cover the upper ones instead. Can you spot which word is missing from each of the rows?

Cockatiel	Cockatoo	Canary	Parrot	Parakeet
Rocket	Explosion	Firework	Gunpowder	Sparkler
Denim	Flannel	Satin	Cashmere	Corduroy

Parrot	Cockatiel	Parakeet	Cockatoo
Gunpowder	Sparkler	Rocket	Firework
Cashmere	Satin	Flannel	Denim

Fact: Identical twins do not have the same shape of brain. The ridges and furrows of our brains are as individual as our fingerprints.

RESULT

5

14	×3	-32	50% of this	×10	+23	Subtract twenty	+9	1/2 of this

1 Can you find an anagram of each of the CAPITALIZED words in order to complete each sentence?

She was in no STATE to _____ it properly.

If he DIGNIFIES it with a response then it will have _____ something profound.

The assistant gave a _____ to where the PROTEIN bars were.

He AUCTIONED off his talent, a result of his _____.

2

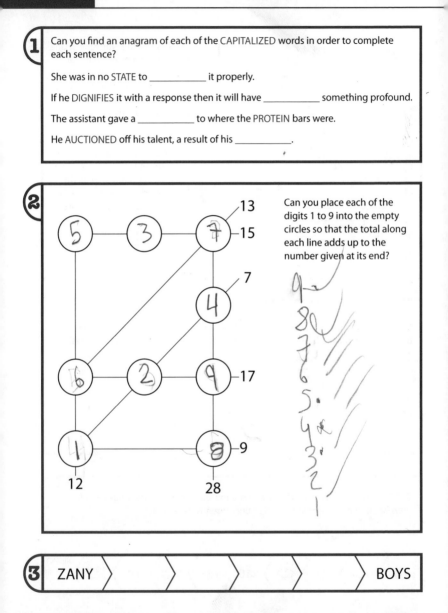

Can you place each of the digits 1 to 9 into the empty circles so that the total along each line adds up to the number given at its end?

3 ZANY 〉 〉 〉 〉 BOYS

Skyscraper is a Sudoku-style logic puzzle, in which the aim is to place the numbers 1 to 6 into every row and column of the grid while obeying the skyscraper constraints around the edge.

In Skyscraper puzzles each number in the completed grid represents a building of that many storeys.

Can you place the buildings in such a way that each given number outside the grid represents the number of buildings that can be seen from that point, looking only at that number's row or column? A building with a higher value always obscures a building with a lower value, and a building with a lower value never obscures a building with a higher value.

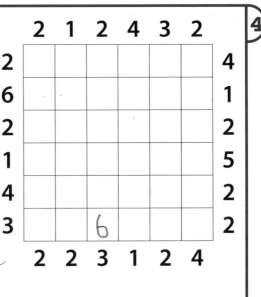

State-dependent recall

Experiments have shown that memory recall is aided by a match between the state we're in when learning and the one we're in when we're trying to remember. Memory researcher Alan Baddeley came up with the most famous demonstration of this effect when he asked divers to learn lists of words either under water or by the side of the pool. As predicted, recall was highest in those individuals who were tested in the same circumstances in which they studied. University psychology students have long claimed that this research supports taking their exams while slightly drunk.

5 ⟩ ×12 ⟩ 50% of this ⟩ ÷10 ⟩ ×3 ⟩ Add twelve ⟩ One third of this ⟩ +37 ⟩ ÷11 ⟩ **RESULT** **5**

1

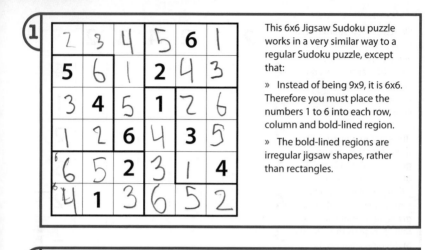

This 6x6 Jigsaw Sudoku puzzle works in a very similar way to a regular Sudoku puzzle, except that:

» Instead of being 9x9, it is 6x6. Therefore you must place the numbers 1 to 6 into each row, column and bold-lined region.

» The bold-lined regions are irregular jigsaw shapes, rather than rectangles.

2 This picture shows 16 matches arranged to form five squares. By moving precisely two matches, can you change the picture to show exactly four squares of the same size, with all matches used to form those squares and none left over? You cannot lie matches directly on top of one another.

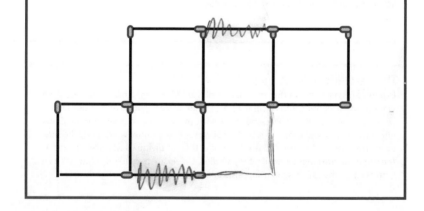

3 YANK 〉 〉 〉 〉 LIMB

4

Each of the following sequences of letters represents an ordered list of real-world initials, such as M T W T F for Monday, Tuesday, Wednesday, Thursday, Friday. Can you work out which letter comes next in each sequence, and why?

R	O	Y	G	B	I
I	V	X	L	C	___
J	J	A	S	O	N
O	T	T	F	F	___
C	D	F	G	H	J

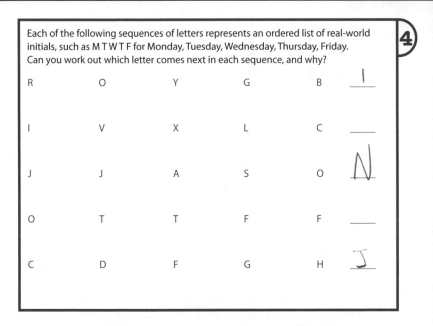

Tools for thinking

Professional thinkers have all sorts of methods for helping them come up with ideas. Some need complete isolation for five hours at a time, others like to work with the buzz of people all around them.

Charles Darwin used to walk miles a day to think, William Gladstone used to chop down trees while pondering. Albert Einstein's daydreams led to the theory of relativity, Winston Churchill used to rearrange cabinet meetings around his afternoon nap and Samuel Taylor Coleridge used the power of daytime napping (in combination with a tincture or two of opium, it's true) to create the famous poem "Kubla Khan". During periods of intense work, Leonardo Da Vinci used to sleep for 15 minutes at a time every four hours.

Although it varies from person to person, hard work (rather than any unifying practice or innate genius) seems to be the common theme.

| **40** | +20 | 1/3 of this | ÷2 | Add forty-eight | -4 | -50% | ÷9 | Multiply by four | **RESULT** **5** |

Music of the (hemi)spheres

All human cultures play and enjoy music. Young infants seem to have an innate preference for consonant over dissonant notes, and will naturally tap along with a rhythm from an early age. In fact, experiments have shown that we start deciding which music we like from before birth – babies played a certain tune while in the womb later like that tune more than a new one. Not only is music universal, but it seems to connect all of us to powerful emotions. All of us can appreciate the products of musical genius in a way that isn't true in other fields. Perhaps Einstein would be better understood if you could hum along to his equations.

There is an attractive but spurious idea that the intelligence behind classical music might rub off on the listeners. This is called the **Mozart Effect**. Ten minutes of Mozart's *Sonata in D major* for two pianos was played to a group of school children about to take a maths test: the children performed noticeably better as compared to those sitting in silence.

But before you order that complete set of concertos for the kids, there's an important lesson to be learned here about what scientists call controls. Yes, listening to Mozart did improve the maths scores. But with this comparison we don't know if the effect was due to not being bored, to being relaxed by the music, to being put in a good mood or whether there is indeed something special about Mozart's music itself.

The evidence is that there is nothing magical about Mozart's music (at least in respect of maths scores). You can get the same improvement in test scores by reading children a story. In fact, kids who enjoy music generally improve more after listening to music and, likewise, kids who prefer stories improve more after listening to stories. The results are determined by the effect of being engaged, and ending up in a better mood: there is nothing intrinsically special about the classical music itself.

The effects of learning to play music, on the other hand, may be very real and very long lasting. Research has shown that children who have been given music lessons have improved their scores in language-based tests and general IQ tests, as well as on maths-based tests and visual-spatial tests: the sort of things that are thought to be processed by the same parts of the brain engaged by music training. These effects aren't just when compared to kids who have not been given music lessons, but in comparison to children given other kinds of after-school lessons, such as drama. One experiment showed that although extra drama lessons improved test scores, the largest improvement was in the music lesson group. Psychologists have suggested that this may be due to the wide range of brain functions engaged by playing music.

To play an instrument with other people you need to concentrate, but also pay attention to other people, use fine motor co-ordination, practise memorization or reading, and all whilst controlling your emotions. Not only is this a considerable range of activities, but music is interesting in that it is uniquely about synchronization. Some researchers have suggested that there is a particular benefit to taking part in making music while young, in that it helps the developing brain learn to coordinate across disparate regions. The benefits of musical training have been supported by brain scans which show growth in the auditory and motor co-ordination areas of the brains of six year olds after just fifteen weeks of weekly keyboard lessons.

Neuropsychologists are taking this logic further and developing music-based therapies for stroke patients. They hope that the unique combination of functions engaged by making and enjoying music can help damaged brains rewire. One particular benefit of music is that in most people it appears to be based in the opposite hemisphere of the brain to language, so musical training may help those who have suffered damage to their language-specialized brain region to retrain their undamaged side of the brain to compensate. Music training is not the quick fix of the Mozart Effect. You need to practise for hours and hours, rather than just passively listen to a CD for ten minutes. But the effects are real and accompanied by the many pleasures of learning a musical skill.

1

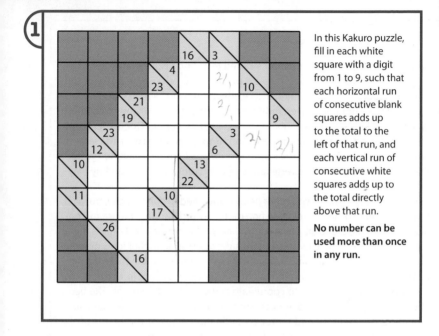

In this Kakuro puzzle, fill in each white square with a digit from 1 to 9, such that each horizontal run of consecutive blank squares adds up to the total to the left of that run, and each vertical run of consecutive white squares adds up to the total directly above that run.

No number can be used more than once in any run.

2 Delete one letter from each pair in order to reveal a word. For example, deleting B and C from "AB CT" would give the word "AT".

GF AI TR RS LT   _____

AE ND OU RT HJ EK LR   _____

DT OU PA HS TU GE YR   _____

3 WOWS ⟩ ⟩ ⟩ ⟩ RACE

Study these pictures of different faces for up to two minutes, then cover them over and try to redraw them on the blank faces below as precisely as possible.

High IQ societies

If you think you are seriously brainy, you might wish to apply to join one of the many "high IQ" societies. Mensa is the best-known and it is open to those who score in the top 2% on a standard supervised intelligence test. So if you think that out of a typical group of 100 people you're probably in the top two on puzzles like the ones in this book, perhaps you should give it a go. If you think you're in the top one out of 30,000 people you could even apply to join the Prometheus Society, the club for people with an IQ above 160.

But why stop there? Perhaps you are one in a million, in which case the society for you is "elite ultra High IQ Society" the Mega Society. One problem with ultra high IQ societies is that their membership tends to be quite small (since they can only recruit from a tiny fraction of the population). Historically, high IQ societies have been dogged by factionalism and debates about the validity of the tests used to determine entry. This perhaps is hardly surprising, bearing in mind that these are groups of people who are keen to mark out their distinctiveness from the rest of the world on the basis of IQ tests...

23	Subtract fifteen	50% of this	√	+11	×3	+37	1/2 of this	÷2	RESULT

5

1

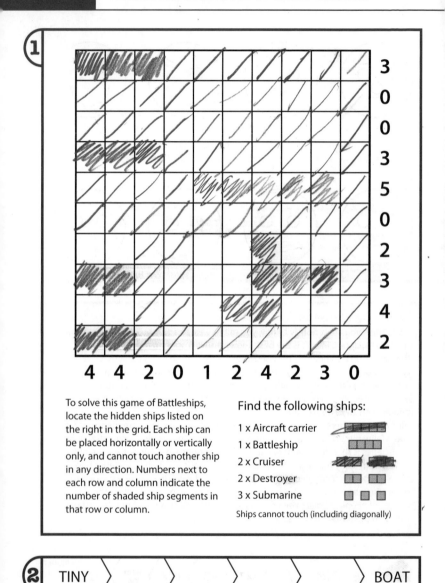

										3
										0
										0
										3
										5
										0
										2
										3
										4
										2

4   4   2   0   1   2   4   2   3   0

To solve this game of Battleships, locate the hidden ships listed on the right in the grid. Each ship can be placed horizontally or vertically only, and cannot touch another ship in any direction. Numbers next to each row and column indicate the number of shaded ship segments in that row or column.

Find the following ships:

1 x Aircraft carrier
1 x Battleship
2 x Cruiser
2 x Destroyer
3 x Submarine

Ships cannot touch (including diagonally)

2 TINY 〉 〉 〉 〉 BOAT

3

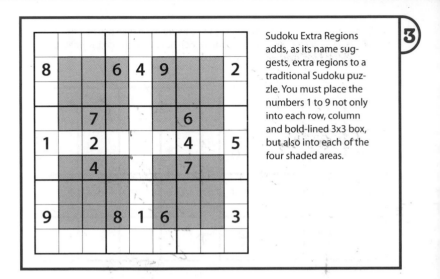

Sudoku Extra Regions adds, as its name suggests, extra regions to a traditional Sudoku puzzle. You must place the numbers 1 to 9 not only into each row, column and bold-lined 3x3 box, but also into each of the four shaded areas.

4

These three boxes follow a visual progression. Which of the three lettered options should come fourth in the sequence?

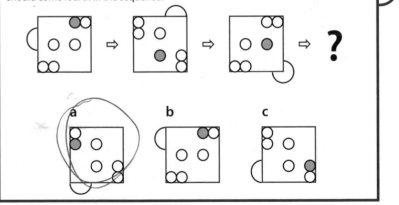

5

| 18 | ÷6 | ×4 | -5 | ×7 | -27 | Add forty-four | 1/2 of this | +25 | RESULT |

1 Study this arrangement of the numbers 1 to 16 for no more than two minutes. When the time is up, cover it over and try to redraw it on the blank grid on the right. Look out for patterns that may help you remember.

5	15	9	3
16	8	1	10
11	4	7	13
2	12	14	6

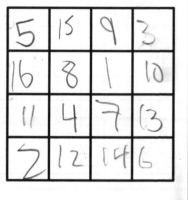

IQ tests

IQ stands for Intelligence Quotient and is supposed to be a way of measuring intelligence. IQ tests were invented to discriminate between children of different abilities at school. All IQ tests are constructed so that the average score is 100 and they have a standard spread so that 68% of people fall within a +/- 15 range, i.e. between 85 and 115. Ninety-five percent of people are supposed to be within the range 70–130, and 99.7% within the range 55–145. The spread works so that it is progressively harder to obtain each extra IQ point as you get further away from 100, so much so that most IQ tests either don't cover or become unreliable for scores higher than 160 (an IQ score which only three people in 100,000 will exceed). Of course, what kinds of questions are included in an IQ test is controversial. Most tests will include reasoning and calculating puzzles like those in this book. Some people claim there are multiple kinds of intelligence, each requiring lots of different tests. What is certainly true is that we can all learn to exploit our strengths and practise to improve our weaknesses.

2 CUTE > MUTE > MATE > MASE > MASK > TASK

3

6	2	8	9	1	5	3	4	7
3	5	4	6	8	7	9	1	2
1	7	9	3	2	4	8	6	5
7	4	3	2	4	1	5	8	6
2	8	6	5	3	9	4	7	1
4	1	5	7	6	8	2	3	9
9	3	2	4	7	6	1	5	8
5	6	1	8	9	3	7	2	4
8	4	7	1	5	2	6	9	3

The rules of Sudoku are very simple: place the numbers 1 to 9 into each row, column and bold-lined 3x3 box. Each number must appear only once in any row, column or box.

4

How many pairs of anagrams can you find among the following words?

PADRES	PYLONS	AUDIOS	STEWED
FAULTY	IMPEDE	ROBOTS	LAMING
BATHED	TWEEDS	CLOSES	SPARED
MALIGN	PERISH	ROGUES	GROUSE

Fact: On average we lose one neuron per second during adulthood. This can be part of our intellectual development: just as a sculptor chips away stone to make a statue, so our brain refines its connections and composition to sharpen our thinking.

5

22	+17	Subtract thirty-one	1/2 of this	+75%	×6	+8	÷5	Fifty percent of this	**RESULT**

39   8   4   7   42   50   10   5

1 Can you complete this number pyramid? Each brick in the pyramid should contain a value equal to the sum of the two blocks directly below it.

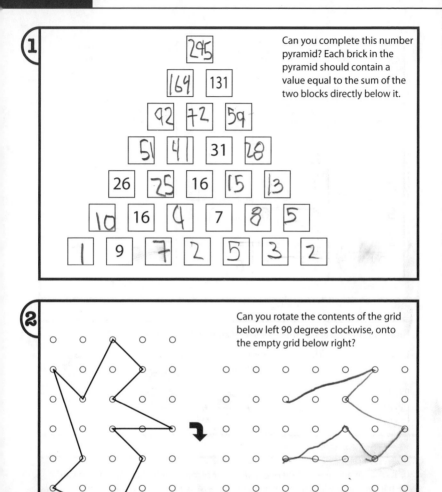

295

169 | 131

92 | 72 | 59

51 | 41 | 31 | 28

26 | 25 | 16 | 15 | 13

10 | 16 | 9 | 7 | 8 | 5

1 | 9 | 7 | 2 | 5 | 3 | 2

2 Can you rotate the contents of the grid below left 90 degrees clockwise, onto the empty grid below right?

3 DARK 〉 DARE 〉 WARE 〉 WARE 〉 WORD 〉 WOOD

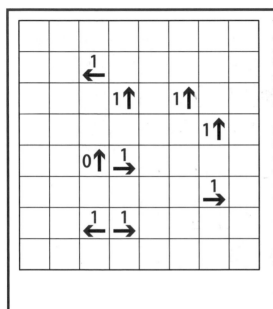

(4)

The aim of Yajilin is to draw a single loop using only horizontal and vertical lines so that the loop does not pass through any square more than once.

Any squares which the loop does not visit must be shaded, but no two of these shaded squares can touch in either a horizontal or vertical direction.

Numbers with arrows indicate the exact number of shaded squares in a given direction in a specific row or column, but not all shaded squares are necessarily identified with arrows.

To sleep, perchance to learn

Professor Matt Walker of the University of Berkeley studies the effect of sleep on learning. His research suggests that having slept well before learning something helps with later recall, and that some of the benefits of learning only arise after sleep.

Interestingly, it seems that the less obvious connections between things may only be encoded in memory during sleep. Other research has shown that some of the benefits of sleep on memory can be gained by a 90-minute nap during the day, rather than requiring a full night's sleep. Which is good news for those of us who like to sleep in the afternoon.

30	50% of this	÷5	+22	Subtract one	÷12	Add thirty-one	1/3 of this	×6	RESULT

15　3　25 24　2　33　11　66

1

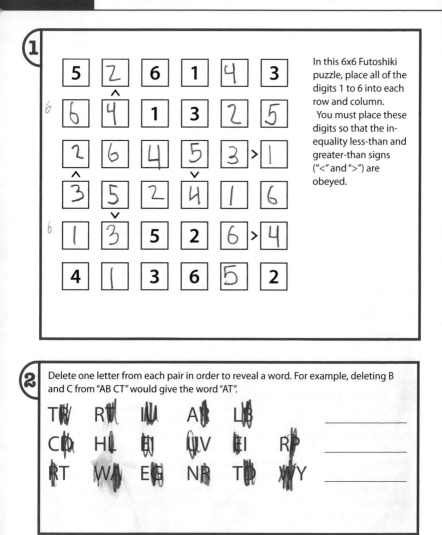

In this 6x6 Futoshiki puzzle, place all of the digits 1 to 6 into each row and column. You must place these digits so that the in-equality less-than and greater-than signs ("<" and ">") are obeyed.

2

Delete one letter from each pair in order to reveal a word. For example, deleting B and C from "AB CT" would give the word "AT".

TW RT IU AR LB _____

CD HL EI UV EI RP _____

RT WA EG NR TD XY _____

3

COLD > COLT > BOLT > BELT > BEET > BEEF

(4)

» If I toss a coin, there is a one in two chance of getting heads, and a one in two chance of getting tails. If I toss a coin three times in a row, what is the likelihood that I get one head and two tails?

$1/3$

» In a drawer I have seven different pairs of socks. If I take socks out of the drawer entirely at random, how many socks do I need to take out to be sure of getting at least two complete pairs?

9

What would Bugs Bunny do?

We all have an innate talent for role-playing. You can use this talent to help you get a fresh perspective on a problem or a situation where you need a creative solution. It works like this: once you feel stuck and you've exhausted thinking about what you should do, call to mind someone else, a real person such as a celebrity or a fictional character, who you think might come up with a good solution. Then imagine you are this person. Ask yourself "What would Bugs Bunny do?", or "What would Oscar Wilde do?", or "What would Buddha do?"

One of the surprising things about our minds is that we can use the idea of thinking as if we were other people to access information that was inside us all along – we didn't get to it because we were stuck in the same old circuits of the self. Of course, if you do get a great idea from imagining you are Bugs Bunny, Al Capone or Buddha, you will probably want to run it past your normal self to double-check that it really is a wise move.

29	-11	50% of this	+21	1/3 of this	+10	÷10	×11	÷2	RESULT

(5)

18   9   30 10 20   2   22 11

1

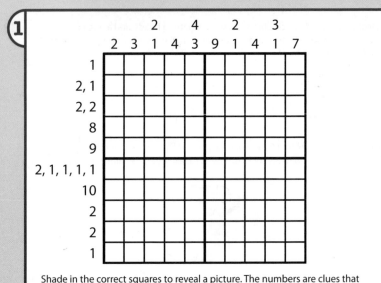

Shade in the correct squares to reveal a picture. The numbers are clues that provide – in order, from the left/top – a list of the length of every sequence of consecutive shaded squares in each row/column respectively. Sequences are separated by one or more empty squares.

2

How many words of three or more letters can you find in this word wheel? Each word must contain the centre letter, plus any selection of the other letters no more than once each.

3

13 + 73 = 86 94 + 11 = 105 3 × 10 = 30

152 ÷ 4 = 38 48 ÷ 2 = 24 16 ÷ 8 = 2

28 + 97 = 125 47 − 20 = 27 10 + 18 = 28

8:50a.m. to 10:00a.m. = $1:10$ 3:55a.m. to 6:35p.m. = $14:40$

1:55a.m. to 3:05p.m. = $1:10$ 12:30a.m. to 5:30a.m. = $5:00$

5:35a.m. to 1:05p.m. = $7:30$ 1:00a.m. to 2:30p.m. = $13:30$

£5700 − £22.30 = 5677.70 £1560 − £345 = 1215

£44 − £4.01 = 39.99 £361 − £22.10 = 338.90

£4 + £3.46 = 7.46 £20400 − £3.57 = 20396.43

4

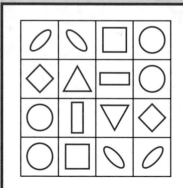

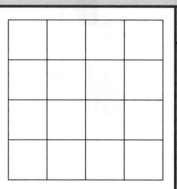

Spend no more than two minutes studying this grid of shapes, then cover it and redraw it as accurately as you can in the empty grid to the right.

1 For each of the three pictures above the line, which of the images below it would result from reflecting the picture in the horizontal line "mirror"?

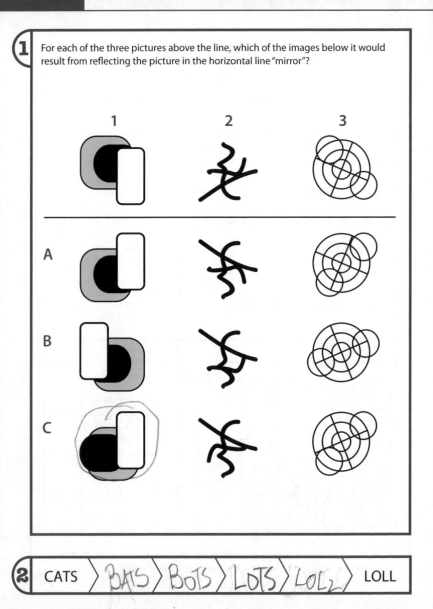

2 CATS BATS BOTS LOTS LOL2 LOLL

3 Cover up the set of words on the right (in blue). Then spend no more than two minutes looking at the list of word-pairs on the left. Once the time is up, cover the word pairs instead. See if you can recall each pair when given just one of the two words.

Popcorn	Cinema	Result
Snack	Supper	Napkin
Decision	Result	Lampshade
Menu	Listing	Outfit
Overall	Outfit	Popcorn
Lampshade	Fitting	Listing
Wallet	Money	Money
Napkin	Handkerchief	Snack

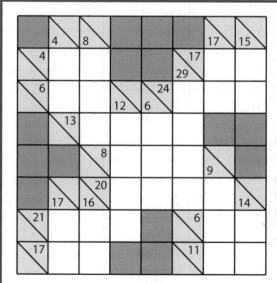

4 In this Kakuro puzzle, fill in each white square with a digit from 1 to 9, such that each horizontal run of consecutive blank squares adds up to the total to the left of that run, and each vertical run of consecutive white squares adds up to the total directly above that run.

No number can be used more than once in any run.

5 43 › -35 › 1/2 of this › ×6 › 50% of this › +23 › 1/5 of this › +57 › -30 › **RESULT** 34

8 4 24 12 357 64 34

1 Cover over the bottom list of words, and then study the upper list for no more than two minutes. When your time is up, uncover the lower list and cover the upper one instead – can you write numbers below the words in order to rearrange them into their original order?

pyramid, monkey, construction, glasses, pineapple, rose, glass, balloon, sock, hand

balloon, construction, glass, glasses, hand, monkey, pineapple, pyramid, rose, sock

2

6	1	2	4	8	5	9	7	3
4	9	3	2	1	7	5	6	8
7	5	8	6	9	3	1	2	4
3	6	7	5	4	1	2	8	9
9	2	1	3	7	8	4	5	6
5	8	4	9	6	2	3	1	7
2	4	9	7	5	6	8	3	1
1	3	6	8	2	4	7	9	5
8	7	5	1	3	9	6	4	2

The rules of Sudoku are very simple: place the numbers 1 to 9 into each row, column and bold-lined 3x3 box. Each number must appear only once in any row, column or box.

3 MAIN > RAIN > LAID > LOID > ROAD

(4)

How many English words can you find in this word square? For each word start on any square and move only to adjacent squares – including diagonals – but without visiting any square more than once. There are at least 82 words to be found, including a nine-letter one.

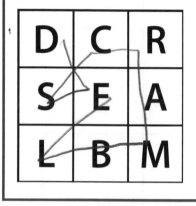

DESCRAMBLE

Neisser's learning limerick

Ulric Neisser is a famous psychologist, who wrote the highly influential book *Cognitive Psychology*. He was an advocate of properly spacing out your practice or learning sessions – as opposed to having long, concentrated practice sessions – and he wrote a limerick celebrating this finding:

You can get a good deal from rehearsal

If it just has the proper dispersal.

You would just be an ass

To do it en masse:

Your remembering would turn out much worsal.

45	Divide by nine	+31	1/6 of this	×10	-32	1/2 of this	+26	÷10	RESULT

5   36   6   60   28   14   40   4

(5) 4

1

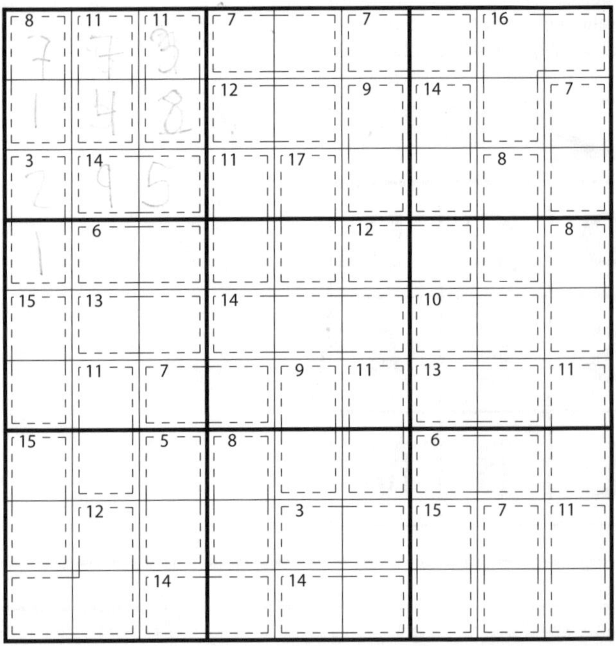

In Killer Sudoku, as in regular Sudoku, the aim is to place the digits 1 to 9 into each row, column and bold-lined 3x3 box.

Additionally, place digits so that the total of each dashed-line cage is the value given at the top-left of that cage. Digits may *not* be repeated within a cage.

2 ROCK > > > > > GAME

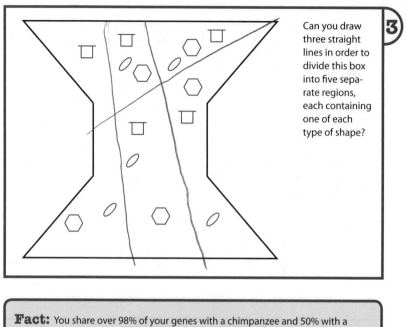

3 Can you draw three straight lines in order to divide this box into five separate regions, each containing one of each type of shape?

Fact: You share over 98% of your genes with a chimpanzee and 50% with a banana. Small changes can clearly make a big difference.

4 David, Sam and Kathy have each been given different toys to play with. The toys are a kite, a truck and a bike, and are coloured red, white or blue.

By reading the following clues, can you work out who was given which toy and what colour it was? Try to do so without making notes.

» Kathy received a wheeled toy.

» The blue truck was given to a boy.

» Dave's toy is red.

DAVID - RED - KITE
SAM - BLUE - TRUCK
CATHY - WHITE - BIKE

5 | 33 | +16 | √ | Multiply by eleven | -36 | Add thirty-nine | Subtract fifty percent | Divide by eight | ×12 | **RESULT** 60 |

49 7 77 41 80 40 5 60

1

7	2	6	5	9	1	3	8	4
8			9	1	6	7		2
		8				7		
9	7	2	4	8	5	6	3	1
			8					3
3	5	1	2	4	8	7	6	9
	9	9	1					8
2			6	5	9	8		7
	8						9	

This 9x9 Jigsaw Sudoku puzzle is solved just like a regular Sudoku puzzle, except that instead of 3x3 boxes you must now place 1 to 9 into each row, column and bold-lined jigsaw region.

2 Can you match each of the following words with one other in order to form a synonym pair? Each word must be used in precisely one pair.

cold   dark   remote   grave   severe

distant   sturdy   unlikely   dim   strong

Fact: One amazing experiment found that people made to wear goggles which turned the world upside down could learn to move around safely and fluidly in just a couple of weeks. They returned to normal once the goggles were taken off.

3 ENDS 〉ANDS〉AIDS〉AIRS〉FIRS〉 FIRM

4

Study the first shape below for no more than two minutes. Then cover it up and try to redraw all of the black lines from memory on the partial copy below it.

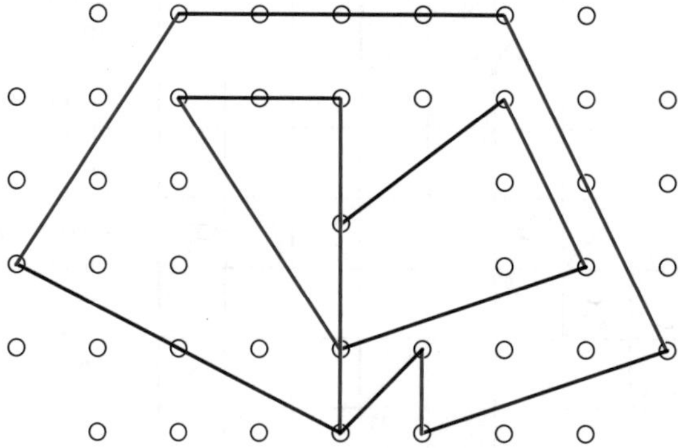

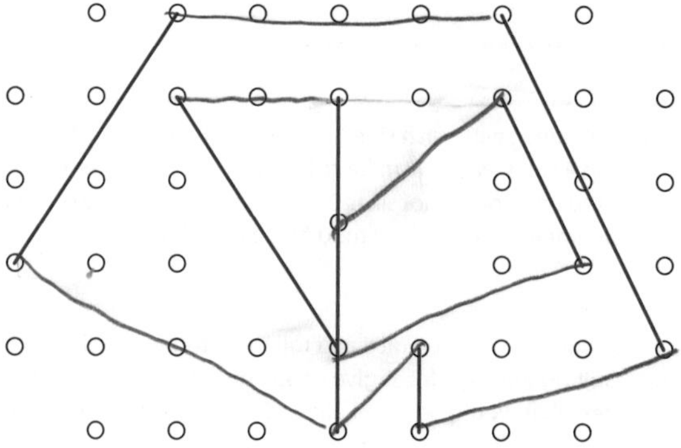

| 20 | 3/5 of this | ×2 | Two thirds of this | Square root of this | ×8 | +50% | Add twenty-three | −35 | RESULT **5** |

36

12 24 16 4 32 48 71 36

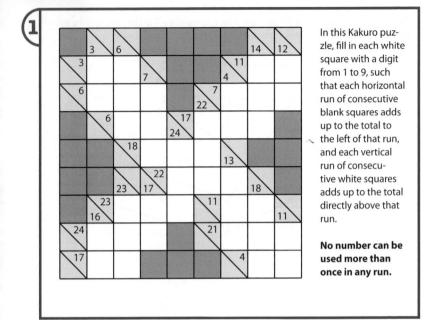

In this Kakuro puzzle, fill in each white square with a digit from 1 to 9, such that each horizontal run of consecutive blank squares adds up to the total to the left of that run, and each vertical run of consecutive white squares adds up to the total directly above that run.

No number can be used more than once in any run.

» I have a square of paper, with each side 10cm in length. The length of its perimeter is 40cm, since it has 4 sides, each 10cm long. If I now cut out and remove four squares, one from each of the four corners, of sizes 2x2cm, 4x4cm, 3x3cm and 1.5x1.5cm, what will be the total perimeter length of my modified piece of paper?

SAME

» If I pick up two ordinary six-sided dice and roll them together, what is the likelihood that the resulting upwards faces give a total of 12? And similarly, if I were to roll three dice together what would be the likelihood of rolling three simultaneous sixes?

36-1   198-1

---

3 DUEL 〉 〉 〉 〉 PAIR

4

This pattern is constructed by following a simple rule. Can you work out what that rule is, and therefore deduce which of the three options (a, b or c) should replace the question mark?

?

a   b   c

Fact: Each neuron in the brain only connects to a tiny proportion of the other neurons in the brain. If each neuron in the brain connected with every other neuron, our brain would be 12.5 miles across.

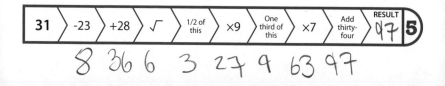

31	-23	+28	√	1/2 of this	×9	One third of this	×7	Add thirty-four	RESULT

5

8   36   6   3   27   9   63   97

Feeding your brain

The fundamental fuels of your brain are oxygen and sugar. Moment by moment these are taken out of your blood and turned by the brain into the electrochemical signals that make up your thoughts. Run out of either, and your thinking will suffer.

Most of the time the body automatically manages the supply of blood and oxygen to the brain. Only rarely will you notice a lack of either of these two things affecting your thinking. A short walk can help raise your blood oxygen levels, which may temporarily boost your brain's performance if you've been sitting still for a long period.

The feeling of being low on sugar is far more common than the feeling of being low on oxygen. Many of us will experience a dip in our thinking abilities in gaps between meals, or if we've been thinking but haven't had a chance to eat when we normally might have done. The solution to this is to have meals of **slow release sugars** (carbohydrates such as pasta, for example) or to take your chances with the obesity and tooth-rot that can result from sugary snacks.

Inadequate hydration levels can also have a severe effect on brain function, but again your body will mostly take care of hydration levels for you, making you thirsty when you need to drink. The idea that we need eight glasses of water a day, or that healthy people can improve their mental performance by drinking more water when they aren't thirsty, is a myth.

The idea probably arose from estimates of how much water the body uses in a day, but we get much of this from food.

In the longer term, your brain needs a variety of vitamins and minerals to function, as well as healthy doses of fatty acids such as those found in fish, seeds and grains. **Fatty acids**, particularly Omega 3 fatty acids, have been in the news recently, and some nutritionalists have suggested that fish oil supplements may be able to boost brain function.

There's no good evidence for this, although there is evidence that supplements can enhance cognitive function in those who are deprived of fish oils or who suffer from various psychiatric conditions such as **schizophrenia**. If you have a healthy balanced diet it is likely that you're getting all the vitamins, minerals and fatty acids you need, and won't benefit from supplements. So, if you do decide to take supplements, remember that once you've redressed a deficit more doesn't equal better, and that it is also possible to overdose on supplements.

Recent research in rats suggests that the benefits of supplements such as fatty acids may be boosted when combined with exercise. These supplements can provide raw materials for building new brain cells, a process that is encouraged by physical activity. Other experiments have shown that rats brought up in enriched environments – basically, living conditions with areas to explore, other rats to interact with and other activities to pursue – have more complex connections between brain cells.

All in all, this suggests that a vital part of feeding your brain is not just the chemicals that you provide via your diet, but also the experiences and ideas you occupy yourself with.

1

Can you complete this number pyramid? Each brick in the pyramid should contain a value equal to the sum of the two blocks directly below it.

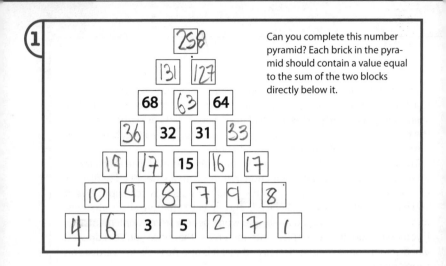

```
              258
           131   127
         68   63   64
       36   32   31   33
     19   17   15   16   17
   10    9    8    7    9    8
  4    6    3    5    2    7    1
```

2

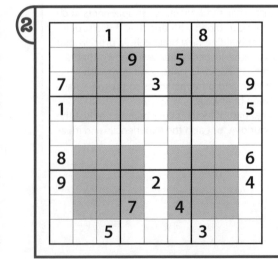

Sudoku Extra Regions adds, as its name suggests, extra regions to a traditional Sudoku puzzle. You must place the numbers 1 to 9 not only into each row, column and bold-lined 3x3 box, but also into each of the four shaded areas.

3 WALK ⟩ WALL ⟩ FALL ⟩ FELL ⟩ FEEL ⟩ FEET

4

Study these pictures of different stick people for up to two minutes, then cover them over and try to redraw them on the partially drawn people below as precisely as possible.

Let sleeping teenagers lie (in)

Sleep is essential for good brain function. When research suggested that the natural tendency of adolescents was to stay up late and get up late, some school boards in the US decided to change school starting times, making them 70 minutes later.

Dr Kyla Wahlstrom at the University of Minnesota studied the effects and found that not only did grades improve, but so did students' daytime alertness, attendance, motivation and positive mood. The later school start time allowed students an average of an extra five hours' sleep over the week.

Of course, they could have got this by going to bed earlier, but it seems that in some circumstances you can't fight biology, and the behaviour of teenagers is one of them.

30	÷10	+21	Subtract ten	+50%	+37	Subtract fifty	1/2 of this	×12	RESULT 48	**5**

3 24 14 21 58 8 4 48

1 To decode this quotation (and the name of its author) you will need to replace each letter with a different one a fixed number of places forwards or backwards in the alphabet. (Wrap around from Z to A or from A to Z when counting.)

ALL TRUTHS ARE EASY TO UNDERSTAND ONCE THEY ARE DIS-
Bmm usvuit bsf fbtz up voefstuboe podf uifz bsf ejt-
COVERED. THE POINT IS TO DISCOVER THEM
dpwfsfe; uif qpjou jt up ejtdpwfs uifn.

                                              GALILEO
                                              Hbmjmfp

ABCDEFGHIJKLMNOPQRSTUVWXYZ

2 Three women went to different classes at the gym last week. Can you work out who went to each class, and on which day? Try to do so without making notes.

» Jennifer went to her cycling practice three days earlier in the week than the yoga class attendee.

» Tuesday's swimming lesson was the day after cycling practice.

» Kate visited earlier in the week than Vanessa.

JEN — CYCLING — MONDAY
KATE — SWIMMING — TUESDAY
VANESSA — YOGA — THURSDAY

Brain landmarks: the amygdala

The amygdala is a brain nucleus which is responsible for processing emotional stimuli and encoding emotional memories. Studies by Portuguese neuroscientist António Damásio have shown that those with damaged amygdalas have trouble making decisions. Even though their rational intellect is intact they feel ambivalent between different choices and their consequences and so end up doing nothing or making arbitrary choices.

3 JUNK 〉 *JUNO* 〉 *JUNE* 〉 *JANE* 〉 *MANE* 〉 MALE

4

In Killer Sudoku, as in regular Sudoku, the aim is to place the digits 1 to 9 into each row, column and bold-lined 3x3 box.

Additionally, place digits so that the total of each dashed-line cage is the value given at the top-left of that cage. Digits may *not* be repeated within a cage.

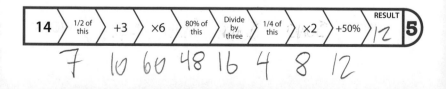

14	1/2 of this	+3	×6	80% of this	Divide by three	1/4 of this	×2	+50%	RESULT
	7	10	60	48	16	4	8	12	12

5

1

```
3  3  2  2  2  3  3  3
2           2  2        2
2        2        3  2
   3        2  3  1        3
3        1  1  3        3
   3  2        2           3
2        0  1              3
3  3  2  1  2  3  2  3
```

Draw a single loop by connecting together the dots so that every numbered square has the specified number of adjacent line segments. Dots can only be joined by straight horizontal or vertical lines. The loop cannot cross or overlap itself in any way.

2 All of the vowels have been eliminated from each of the following four words. Can you work out what the original set of words was?

bfsctry

yngstr   YOUNGSTER

hppnstnc

ndrstndbl   UNDERSTANDABLE

3 KING ⟩ KIND ⟩ WIND ⟩ ⟩ WORM

These three boxes follow a visual progression. Which of the three lettered options should come fourth in the sequence?

4

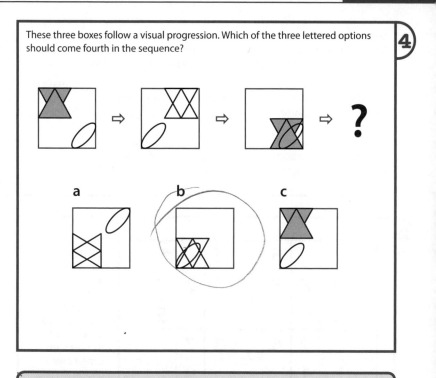

Brain fuel

Your brain runs on oxygen and sugar. Boosting levels of both can improve performance in the short term. Light exercise will get slightly more oxygen to the brain temporarily – taking a brisk walk before sitting down to learn something might put you in a better frame of mind.

Sugar is released continuously as your stomach breaks down your meals. You definitely shouldn't live off sugary snacks for the sake of your brain, but if you are suffering from a blood sugar dip between meals there's nothing like a sugary snack to give you a sharp increase in blood sugar and keep your brain firing on all cylinders.

| 11 | ×9 | 2/3 of this | +1 | -61 | +50% | ÷3 | ×15 | +40% | RESULT 63 |

5

99 66 67 6 9 3 45 63

1 Cover over the bottom three rows of words and then spend two minutes looking at these first three rows. When the time's up, reveal the lower rows and cover the upper ones instead. Can you spot which word is missing from each of the rows?

Savannah	Steppe	Desert	Plain	Grassland
Helium	Potassium	Nitrogen	Oxygen	Carbon
Chocolate	Candy	Sweet	Jellybean	Fudge

Desert	Plain	Savannah	Grassland
Oxygen	Carbon	Potassium	Helium
Fudge	Sweet	Jellybean	Chocolate

2

			6		5			
	1	6	8		9	2	7	
	7							5
		2	5		3	7		
		1					9	
		4	9		8	3		
	2						9	
	6	5	1		7	4	8	
			2		6			

The rules of Sudoku are very simple: place the numbers 1 to 9 into each row, column and bold-lined 3x3 box. Each number must appear only once in any row, column or box.

3 MOON ⟩ ⟩ ⟩ ⟩ DUSK

4

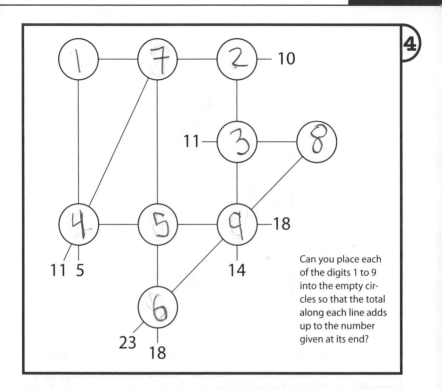

Can you place each of the digits 1 to 9 into the empty circles so that the total along each line adds up to the number given at its end?

The 10% myth

There's a myth that we use only 10% of our brains. This is false: we use all of our brains. In fact, neuroscientists have shown that brain cells which don't get used die, so it would therefore be impossible for you to have unused bits of brain.

The reason this myth has become so widespread is that, like all myths, it does at least point towards a truth. In this case, to the idea that we have unused brain capacity. Whoever you are, your brain has the capacity to learn to do new things, to have new experiences and to gain new skills.

8	-50%	+50%	×4	÷8	+18	2/3 of this	×7	Subtract thirty-six	RESULT

6 24 3 21 14 9 8 62

5

①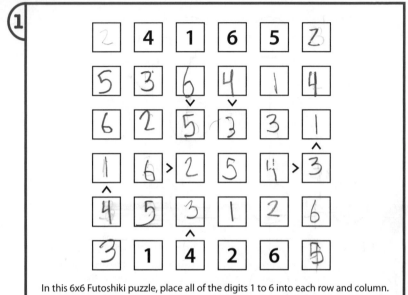

In this 6x6 Futoshiki puzzle, place all of the digits 1 to 6 into each row and column. You must place these digits such that the inequality less-than and greater-than signs ("<" and ">") are obeyed.

Weird brains: the tunicate

What is your brain for? You might have your own opinions, but biologists have a simple answer: to move your body around. Things that don't make complex movements quite simply don't have brains.

The proof of this can be seen in the tunicate, or sea slug. These aquatic creatures are born with brains, and swim around for the first half of their lives. However, when they reach adulthood they find a rock to fix themselves to and they never move again. Then, because they have no more need for it, they digest their own brains for food.

Like they say: use it or lose it.

② COWS 〉 ROWS 〉 ROWE 〉 LOWE 〉 LOVE 〉 LIVE

3

Using each of the following numbers and signs only once each, can you reach a total of 117?

2	2	5	7	25
+	+	×	×	

You can use as many brackets as you like – for example given 1, 2, 2, 3, + and × you could have (2+2) × (1+3) for a total of 16.

4

How good is your memory for detail? Spend no more than two minutes studying these two unusual sentences, then cover them up and see how accurately you can recall them – word for word, punctuation mark for punctuation mark. You might well find it harder than you expect!

» Throughout the entirety of mankind's sentience – from moments carved in stone to the lost thoughts of a silent hermit – this level of manifold genius had announced itself but once before.

» The diaphanous texture hung in the sky, glistening with the power of a million tiny stars; a heavenly dancer in the magnificent firmament of celestial light – an empyrean reminder of the ravishing mystery of nature.

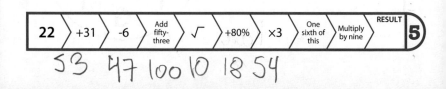

22	+31	-6	Add fifty-three	√	+80%	×3	One sixth of this	Multiply by nine	RESULT

5

53 47 100 10 18 54

1

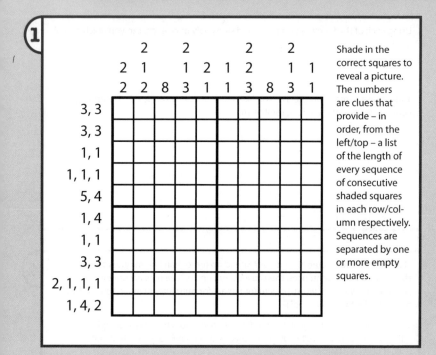

Shade in the correct squares to reveal a picture. The numbers are clues that provide – in order, from the left/top – a list of the length of every sequence of consecutive shaded squares in each row/column respectively. Sequences are separated by one or more empty squares.

2 How many words of three or more letters can you find in this word wheel? Each word must contain the centre letter, plus any selection of the other letters no more than once each.

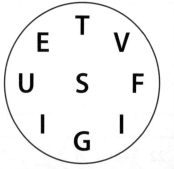

3

34 ÷ 2 = $\boxed{17}$ 19 + 68 = $\boxed{87}$ 14 × 11 = $\boxed{144}$

40 − 12 = $\boxed{28}$ 78 ÷ 3 = $\boxed{26}$ 14 × 5 = $\boxed{70}$

56 − 8 = $\boxed{48}$ 24 + 29 = $\boxed{53}$ 6 × 5 = $\boxed{30}$

4:15a.m. to 5:55a.m. = $\boxed{1:40}$ 5:10a.m. to 4:55p.m. = $\boxed{11:45}$

7:50a.m. to 2:15p.m. = $\boxed{6:25}$ 3:10a.m. to 6:50p.m. = $\boxed{15:40}$

5:00a.m. to 11:55a.m. = $\boxed{6:55}$ 1:00a.m. to 3:15a.m. = $\boxed{2:15}$

£49100 − £1.20 = $\boxed{49098.80}$ £28800 − 65p = $\boxed{28799.35}$

£4330 − £29.90 = $\boxed{4300.10}$ £43.50 + £1.51 = $\boxed{41.99}$

£320 + £204 = $\boxed{524}$ £1510 − £2.39 = $\boxed{1507.61}$

4

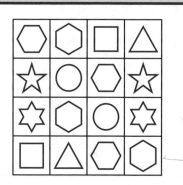

Spend no more than two minutes studying this grid of shapes, then cover it and redraw it as accurately as you can in the empty grid to the right.

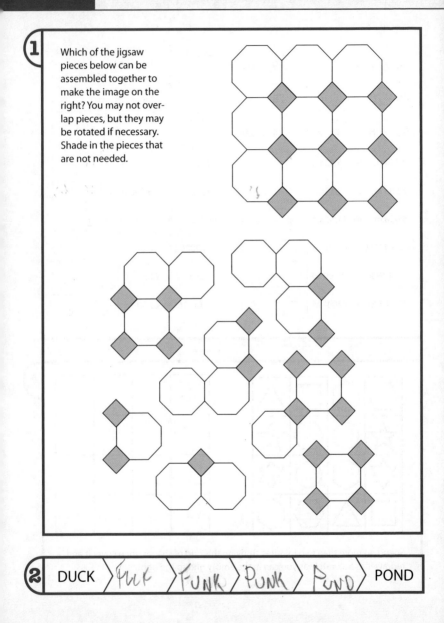

1 Which of the jigsaw pieces below can be assembled together to make the image on the right? You may not overlap pieces, but they may be rotated if necessary. Shade in the pieces that are not needed.

2 DUCK ⟩ FUCK ⟩ FUNK ⟩ PUNK ⟩ PUND ⟩ POND

Fact: Babies have many more interconnections between their neurons than adults. As we learn the skills of life, useful connections are strengthened and useless connections are pruned away.

3

Delete one letter from each pair in order to reveal a word. For example, deleting B and C from "AB CT" would give the word "AT".

AA PR EA XB

DT EI SW TI EA DW

AP DR EO CB IE DE

APEX

TESTED

_____

4

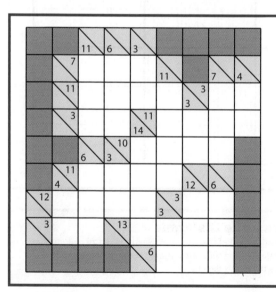

In this Kakuro puzzle, fill in each white square with a digit from 1 to 9, such that each horizontal run of consecutive white squares adds up to the total to the left of that run, and each vertical run of consecutive white squares adds up to the total directly above that run.

No number can be used more than once in any run.

---

36 〉 50% of this 〉 −14 〉 ×7 〉 ÷4 〉 +19 〉 Divide by two 〉 +52 〉 3/5 of this 〉 **RESULT** **5**

1

Here's another Killer Sudoku for you to try: see **Day 2** for instructions.

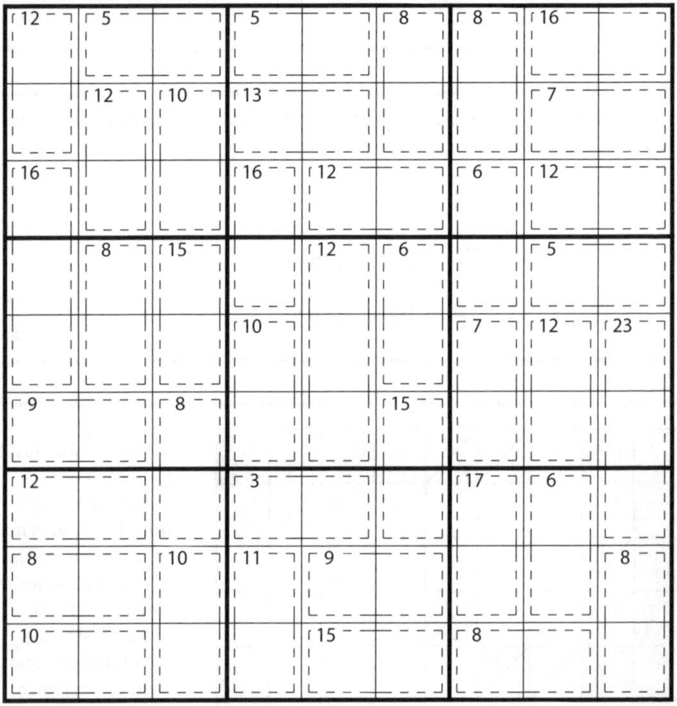
12 5 5 8 8 16
12 10 13 7
16 16 12 6 12
8 15 12 6 5
10 7 12 23
9 8 15
12 3 17 6
8 10 11 9 8
10 15 8

Brain landmarks: the thalamus

The thalamus is a relay station, part of the subcortex. Nearly all sensory information passes through here before entering the cortex. The exception is olfactory (smell) information, which enters the cortex directly.

2

LONG > BONG > BONE > BINE > BITE > KITE

3

For each of the three pictures on the left, which of the images on the right would result from rotating the picture in the way shown by the arrow – 90 degrees anti-clockwise, 180 degrees and 90 degrees clockwise respectively?

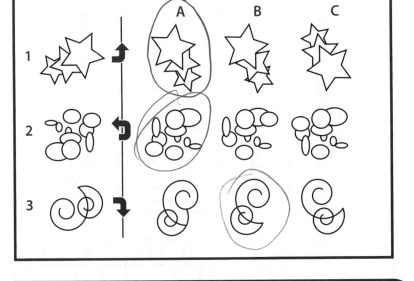

A   B   C

1

2

3

4

Cover up the set of words on the right (in blue). Then spend two minutes looking at the list of word-pairs on the left. Once the time is up, cover the word-pairs instead. See if you can recall each pair when given just one of the two words.

Sudoku	Nurikabe	Preparation
Dominoes	Cards	Twenty
Queen	Ace	Sudoku
Twenty	Seventy	Cards
Back	Forwards	Forwards
Rear	Behind	Ace
Jumping	Squatting	Understand
Practice	Preparation	Jumping
Understand	Digest	Behind

5

8	Multiply by seven	+17	−35	50% of this	+26	×2	30% of this	One third of this	RESULT

56   73   38   19   45   90   27   9

1

6	2	0	0	1	3	6	5
4	4	6	4	4	1	2	3
0	5	1	5	3	3	3	5
0	6	6	2	0	3	1	6
0	4	1	2	4	4	1	0
5	1	5	5	5	2	0	4
3	3	1	6	6	2	2	2

Can you place a full set of dominoes into the grid above, where "0" represents a blank? Each domino will occur exactly once in the finished puzzle.

You can use the chart on the right to keep track of which dominoes you have already placed.

	0	1	2	3	4	5	6
6							
5							
4							
3							
2							
1							
0							

2　LOST 〉 LOST 〉 CALL 〉 CALL 〉 CALL 〉 CALL

3

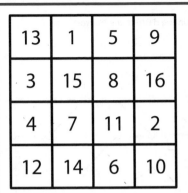

13	1	5	9
3	15	8	16
4	7	11	2
12	14	6	10

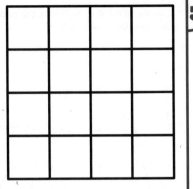

Study this arrangement of the numbers 1 to 16 for no more than two minutes. When your time is up, cover it up and try to redraw it on the blank grid. Look out for patterns that may help you remember.

Brain landmarks: the frontal lobes

The frontal lobes, part of the cortex at the front of the brain, are thought to be responsible for planning of actions, mental scheduling and strategizing, and inhibition of automatic responses.

4

Can you put the results of each of the following rows of sums in ascending order? The first one has been done for you, as an example.

a	b	c	d	e	
1 + 3	2 + 1	3 + 4	7 + 2	1 + 1	ebacd
14 + 12	3 + 7	15 + 14	19 + 3	2 + 40	BDACE
34 x 5	5 x 9	12 x 6	17 x 12	10 x 4	EBCAD
143 - 50	196 - 72	203 - 64	98 - 3	321 - 123	ADBCE

RESULT

5

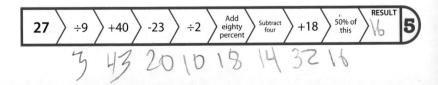

| 27 | ÷9 | +40 | -23 | ÷2 | Add eighty percent | Subtract four | +18 | 50% of this | 16 |

3 43 20 10 18 14 32 16

1 Can you reflect all of the lines in this grid in the dashed-line "mirror" that runs down the middle?

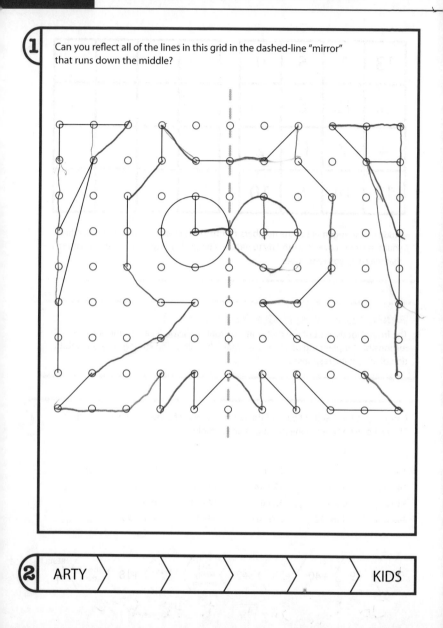

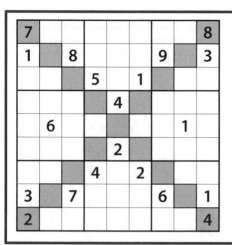

3

Sudoku-X adds one extra rule to a traditional Sudoku puzzle: not only must you place the numbers 1 to 9 into each row, column and bold-lined 3x3 box, but also into each of the two main diagonals (shaded on the puzzle).

The importance of forgetting

Although there are memory champions and people with extraordinary memories, all of us forget things fairly regularly. It can't be avoided. Forgetting is a normal part of life. It is built into the way our memories work for a reason; imagine how impossible thinking would be if you could not clear out old thoughts or if once you'd learnt something you could never alter the way you thought about it, or change your perspective about it.

4

Can you match each of the following words with one other in order to form a synonym pair? Each word must be used in precisely one pair.

pleased	executing	apparent
joyful	obliged	performing
willing	happy	deducting
blithe	seeming	taking

5

17	+53	80% of this	1/2 of this	50% of this	×7	-20	÷3	×2	RESULT

70 56 28 14 98 78 26 52

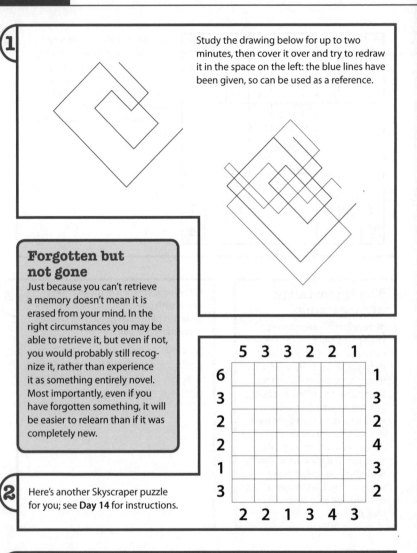

1 Study the drawing below for up to two minutes, then cover it over and try to redraw it in the space on the left: the blue lines have been given, so can be used as a reference.

Forgotten but not gone

Just because you can't retrieve a memory doesn't mean it is erased from your mind. In the right circumstances you may be able to retrieve it, but even if not, you would probably still recognize it, rather than experience it as something entirely novel. Most importantly, even if you have forgotten something, it will be easier to relearn than if it was completely new.

2 Here's another Skyscraper puzzle for you; see **Day 14** for instructions.

	5	3	3	2	2	1	
6							1
3							3
2							2
2							4
1							3
3							2
	2	2	1	3	4	3	

3 MOST > HOST > POST > POSS > PISS > PIGS

4

Four people have popped out to buy just one item each at different food stores. Can you work out who bought what item where?

- Neither woman went to Rapidbuy or Fastmart.
- Sandra did not buy the milk or tomatoes.
- Fastmart sold the marzipan, but not to Tom.
- Neither the tortilla chips nor the tomatoes were bought in Quickstop.

Person	Store	Purchase

People:
Sandra, Sophie, Tom, Tony

Stores:
Fastmart, Quickstop, Rapidbuy, Speedyshop

Purchase:
Marzipan, Milk, Tomatoes, Tortilla Chips

You might find this chart helpful when completing this puzzle – place ticks and crosses to indicate what you have deduced.

		Store				Purchase			
		Fastmart	Quickstop	Rapidbuy	Speedyshop	Marzipan	Milk	Tomatoes	Tortilla Chips
Person	Sandra								
	Sophie								
	Tom								
	Tony								
Purchase	Marzipan								
	Milk								
	Tomatoes								
	Tortilla Chips								

The art of sudoku

In November 2004 *The Times* published its first Sudoku puzzle, kick-starting a worldwide phenomenon. Sudoku puzzles have since appeared in almost every newspaper and magazine, rivalling and even surpassing crosswords for popularity. Sudoku requires no common language skills or general world knowledge, and – despite surface appearances – absolutely no mathematics. The beauty of Sudoku stems from its incredible simplicity. Placing the numbers 1 to 9 into each row, column and 3x3 box may sound like a simple task, but this lack of apparent complexity conceals an incredible depth of logic.

Anyone can solve a Sudoku puzzle if they spend long enough on it, particularly if they are willing to make a few guesses. But Sudoku should never require guesswork, and the best players can conquer almost any puzzle in under ten minutes. So how do they do this? Solving Sudoku efficiently is a good test of not just logic but also your memory and visual processing: remember the numbers you are placing and see what effect they have on the rest of the grid, and practise scanning regions quickly so you can eyeball missing digits instantly.

Make sure you consider rows, columns and boxes equally, looking out for regions which are nearly full and targeting these first, as well as numbers which are already placed frequently in the grid. A common temptation is to write in all possible candidates for each square, filling the grid with small "pencilled-in" numbers. Unfortunately this typically leads to information overload, obscuring key facts – it's much better to reserve note-taking in the grid for those numbers and regions most likely to provide progress – at least until you get completely stuck! For example, try only making pencilmarks for numbers with just two or perhaps three possible fits in a region.

» Hidden singles Sudoku puzzles vary significantly in difficulty, but all puzzles require one simple solving ability: searching each row, column and 3x3 box for numbers which aren't yet in that region but can fit in only a single square, and therefore must be placed there. Sudoku fans call this method "hidden singles", and it is the most basic – and intuitive – of solving techniques. The vast majority of puzzles have a few such deductions you can make right away, so look for these before resorting to the more complex techniques below.

» Region intersections Pick any row or column and overlapping 3x3 box, and you'll see three intersecting squares. This overlap is often the key to solving Sudoku, since any number which occurs only in that overlap for one of the two regions can be eliminated from the other. This is because we can't repeat a digit in a region. Limiting the number of pencilmarks typically makes it much easier to spot intersections.

» Naked singles A naked single is a square where only one number can fit. As such, they're logically very simple but can be extremely difficult to spot, unless you actually do go ahead and write all possible pencilmarks in. Unfortunately many published Sudoku come from poor-quality computer generators which consider naked singles easy to find, based on their logical simplicity, which is generally not true for a human solver. A good tip is to only buy Sudoku books and magazines from named authors who typically provide fairer difficulty ratings.

» Naked sets One technique which instantly makes almost any puzzle more difficult is that of naked sets. This technique involves finding a set of 2, 3 or occasionally 4 squares in a region which can contain only that number of different digits – these digits can then be eliminated from the rest of the region they are in, since they must go in these squares. Naked pairs are by far the most common type of naked set.

» Hidden sets These are the logical inverse of naked sets, and are much harder to spot. They require you to find 2, 3 or (extremely rarely) 4 different digits in that number of squares in a region which do not occur anywhere else in that region – any other candidates in those squares can then be eliminated.

Check out *The Logic of Sudoku* (see Resources section) or the website www.sudopedia.org for descriptions of further solving methods.

1 By choosing one number from each ring of this dartboard, can you find three segments whose values add up to a total of 80? And can you do the same thing for a total of 65?

For example, to reach a total of 34 you would take 13 from the outer ring, 8 from the middle ring and 13 from the inner ring.

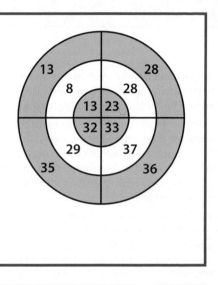

Rice: a distant cousin

Humans have an estimated 22,000 genes – the same number as a rat and about 60% of the number of genes in rice. Evidently something more than just the number of genes is responsible for our wonderful brains.

2 Can you draw three straight lines in order to divide this box into five separate regions, each containing one of each type of shape?

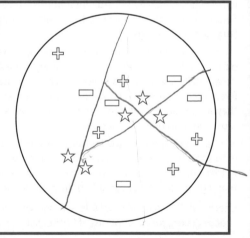

3 LAND 〉   〉   〉   〉 HOGS

4

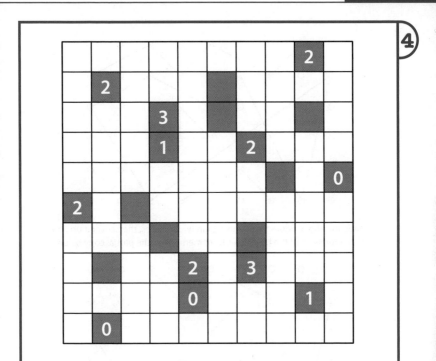

Here is another Light Up puzzle for you to try. See **Day 11** for instructions.

Brain landmarks: the cerebellum

The cerebellum, an ancient and still mysterious structure at the rear and base of the brain, seems to be involved in many motor, sensory and cognitive functions; it contains around half the cells in the brain.

29	+39	-8	1/2 of this	÷10	×5	÷3	Multiply by two	90% of this	RESULT
	68	60	30	3	15	5	10	9	9

5

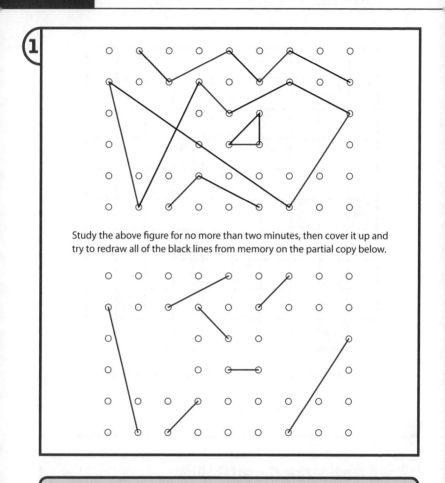

Study the above figure for no more than two minutes, then cover it up and try to redraw all of the black lines from memory on the partial copy below.

Fact: Our closest relatives in the animal world are chimpanzees, followed by the other apes and monkeys. After them, our next nearest branches in the extended family tree are the rodents: tree shrews, rabbits and ordinary mice and rats.

2 CORE ⟩ ⟩ ⟩ ⟩ SUMS

3

In this Kakuro puzzle, fill in each white square with a digit from 1 to 9, such that each horizontal run of consecutive blank squares adds up to the total to the left of that run, and each vertical run of consecutive white squares adds up to the total directly above that run.

No number can be used more than once in any run.

4

For each of the three pictures above the line, which of the images below would result from reflecting the picture in the horizontal line "mirror"?

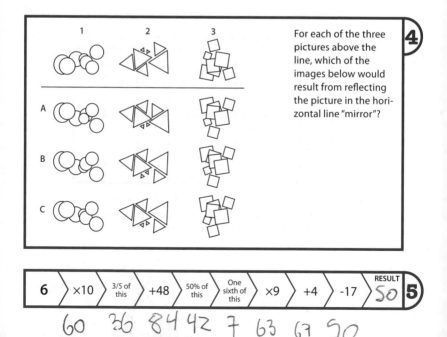

5

6	×10	3/5 of this	+48	50% of this	One sixth of this	×9	+4	-17	RESULT

60   36   84   42   7   63   67   50

1

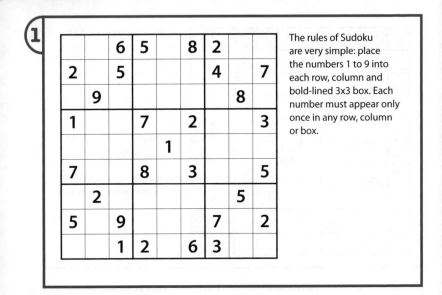

		6	5		8	2		
2		5				4		7
	9						8	
1			7		2			3
				1				
7			8		3			5
	2						5	
5		9				7		2
		1	2		6	3		

The rules of Sudoku are very simple: place the numbers 1 to 9 into each row, column and bold-lined 3x3 box. Each number must appear only once in any row, column or box.

2

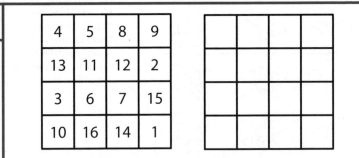

4	5	8	9
13	11	12	2
3	6	7	15
10	16	14	1

Study this arrangement of the numbers 1 to 16 for no more than two minutes. When your time is up, cover it over and try to redraw it on the blank grid. Look out for patterns that may help you remember.

3   FIRE 〉 〉 〉 〉 COWS

By cracking the code, can you complete this crossword grid? Each of the 26 letters of the alphabet has a different numerical value, which you can write down in the box at the bottom once you've worked it out. Start by examining the "I", "U" and "X". As you allocate each letter to a number, cross the letter off the list running down the side of the grid.

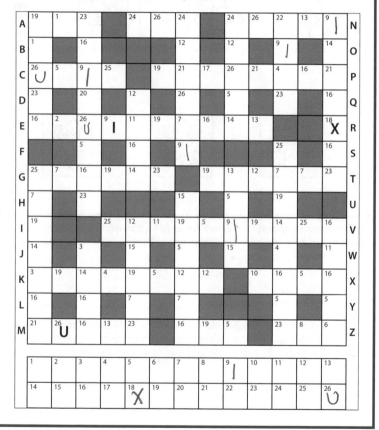

	1	2	3	4	5	6	7	8	9 I	10	11	12	13
	14	15	16	17	18 X	19	20	21	22	23	24	25	26 U

1 These three boxes follow a visual progression. Which of the three lettered options should come fourth in the sequence?

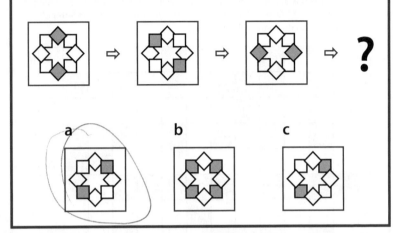

a   b   c

2 » If this year is a leap year, and I ask a friend to pick a truly random date from this entire calendar year, what is the likelihood that she picks a date in the two months of June or July?

» In my garden I have an L-shaped plot which I wish to build a fence around. The plot consists of a 5m square with a cut-out corner that is 1m square. If I can place fence posts no more than 2m apart, what is the minimum number of fence posts I require?

3 DOWN 〉   〉   〉   〉 TIME

④

Here is another Killer Sudoku. For instructions, see **Day 2**.

Electrical brainstorming

American physician Roberts Bartholow was the first to directly show that electrical activity on the surface of the brain controlled the body. In 1874, Bartholow was able to provoke movements of the body and limbs of patient Mary Rafferty by inserting electrodes through a hole in her skull.

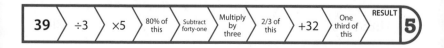

| 39 | ÷3 | ×5 | 80% of this | Subtract forty-one | Multiply by three | 2/3 of this | +32 | One third of this | RESULT |

1 Three boys visited the market to buy a bag of fruit or vegetables. Can you work out what each boy bought, and how much it weighed? Try to do so without making notes.

» Jim did not buy the lightest bag.

» The apples weighed twice as much as the bananas.

» The potatoes were the heaviest item.

» Jim and Bill's purchases weighed as much together as Doug's six kilogram bag did on its own.

2

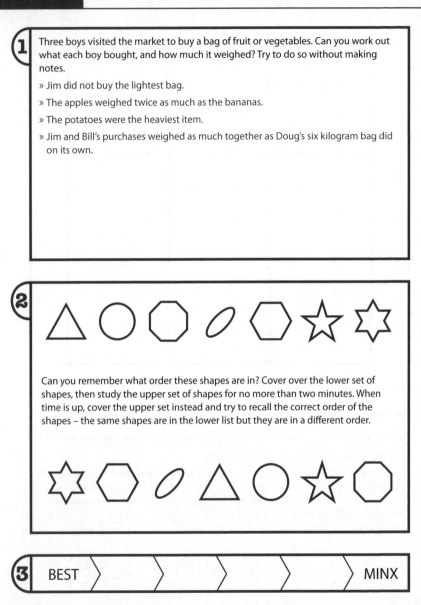

Can you remember what order these shapes are in? Cover over the lower set of shapes, then study the upper set of shapes for no more than two minutes. When time is up, cover the upper set instead and try to recall the correct order of the shapes – the same shapes are in the lower list but they are in a different order.

3 BEST 〉 〉 〉 〉 MINX

1					4
	3				
			3		
3		6			
	1		3		3

To solve this Nurikabe, shade in certain squares so that every given number in the puzzle remains as part of a continuous unshaded area of the stated number of squares. There can be only one number per unshaded area. Shaded squares cannot form any solid 2x2 (or larger) areas, and together all the shaded squares must form one single continuous area. White areas cannot touch each other in either a horizontal or vertical direction.

4

Maps in the brain

In 1951 Wilder Penfield demonstrated that sensations from the body are represented by your brain in an ordered map, so that feelings from adjacent body parts are processed by adjacent brain parts. This body map in the brain is also intelligently distorted, so that more space is devoted to the most sensitive parts of the body, such as the hands and lips.

You can't tell the diffence between two fingers pressed on the middle of your back four centimetres apart and just one finger pressed there, but you can tell the difference between two pins pressed four millimeters apart in the middle of your palm. That's because even though your palm is smaller, it has far more neural territory devoted to its sensations. Should you try this out, it will make a difference whether you do it across the mid-line (the spine) or place the fingers vertically, one above the other.

More recent experiments have shown that this body map is constantly adjusting depending on the inputs it receives. If you lose a finger, the part of the map devoted to representing that finger is taken over by neighbouring fingers. If you practise the piano, the finger parts of the map initially enlarge, and then grow more sensitive, resolving a higher degree of detail than before. Maps have been found in all parts of the brain, representing everything from visual motion to auditory tones to complex limb movements. As we practise a particular skill these maps refine and grow to create the necessary neural resources needed to support the detailed perception and skilled behaviour required.

| 40 | +12 | -7 | ÷5 | 1/3 of this | ×11 | +62 | 80% of this | ÷2 | RESULT **5** |

1

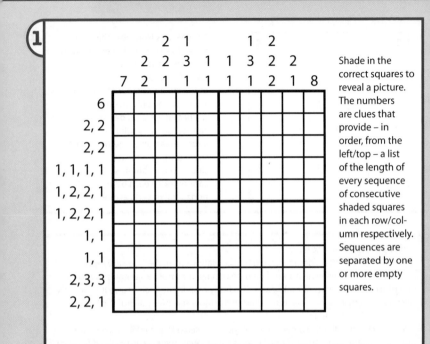

Shade in the correct squares to reveal a picture. The numbers are clues that provide – in order, from the left/top – a list of the length of every sequence of consecutive shaded squares in each row/column respectively. Sequences are separated by one or more empty squares.

2 How many words of three or more letters can you find in this word wheel? Each word must contain the centre letter, plus any selection of the other letters no more than once each.

3

45 − 19 = ☐   156 ÷ 3 = ☐   57 + 28 = ☐

18 ÷ 6 = ☐   86 − 9 = ☐   108 ÷ 4 = ☐

8 × 11 = ☐   18 + 53 = ☐   192 ÷ 6 = ☐

2:50a.m. to 3:35a.m. = ☐ : ☐   2:45a.m. to 10:45p.m. = ☐ : ☐

7:15a.m. to 9:45a.m. = ☐ : ☐   5:30a.m. to 10:05a.m. = ☐ : ☐

6:55a.m. to 8:40p.m. = ☐ : ☐   4:10a.m. to 11:10p.m. = ☐ : ☐

£3570 − £2 = ☐   £445 + £3270 = ☐

£40700 − £404 = ☐   £95 + £190 = ☐

£9400 − £600 = ☐   £222 − £3.52 = ☐

4

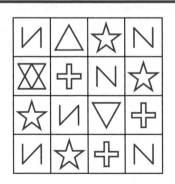

Spend no more than two minutes studying this grid of shapes, then cover it and redraw it as accurately as you can in the empty grid to the right.

1 Can you find the missing word that will complete the sentence? Each one is an anagram of the word in CAPITAL letters.

1. The MEDICATED insects still _____ the crop.

2. The _____ were STATIONED at the clinic.

3. This was a place for the _____ , not an appointed SELECTOR.

4. The Christmas TINSEL lay _____ on the tree.

Thinking habits: Descartes

René Descartes was one of history's great geniuses and was said to be very fond of lying in bed until the afternoon. He apparently came up with the idea of x and y co-ordinates while looking up at a spider on the square ceiling above his bed. He died in 1650: after getting up early in the morning to give the Queen of Sweden philosophy lessons, he caught a cold from which he never recovered.

2 Can you put the results of each of the following rows of sums in ascending order? You will almost certainly find it easiest to estimate some of the values, rather than calculate them all. The first one has been done for you, as an example.

a	b	c	d	e	
1 + 3	2 + 1	3 + 4	7 + 2	1 + 1	ebacd
73 x 3	99 x 3	54 x 5	66 x 6	23 x 20	_____
1458 + 2845	3501 + 7435	9634 + 974	1584 + 2567	8743 + 2304	_____
1.5 x 70	2.5 x 35	2.2 x 90	3 x 40	5 x 5.5	_____

3 HOME ⟩ ⟩ ⟩ ⟩ FARM

4

				1				
		8				5		
		3		2				
7								4
		4				3		
5								6
		6		4				
		7				9		
			8					

Sudoku Extra Regions adds, as its name suggests, extra regions to a traditional Sudoku puzzle. You must place the numbers 1 to 9 not only into each row, column and bold-lined 3x3 box, but also into each of the four shaded areas.

Learning for tests

When checking your memory for things you might be tested on, keep studying until you have recalled each item successfully more than once. To be able to recall something just once is no guarantee that you'll be able to do it again.

82	Divide by two	+16	-51	Multiply by thirteen	+50%	-25	1/2 of this	Add forty-eight	RESULT 5

1 Study this picture for up to two minutes, then cover it over and try to redraw it below. The blue square is already given so can be used as a reference.

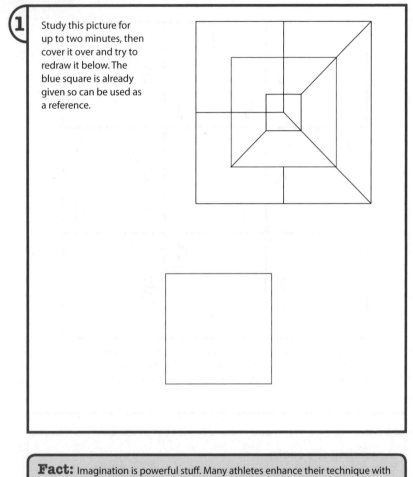

Fact: Imagination is powerful stuff. Many athletes enhance their technique with visualization training, and research has shown that mental practice can improve skills in many of the same ways as real physical practice.

2 LOCH 〉 〉 〉 〉 GATE

3

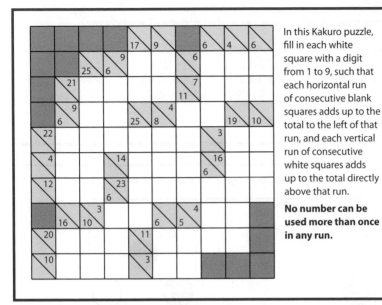

In this Kakuro puzzle, fill in each white square with a digit from 1 to 9, such that each horizontal run of consecutive blank squares adds up to the total to the left of that run, and each vertical run of consecutive white squares adds up to the total directly above that run.

No number can be used more than once in any run.

4

Using each of the following numbers and signs only once, can you reach a total of 619?

1	2	3	7	25	100
+	-	-	×	×	

You can use as many brackets as you like – for example given 1, 2, 2, 3, + and × you could have (2+2) × (1+3) for a total of 16.

72 ÷4 | 50% of this | ×11 | 1/3 of this | +75 | Subtract ninety-seven | ×16 | ÷11 | **RESULT** **5**

1 How many pairs of anagrams can you find among the following words?

MEDITATES   FURNISHED   ESTIMATED   UNRELATED
PADDOCKED   ELECTRIFY   REPEALING   FLASHIEST
SUCTIONED   RELATIVES   UNALTERED   SIGNATORY
GYRATIONS   SEDUCTION   FAITHLESS   VERSATILE

2 Here is another Masyu for you to try. For instructions, see **Day 8**.

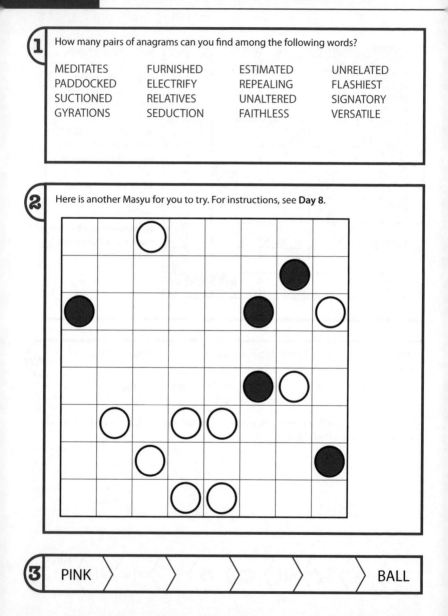

3 PINK 〉   〉   〉   〉 BALL

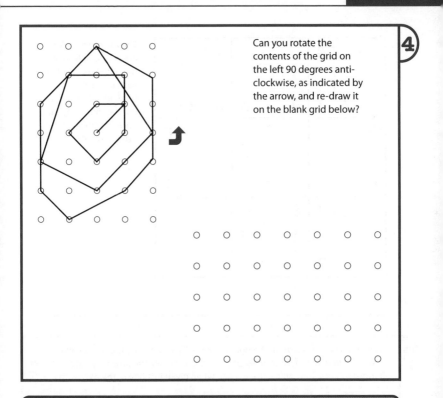

Can you rotate the contents of the grid on the left 90 degrees anti-clockwise, as indicated by the arrow, and re-draw it on the blank grid below?

Varied learning

You may have heard about "visual learners" and "auditory learners" and the differences between them. Or maybe that people are either sensers, intuitors, thinkers or feelers. The truth is that everybody learns differently, and finding a learning style that is good for you is important work. Unfortunately, there's no system that works unerringly for everyone, and none that can be proven to improve teaching more than any of the others. That is, it is important for teachers to vary their style of teaching, but there is no fixed set of rules on how they should do this.

| 36 | ÷3 | ×4 | One half of this | Divide by four | Add sixty-eight | 50% of this | -20 | +32 | RESULT |

1

		4				7		
			7		8			
	7	1	4		5	3	2	
5				4				8
6				3				1
	2	7	8		6	4	3	
			1		3			
		3				8		

The rules of Sudoku are very simple: place the numbers 1 to 9 into each row, column and bold-lined 3x3 box. Each number must appear only once in any row, column or box.

2 Cover up the set of words on the right (in blue). Then spend no more than two minutes looking at the list of word-pairs on the left. Once the time is up, cover the left set instead. See if you can recall each pair when given just one of the two words.

Apple	Kiwi	Pliable
Allude	Refer	Odour
Yes	Agreement	Sienna
Donkey	Zebra	Refer
Yellow	Sienna	Yes
Halitosis	Odour	Donkey
Congruity	Sense	Apple
Pliable	Editable	Congruity

3 PLAY ⟩   ⟩   ⟩   ⟩ TENT

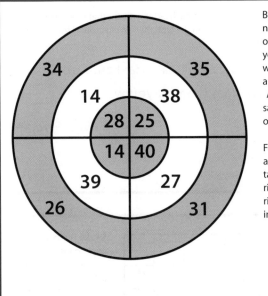

By choosing exactly one number from each ring of this dartboard, can you find three segments whose values add up to a total of 100?
And can you do the same thing for a total of 75?

For example, to reach a total of 65 you would take 26 from the outer ring, 14 from the middle ring and 25 from the inner ring.

④

Technology and IQ

Many people worry that modern technology is making us more stupid. With computers that check our spelling for us and sat navs which can guide us around town, it's clear that some basic skills are being made easier by technology. What isn't clear is whether we are getting any less intelligent overall. But this is nothing new. Throughout history, people have always worried about the effects of new technology on our minds. In the fourth century BC the philosopher Plato wrote about the negative effects that writing would have on people's memories and moral character, and in the seventeenth century, when printed books and journals first became popular in England, there were complaints about the "sullen silence" that overtook coffee houses, and fears that people would forget how to socialize by talking to each other.

| 67 | Add fifty-four | -90 | Multiply by six | -17 | ÷13 | Add sixty-three | 1/2 of this | +50% | RESULT ⑤ |

1 Try decoding this quotation by replacing each letter with another one a fixed number of places forwards/backwards in the alphabet. (Wrap around from Z to A or from A to Z when counting.)

Whh iu heba E'ra swjpaz pk xa okiaxkzu. Xqp E oaa

jks E odkqhz dwra xaaj ikna olayebey.

Fwja Swcjan

2

Sikaku is a Japanese shape-placing number puzzle with just one simple aim: draw rectangles on the existing grid lines so that each square in the grid ends up in exactly one rectangle, and so that each rectangle contains precisely one number. The number inside each rectangle must be equal to the number of grid squares inside that rectangle.

3 RAVE ⟩ ⟩ ⟩ ⟩ GIRL

4

Which of the jigsaw pieces below can be assembled together to make the image at the top? You may not overlap pieces, but they may be rotated if necessary. Shade in the pieces that are not needed.

| 100 | ÷2 | 1/2 of this | Add sixty-four | Subtract forty-five | +48 | Subtract forty-six | 50% of this | ×7 | RESULT **5** |

The ageing brain

It is perfectly possible to get to the age of 100 with a fully healthy brain. Although many older people suffer brain injuries from strokes, or diffuse damage due to **dementia**, this doesn't happen to everyone. Even though the plasticity of the brain reduces in old age, at every age we can learn new facts and learn to do new things.

Most excitingly, research has shown that it is possible to prepare your brain for a healthy old age. You can prevent or slow a decline in your mental sharpness by establishing the learning habit early and keeping it up as you get older. Lots of research into mental function in old age focuses on dementia, which is obviously a very serious form of cognitive decline. Dementia affects a high proportion of the very old, but those with the most education and those with intellectually challenging jobs are the most likely to avoid it. A 2007 study of twins, who shared the same genes and family background, demonstrated that if one twin of a pair went to university they were less likely to suffer from dementia than the twin who didn't, suggesting that education genuinely helps, and is not just a spurious prejudicial association due to wealth or class.

Physical activity also has a significant protective effect against mental decline in old age. It doesn't matter how old you start, exercising will help keep you mentally fit. The strongest benefit is for those who exercise in their youth and keep active. Exercise helps build and maintain a healthy blood supply to the brain, which ensures the basic fuels of sugar and oxygen. Exercise reduces your risk of stroke, which can obviously have a severe effect on your mental faculties. For this reason, treating **hypertension** early is a major factor for keeping an older brain healthy.

On a related note, stress also appears to contribute to the risk of dementia. One study found that those with a susceptibility to distress were twice as likely to suffer from **Alzheimer's disease**. Our earlier lives are an important preparation for maintaining a healthy brain in older age. We know that an active, socially and intellectually engaged youth leads to a denser and richer set of neuronal connections. In old age, these rich connections offer protection against the injuries and general deterioration of the brain. In effect, by training your brain when you are young, you build up cognitive resources that will make your brain resilient in old age.

It is never too late to start, however. Brain training, and other forms of mental activity, have benefits when practised in old age. As with brain training when young, it is difficult to find single activities which have **far transfer** – a range of multiple benefits – across a wide range of cognitive abilities, and the advantages of brain training often disappear if the exercise is not kept up.

One promising study found that older people who played a **strategy videogame** for just 24 hours spread across 8 weeks had improved their planning and scheduling abilities, something that is particularly vulnerable to decline in old age. Another approach to brain training in old age is to build up a well-rounded programme that engages you physically and socially, not just intellectually. The benefit of this holistic approach is that it is easier to make the activities intrinsically rewarding.

Motivation is very important for any brain training programme. Even if we could train our brains by spending two hours a day doing a boring computer training task, most people simply wouldn't be able to find the motivation to do it. An activity programme that involves meeting people and learning meaningful skills, such as crafts, is much more likely to keep people involved and hence training their brains.

It is probably for this reason that one study found that the following activities were best for avoiding dementia in old age: reading, playing board games, practising musical instruments, and dancing. All of these are intellectually stimulating. All (apart from reading) involve social contact and physical activity. And, furthermore, they are fun.

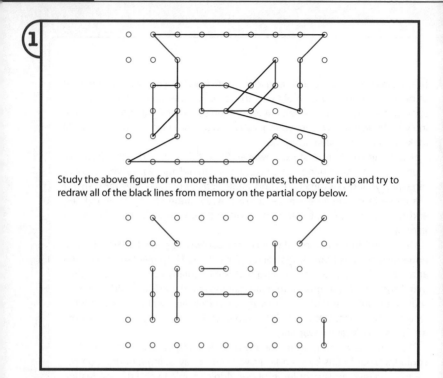

1 Study the above figure for no more than two minutes, then cover it up and try to redraw all of the black lines from memory on the partial copy below.

2 What number should come next in each of these three separate mathematical progressions?

243	81	27	9	3		____
161	144	127	110	93		____
1	2	2	4	8	32	____

3 BARE ＞ ＞ ＞ ＞ DESK

Here is another Kakuro puzzle for you to try. See **Day 4** for instructions.

| 85 | -21 | ÷2 | One half of this | +90 | 50% of this | -10 | ×2 | +16 | **RESULT** 5 |

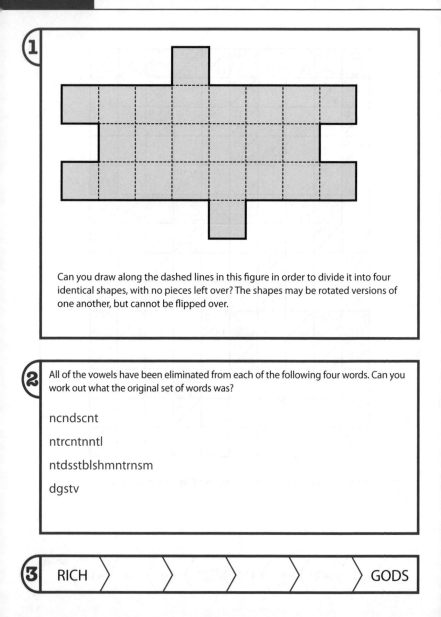

1

Can you draw along the dashed lines in this figure in order to divide it into four identical shapes, with no pieces left over? The shapes may be rotated versions of one another, but cannot be flipped over.

2 All of the vowels have been eliminated from each of the following four words. Can you work out what the original set of words was?

ncndscnt

ntrcntnntl

ntdsstblshmntrnsm

dgstv

3 RICH 〉 〉 〉 〉 GODS

④

In Killer Sudoku, as in regular Sudoku, the aim is to place the digits 1 to 9 into each row, column and bold-lined 3x3 rectangle.

Additionally, place digits so that the total of each dashed-line cage is the value given at the top-left of that cage. Digits may *not* be repeated within a cage.

The extended mind hypothesis

The "extended mind hypothesis" is the idea that we utilize objects in the world as part of our thinking – not as abstracted, separate entities. The mind and the environment act as a "coupled system". One simple example might be the act of leaving your keys by the door so you notice them before you leave.

| 42 | Fifty percent of this | Divide by seven | ×9 | +61 | -31 | +67 | ÷2 | 1/2 of this | RESULT **5** |

1

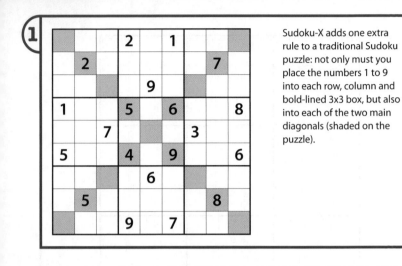

Sudoku-X adds one extra rule to a traditional Sudoku puzzle: not only must you place the numbers 1 to 9 into each row, column and bold-lined 3x3 box, but also into each of the two main diagonals (shaded on the puzzle).

2

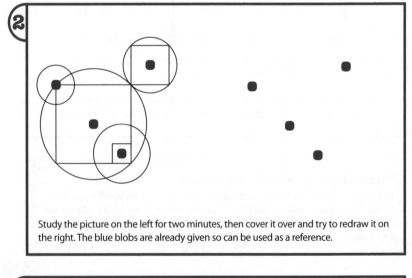

Study the picture on the left for two minutes, then cover it over and try to redraw it on the right. The blue blobs are already given so can be used as a reference.

3 BLUE 〉 〉 〉 〉 MOAT

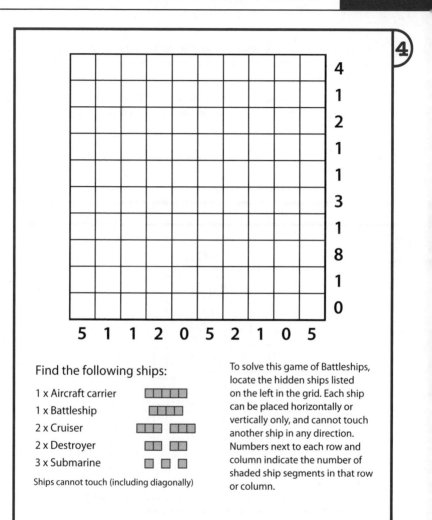

4

Grid column totals (bottom): 5 1 1 2 0 5 2 1 0 5

Grid row totals (right): 4 1 2 1 1 3 1 8 1 0

Find the following ships:

1 x Aircraft carrier
1 x Battleship
2 x Cruiser
2 x Destroyer
3 x Submarine

Ships cannot touch (including diagonally)

To solve this game of Battleships, locate the hidden ships listed on the left in the grid. Each ship can be placed horizontally or vertically only, and cannot touch another ship in any direction. Numbers next to each row and column indicate the number of shaded ship segments in that row or column.

| 9 | Multiply by eleven | -4 | -60% | ×3 | +49 | -6 | +7 | ÷2 | RESULT 5 |

1

How good are you at remembering related words? Study this set of words for no more than two minutes, then cover it over and see how many you can recall correctly.

| Rose | Turquoise | Burgundy | Cyan | Amethyst |
| Cream | Peach | Magnolia | Khaki | Navy |

2

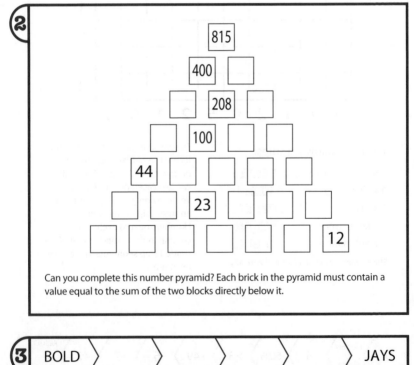

Can you complete this number pyramid? Each brick in the pyramid must contain a value equal to the sum of the two blocks directly below it.

3 BOLD ⟩ ⟩ ⟩ ⟩ JAYS

Brain landmarks: the basal ganglia

The basal ganglia, a group of subcortical brain nuclei, are responsible for learning and executing sequences of actions, especially those that have been practised, so that they become automatic.

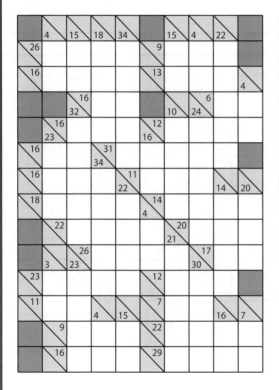

4

In this Kakuro puzzle, fill in each white square with a digit from 1 to 9, so that each horizontal run of consecutive blank squares adds up to the total to the left of that run, and each vertical run of consecutive white squares adds up to the total directly above that run.

No number can be used more than once in any run.

95 〉 3/5 of this 〉 ÷3 〉 Add fifty-eight 〉 −37 〉 ×4 〉 20% of this 〉 5/8 of this 〉 +45% 〉 **RESULT** **5**

1 Delete one letter from each pair in order to reveal a word. For example, deleting B and C from "AB CT" would give the word "AT".

AU	MN	EF	AE	IO	RS			_____
ST	PW	IU	SM	ST	AE	MD		_____
PR	AI	MN	MN	AE	CD	LM	AE	_____

2 Three of the "shape nets" below fold up into identical cubes, while the fourth is slightly different. Which shape net is the odd one out?

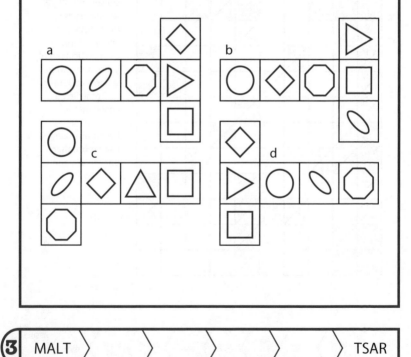

3 MALT 〉 〉 〉 〉 TSAR

4

The aim of Yajilin is to draw a single loop using only horizontal and vertical lines so that the loop does not pass through any square more than once.

  Any squares which the loop does not visit must be shaded, but no two of these shaded squares can touch in either a horizontal or vertical direction.

  Numbers with arrows indicate the exact number of shaded squares in a given direction in a specific row or column, but not all shaded squares are necessarily identified with arrows.

The growth of the human brain

The explosion in human brain size began about two million years ago. Since then our brain has evolved, growing to over twice the size of the brain of our earliest human ancestors.

73	−49	−25%	1/2 of this	√	×15	Sixty percent of this	Multiply by five	−79	RESULT
									5

1

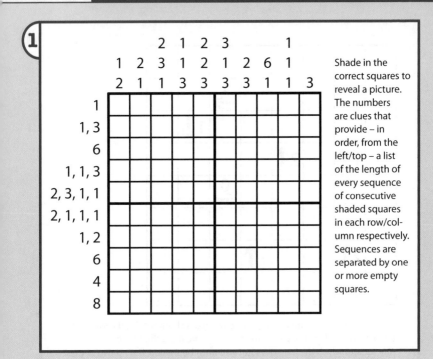

Shade in the correct squares to reveal a picture. The numbers are clues that provide – in order, from the left/top – a list of the length of every sequence of consecutive shaded squares in each row/column respectively. Sequences are separated by one or more empty squares.

2 How many words of three or more letters can you find in this word wheel? Each word must contain the centre letter, plus any selection of the other letters no more than once each.

3

$88 - 7 =$ ☐ $29 + 26 =$ ☐ $156 \div 12 =$ ☐

$49 - 20 =$ ☐ $24 - 21 =$ ☐ $8 \div 2 =$ ☐

$24 + 83 =$ ☐ $8 \times 11 =$ ☐ $93 - 20 =$ ☐

10:30a.m. to 8:00p.m. = ☐ : ☐   1:40a.m. to 12:05p.m. = ☐ : ☐

10:05a.m. to 4:30p.m. = ☐ : ☐   7:35a.m. to 2:20p.m. = ☐ : ☐

7:00a.m. to 10:20a.m. = ☐ : ☐   9:10a.m. to 9:40p.m. = ☐ : ☐

£41.80 + £43600 = ☐   £42 + £1200 = ☐

£800 − £630 = ☐   £37800+ £319 = ☐

£1750 + £3.42 = ☐   £3340 + £29 = ☐

4

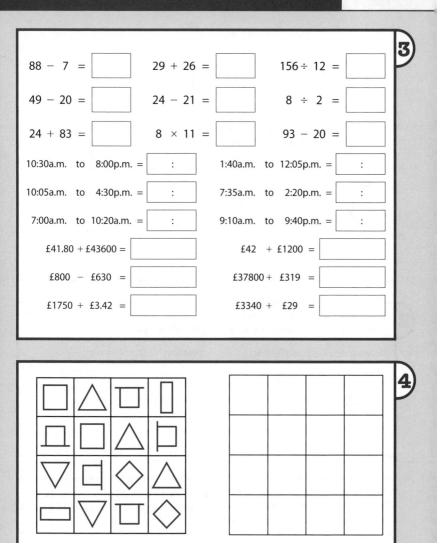

Spend no more than two minutes studying this grid of shapes, then cover it and redraw it as accurately as you can in the empty grid to the right.

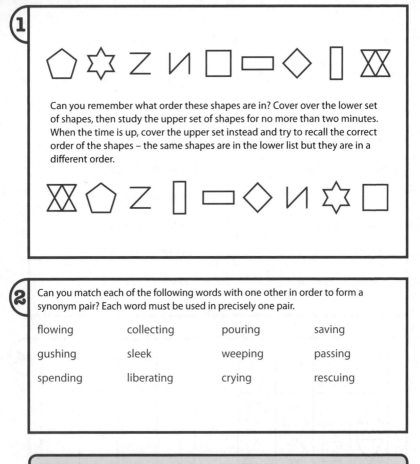

1

Can you remember what order these shapes are in? Cover over the lower set of shapes, then study the upper set of shapes for no more than two minutes. When the time is up, cover the upper set instead and try to recall the correct order of the shapes – the same shapes are in the lower list but they are in a different order.

2 Can you match each of the following words with one other in order to form a synonym pair? Each word must be used in precisely one pair.

flowing	collecting	pouring	saving
gushing	sleek	weeping	passing
spending	liberating	crying	rescuing

Fact: Each brain cell is connected to many others – perhaps an average of 10,000 others. That's over 150,000 kilometres of wiring, enough to stretch around the Earth four times.

3 SKID ⟩ ⟩ ⟩ ⟩ PARK

④

Toroidal Sudoku is a devious twist on a regular Sudoku puzzle, replacing each of the 3x3 boxes with jigsaw-shaped regions which wrap around the edges of the puzzle.

Where a region flows off the side of the puzzle it continues in the square directly opposite in the same row or column. Can you place the numbers 1 to 9 into each row, column and toroidal region? You may find it helpful to start by shading each region with a different colour.

| 31 | -12 | Multiply by seven | Add fifty-one | ÷2 | 50% of this | 1/2 of this | ×5 | -34 | RESULT 5 |

1

14	21	4	20	15
22	1	5	2	23
10	11	7	9	8
18	12	3	13	24
17	19	6	25	16

Study this arrangement of the numbers 1 to 25 for no more than two minutes. When the time is up, cover it over and try to redraw it on the blank grid. Look out for patterns that may help you remember.

2

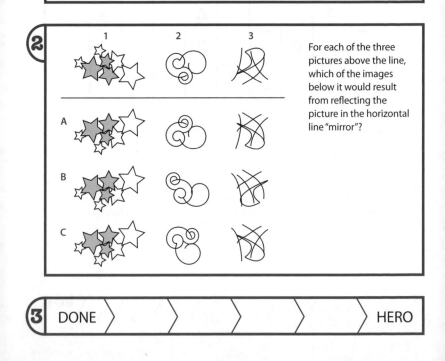

For each of the three pictures above the line, which of the images below it would result from reflecting the picture in the horizontal line "mirror"?

3

DONE 〉 〉 〉 〉 HERO

④

14	10	12	9	9	9	11	15	
							8	
5	7		18			14	6	
		15	22	12			10	6
15	7					6		
		7	11				17	9
9			15			14		
13		11	5	11	14		7	12
10								

Here is another Killer Sudoku for you to try. See **Day 2** if you need a reminder
of the instructions.

Which side are you on?

While many of our abilities rely on both sides of the brain, some appear to have a
relative specialization for one half or the other. Language, for example, seems to rely
most heavily on the left side of most people's brains.

| 89 | -12 | Divide by seven | ×17 | ÷11 | Add fifty-eight | 40% of this | 1/5 of this | ×10 | RESULT 5 |

1 These three boxes follow a visual progression. Which of the three lettered options should come fourth in the sequence?

a   **b**   **c**

2 Can you find an anagram of each of the CAPITALIZED words in order to complete each sentence?

» Hidden in the DRAWERS were the promised _____.

» He was REFINING how to _____ the rules without detection.

» She UNBURDENS herself about how she became _____.

» Posing for the statue, he _____ in the PROUDEST way.

3 YAKS 〉 〉 〉 〉 DUDE

Videogames can be good for you...

Videogames are a form of brain training: studies have shown that playing action videogames increases gamers' ability to pay attention to multiple things at once, and trains them to recover more quickly from distraction.

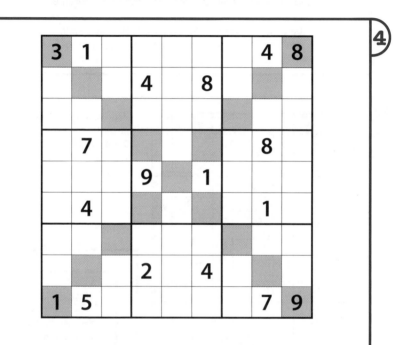

Sudoku-X adds one extra rule to a traditional Sudoku puzzle: you must place the numbers 1 to 9 not only into each row, column and bold-lined 3x3 box, but also into each of the two main diagonals (shaded on the puzzle).

71	-15	÷14	+60	Twenty-five percent of this	3/4 of this	75% of this	×11	Subtract seventy-seven	RESULT
									5

1 Cover over the bottom list of words, and then study the upper list for two minutes. When time is up, uncover the lower list and cover the upper one instead – can you write numbers next to the words in order to rearrange them into their original order?

problem, sliding, football, sunshine, newspaper,
president, economy, crossword, balcony, summertime

balcony, crossword, economy, football, newspaper,
president, problem, sliding, summertime, sunshine

2

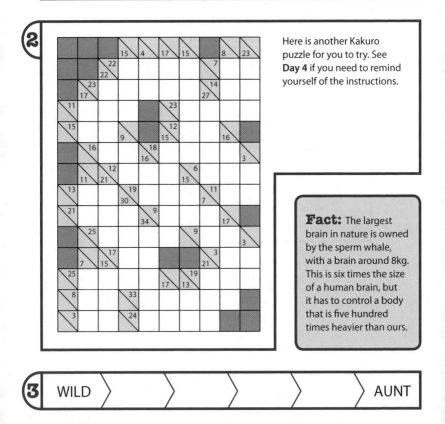

Here is another Kakuro puzzle for you to try. See **Day 4** if you need to remind yourself of the instructions.

Fact: The largest brain in nature is owned by the sperm whale, with a brain around 8kg. This is six times the size of a human brain, but it has to control a body that is five hundred times heavier than ours.

3   WILD 〉　　〉　　〉　　〉 AUNT

Three healthcare professionals are comparing their week's work. Can you work out who does what job, which day of the week they had the most patients, and how many patients that was?

» The optician had twice as many patients on their busiest day as Jane did.

» Peter's busiest day was later in the week than the dentist's.

» Susan did not have the greatest number of patients.

» The professional who saw no more than seven patients in a day did not have their busiest day on Monday.

People: Jane, Peter, Susan
Jobs: Dentist, Doctor, Optician

Busiest day: Monday, Tuesday, Wednesday
Most patients in a day: 7, 14, 18

Job	Person	Day	Patients

You might find the chart on the right helpful when completing this puzzle – place ticks and crosses to indicate what you have deduced.

		Person			Day			Patients		
		Jane	Peter	Susan	Monday	Tuesday	Wednesday	7	14	18
Job	Dentist									
	Doctor									
	Optician									
Patients	7									
	14									
	18									
Day	Monday									
	Tuesday									
	Wednesday									

| 47 | +92 | -18 | ÷11 | -4 | 3/7 of this | ×2 | +98 | 1/4 of this | **RESULT** **5** |

1 Cover over the bottom three rows of words and then spend no more than two minutes looking at the first three rows. When time is up, reveal the lower rows and cover the upper ones instead. Can you spot which word is missing from each of the rows?

Cheese	Salami	Tomato	Bacon	Egg	Beef
Racquet	Net	Umpire	Player	Line	Score
Brisk	Nimble	Hasty	Fleet	Agile	Zoom

Tomato	Egg	Bacon	Salami	Cheese
Net	Racquet	Line	Player	Umpire
Zoom	Agile	Brisk	Nimble	Hasty

2

7								8
2	9						4	5
		2				9		
		8	7	3	9	1		
		5				8		
5	8						3	6
4								9

This Jigsaw Sudoku puzzle works in a very similar way to a regular Sudoku puzzle (see **Day 7**), except that the bold-lined regions are irregular jigsaw shapes rather than squares.

3 SAME 〉 〉 〉 〉 FOOT

By cracking the code, can you complete this crossword grid? Each of the 26 letters of the alphabet has a different numerical value, which you can write down in the box at the bottom once you've worked it out. Start by examining the "N", "W" and "L". As you allocate each letter to a number, cross the letter off the list running down the sides of the grid.

| 55 | ▷ -35 | ▷ +50% | ▷ Eighty percent of this | ▷ ÷6 | ▷ Multiply by sixteen | ▷ -7 | ▷ +33 | ▷ 1/2 of this | ▷ **RESULT** 5 |

A recipe for genius

In Roman myth, "genius" was a guiding spirit or inspiration. Nowadays we use the word to describe extraordinary ability in sports, the arts or science. Genius is more than just incredible talent or expertise. For someone to be described as a genius, they must also have a creative vision, the ability to surprise. "Talent hits a target no one else can hit; genius hits a target no one else can see," said **Schopenhauer**.

For a long time the dominant view of genius was that it was unpredictable, something that affected a few unique individuals who were as different from the rest of us as humans are from monkeys. The good news is that research into geniuses suggests that they are made, not born. The bad news is that what lies behind most geniuses is hard work. And not just a bit of hard work: an extraordinary degree of hard work over many years. The psychologist Benjamin Bloom proposed a **ten thousand hour rule**, named after the amount of practice all true experts seemed to need to achieve mastery in their field. Ten thousand hours is about three hours a day, or twenty hours a week, for ten years. Even child prodigies such as Mozart don't seem to produce the works that win them the accolade genius until they've put in this amount of practice.

Genius may appear innate because the amount of practice required means that it helps to start early. Not only does this mean you have more time to fit your ten thousand hours of it in, but you are also young enough not to have the distractions of adult life to diminish your motivation or fill up your time.

Another ingredient of genius is having a mentor during the development of your skills. Again, child prodigies usually have a tutor, often a parent, who encourages them and guides their practice. Adult geniuses tend to be surrounded by a community of other talented individuals, with whom they can share and develop ideas. What isn't required of a genius is an especially high IQ. One study of chess grand masters, for example, showed that although they had above-average IQs (in the 115–130 range), they weren't as exceptional in IQ terms as their chess ability would imply. A reverse study looked at the achievements of pupils in a high-IQ school in America, where the average pupil had an IQ of 157. Although pupils from this school often went on to be high achievers, there were no Nobel prizes or other significant markers of genius, despite the exceptional rarity of their IQ scores.

Genius is often restricted to a single domain: many of us could probably beat **Tiger Woods** at chess, or **Gary Kasparov** at golf. Looked at like this, genius is as much about a good match between the skills you've practised and things society finds valuable. Learning to read and write fluently probably takes about ten thousand hours: in different times or different cultures the ability to read and write fluently might be regarded as a sign of genius, but here and now it is regarded as commonplace.

Even inventors and creative geniuses may not be that unlike the rest of us. Many great inventions are discovered simultaneously by different people or groups who are unaware of each other. Genius may even just be having more ideas than everyone else, not necessarily better ones. And how do you have more ideas? You've guessed it – by working harder than everyone else.

So the real meaning of genius may not ultimately be that different from that captured by the Roman use of the word. Very few of us are able or willing or curious enough to put in the effort to turn these into something truly remarkable. Those who are have access to some secret of motivation that lets them practise and maintain their focus for long hours after most of us have given up. That may just be the true spirit of genius.

1

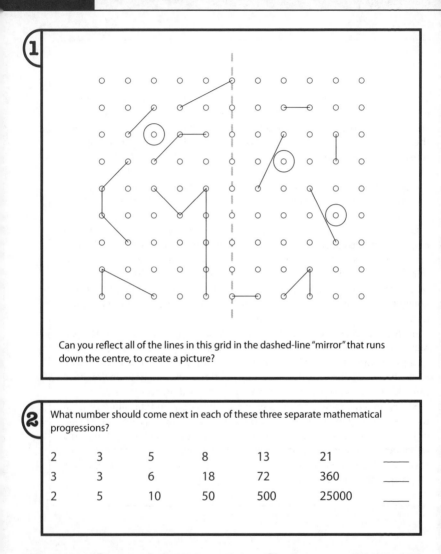

Can you reflect all of the lines in this grid in the dashed-line "mirror" that runs down the centre, to create a picture?

2 What number should come next in each of these three separate mathematical progressions?

2	3	5	8	13	21	____
3	3	6	18	72	360	____
2	5	10	50	500	25000	____

3 NEXT 〉 〉 〉 〉 GONE

4

Killer Sudoku-X brings the diagonal regions of Sudoku-X to Killer Sudoku. In Killer Sudoku-X, the aim is to place the digits 1 to 9 into each row, column and bold-lined 3x3 rectangle, and each of the two main diagonals (shaded).

Additionally, place digits so that the total of each dashed-line cage is the value given at the top-left of that cage. **Digits may not be repeated within a cage.**

| 29 | Add sixty-six | -68 | 2/3 of this | ×7 | ÷6 | Add forty-four | ÷5 | ×12 | RESULT **5** |

1

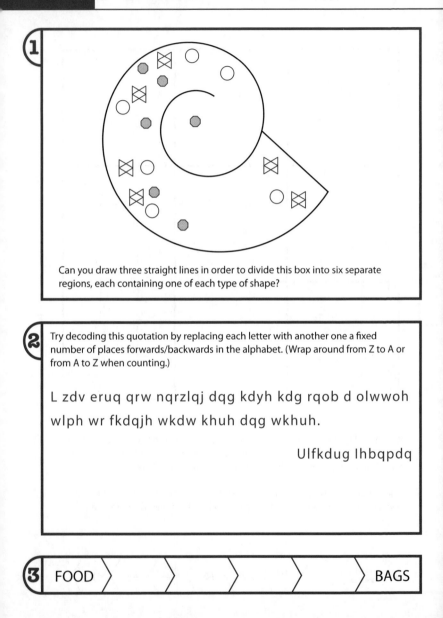

Can you draw three straight lines in order to divide this box into six separate regions, each containing one of each type of shape?

2 Try decoding this quotation by replacing each letter with another one a fixed number of places forwards/backwards in the alphabet. (Wrap around from Z to A or from A to Z when counting.)

L zdv eruq qrw nqrzlqj dqg kdyh kdg rqob d olwwoh wlph wr fkdqjh wkdw khuh dqg wkhuh.

Ulfkdug Ihbqpdq

3 FOOD ⟩ ⟩ ⟩ ⟩ BAGS

4

		8				4		
	6		3	2	7		5	
5								7
			6	1	2			
2								8
			9	8	5			
1								5
	9		8	7	3		6	
		6				9		

Here is another traditional Sudoku. See **Day 7** for instructions.

You need trepanation like you need a hole in your head

Brain injuries are mentioned in the world's first medical text, an ancient Egyptian papyrus manuscript which is around 3700 years old – and which is thought to be based on records that go back a further 1000 years. The oldest surgical procedure for which we have evidence is that of trepanation – drilling or scraping a hole in the skull. The practice is at least 7000 years old and is, rather worryingly, still practised today by a dedicated few, who believe it enhances brain function and mental health.

| 11 | Multiply by eight | 1/2 of this | +80 | 25% of this | Subtract sixteen | +84 | 1/3 of this | -9 | RESULT **5** |

1 By choosing exactly one number from each ring of this dartboard, can you find three segments whose values add up to a total of 111? And can you do the same thing for a total of 66?

For example, to reach a total of 135 you would take 39 from the outer ring, 47 from the middle ring and 49 from the inner ring.

2 How good is your memory for detail? Spend no more than two minutes studying these two unusual sentences, then cover them over and see how accurately you can recall them – word for word, punctuation mark for punctuation mark. You may find it harder than you expect.

» Indescribable and yet somehow familiar; majestic yet undeniably alien: it was either the manifestation of an elaborate hoax or the teetering edge of an incipient insanity.

» Ripped through time and with the scars to show it, brutally dislodged from the fabric of space itself – the entity (whatever it was) was certainly Not Known.

3 WARM 〉 〉 〉 〉 NEST

The brain – an orchestra, not a soloist

Next time you read a media report that identifies something like "love" or "learning" with a particular part of the brain, remember that the whole brain is involved in almost everything we do. No single part plays alone, although they do sometimes play louder than others.

In this 6x6 Futoshiki puzzle, place all of the digits 1 to 6 into each row and column. You must place these digits so that the less-than and greater-than signs ("<" and ">") are obeyed.

| 39 | 1/3 of this | Multiply by thirteen | -100 | Divide by three | ×4 | 1/2 of this | +50 | 75% of this | RESULT |

1   How many pairs of anagrams can you find in the following set?

LEGENDS	WORRIED	SCENTED	PATENTS
WINDOWS	BOARDER	SCANTER	CANTERS
LOUDEST	WORDIER	STILTED	DESCENT
EFFORTS	TOUSLED	SLITTED	BROADER

2   Study this picture for up to two minutes, then cover it over and try to redraw it below. The blue star is already given so can be used as a reference.

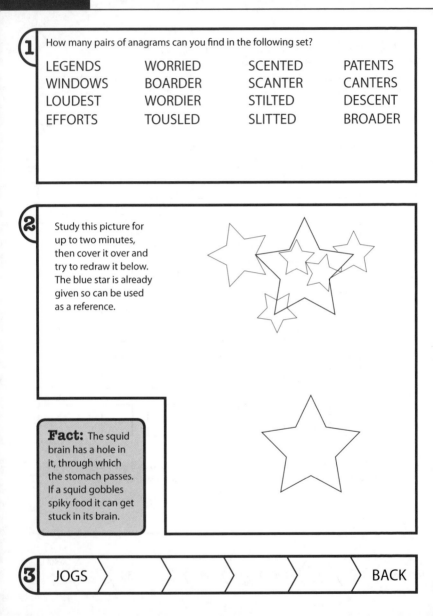

Fact: The squid brain has a hole in it, through which the stomach passes. If a squid gobbles spiky food it can get stuck in its brain.

3   JOGS   ⟩   ⟩   ⟩   ⟩   BACK

(4)

3	0	5	2	6	3	4	2
3	4	5	2	1	5	5	0
4	1	0	6	2	2	6	4
3	1	4	3	5	2	5	0
1	4	0	0	0	1	4	6
6	4	0	6	3	5	2	6
1	1	3	6	1	3	2	5

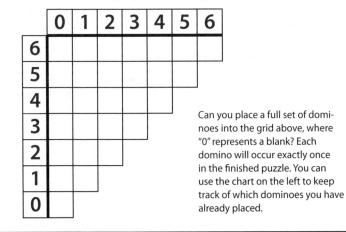

	0	1	2	3	4	5	6
6							
5							
4							
3							
2							
1							
0							

Can you place a full set of dominoes into the grid above, where "0" represents a blank? Each domino will occur exactly once in the finished puzzle. You can use the chart on the left to keep track of which dominoes you have already placed.

| 20 | -60% | One half of this | ×13 | ÷4 | ×5 | Add eighty percent | 1/3 of this | +45 | **RESULT** 5 |

1 If you were to lay these two images one on top of the other, how many circles would there be?

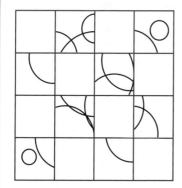 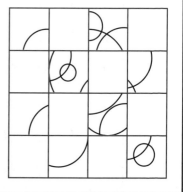

Brain landmarks: the hypothalamus

The hypothalamus, a subcortical brain structure, regulates the essentials of life. Neuroscientists joke that in lower animals it controls the four Fs: fighting, feeding, fleeing and mating.

2 All of the vowels have been eliminated from each of the following four words. Can you work out what the original set of words was?

ncngrs

tlprttn

xpcttn

pqr

3 CHIC 〉 〉 〉 〉 BORE

④

Here is another Kakuro puzzle for you to try. For instructions, see
Day 4.

| 39 | 2/3 of this | +62 | ÷11 | ×14 | +75% | -32 | +33 | Subtract seventy-nine | RESULT 5 |

1

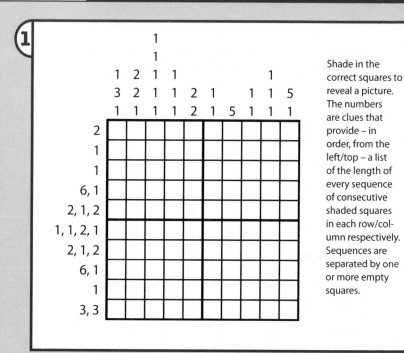

Shade in the correct squares to reveal a picture. The numbers are clues that provide – in order, from the left/top – a list of the length of every sequence of consecutive shaded squares in each row/column respectively. Sequences are separated by one or more empty squares.

2 How many words of three or more letters can you find in this word wheel? Each word must contain the centre letter, plus any selection of the other letters no more than once each.

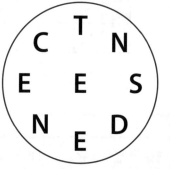

3

13 × 8 = ☐   85 − 15 = ☐   64 + 8 = ☐

11 × 12 = ☐   12 × 7 = ☐   24 + 37 = ☐

57 ÷ 3 = ☐   54 + 8 = ☐   94 − 10 = ☐

1:15a.m. to 10:10p.m. = ☐:☐   2:35a.m. to 5:15p.m. = ☐:☐

6:10a.m. to 6:30p.m. = ☐:☐   12:15a.m. to 2:05p.m. = ☐:☐

7:00a.m. to 3:55p.m. = ☐:☐   5:05a.m. to 11:20a.m. = ☐:☐

£7 + £160 = ☐   £3360 − £3.68 = ☐

£49 − £11.20 = ☐   £177 − £2.35 = ☐

£42600 + 20p = ☐   £9.40 − £2.87 = ☐

4

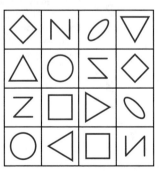

Spend no more than two minutes studying this grid of shapes, then cover it and redraw it as accurately as you can in the empty grid to the right.

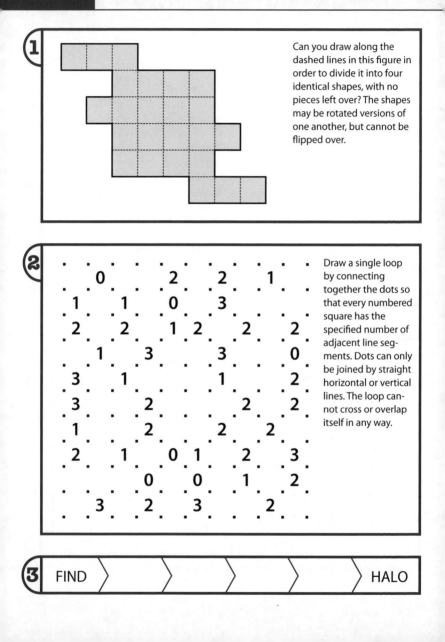

1 Can you draw along the dashed lines in this figure in order to divide it into four identical shapes, with no pieces left over? The shapes may be rotated versions of one another, but cannot be flipped over.

2 Draw a single loop by connecting together the dots so that every numbered square has the specified number of adjacent line segments. Dots can only be joined by straight horizontal or vertical lines. The loop cannot cross or overlap itself in any way.

3 FIND 〉 〉 〉 〉 HALO

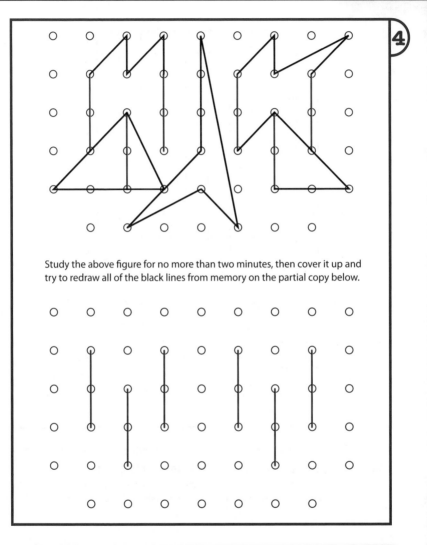

Study the above figure for no more than two minutes, then cover it up and try to redraw all of the black lines from memory on the partial copy below.

130 〉 Divide by five 〉 Nine thirteenths of this 〉 ×4 〉 Add one hundred and seventy-one 〉 Two thirds of this 〉 -44 〉 +53 〉 -22 〉 **RESULT** 5

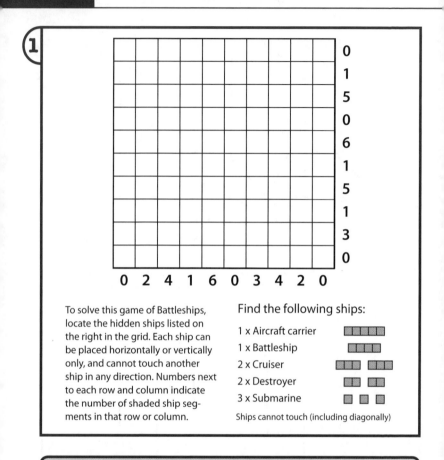

1

```
                                        0
                                        1
                                        5
                                        0
                                        6
                                        1
                                        5
                                        1
                                        3
                                        0
   0  2  4  1  6  0  3  4  2  0
```

To solve this game of Battleships, locate the hidden ships listed on the right in the grid. Each ship can be placed horizontally or vertically only, and cannot touch another ship in any direction. Numbers next to each row and column indicate the number of shaded ship segments in that row or column.

Find the following ships:

1 x Aircraft carrier
1 x Battleship
2 x Cruiser
2 x Destroyer
3 x Submarine

Ships cannot touch (including diagonally)

Brain landmarks: the nucleus accumbens

The nucleus accumbens, part of the subcortex, is a key part of the circuitry in the brain for learning about rewards. Addictive drugs seem to have their effect here.

2 PAST 〉 〉 〉 〉 WEEK

			3	2	1			
		7				5		
	2						4	
7			9		4			8
		5	2		3	1		
9			6		7			4
	1						2	
		6				8		
			4	6	5			

The rules of Sudoku are very simple: place the numbers 1 to 9 into each row, column and bold-lined 3x3 box. Each number must appear only once in any row, column or box.

4

C	O	G
N	U	N
F	S	I

How many English words can you find in this word square? For each word, start on any square and move only to adjacent squares – including diagonals – but without visiting any square more than once. There are at least 26 words to be found, including a nine-letter one.

RESULT
5

| 95 | Sixty percent of this | +118 | -106 | 2/3 of this | Multiply by five | One half of this | Divide by five | +87 |

1 Cover up the set of words on the right (in blue). Then spend no more than two minutes looking at the list of word-pairs on the left. Once the time is up, cover the word-pairs instead. See if you can recall each pair when given just one of the two words.

Consternation	Confusion	Antediluvian
Implacable	Immovable	Downing
Downing	Feathering	Confusion
Pleasing	Amusing	Amusing
Destructive	Breaking	Destructive
Obfuscate	Obscure	Immovable
Dental	Oral	Builder
Transitive	Moving	Obscure
Builder	Constructor	Moving
Ancient	Antediluvian	Oral

2

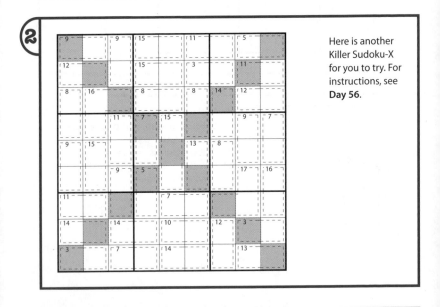

Here is another Killer Sudoku-X for you to try. For instructions, see **Day 56**.

3 NEAT 〉 〉 〉 MAZE

For each of the three pictures below, which of the images below would result from rotating the picture in the way shown by the arrow – 90 degrees anti-clockwise, 180 degrees and 90 degrees clockwise respectively?

4

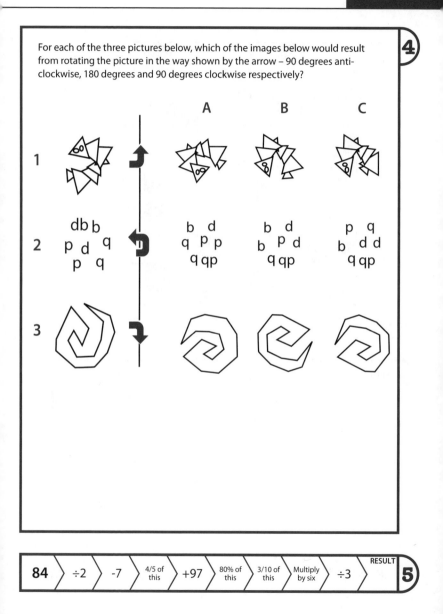

A   B   C

1

2

db b
p d q
p q

b d
q P p
q qp

b d
b P d
q qp

p q
b d d
q qp

3

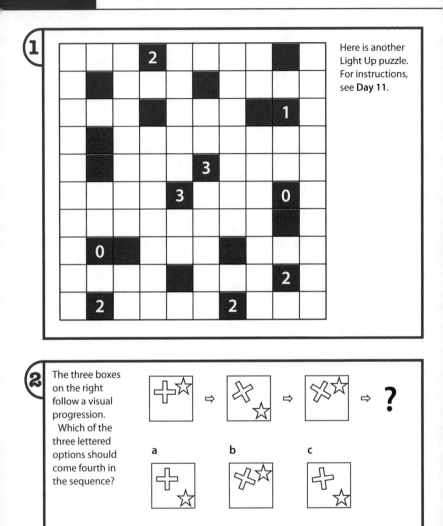

1 Here is another Light Up puzzle. For instructions, see **Day 11**.

2 The three boxes on the right follow a visual progression.
Which of the three lettered options should come fourth in the sequence?

a   b   c

3 RUNS 〉 〉 〉 〉 WILD

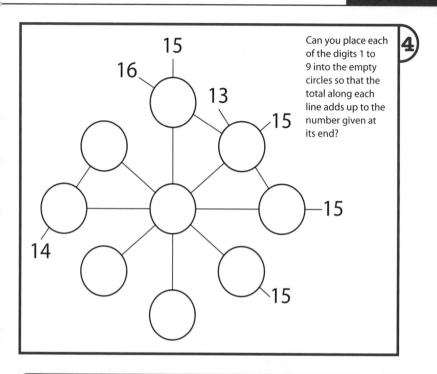

4

Can you place each of the digits 1 to 9 into the empty circles so that the total along each line adds up to the number given at its end?

15

16

13

15

15

14

15

Einstein's brain

After his death, Einstein's brain was preserved and was the subject of several investigations. Neuroscientists hoped to be able to locate the source of his unique genius in some physical difference in his brain. The results of these studies have been disappointingly – or perhaps reassuringly – undramatic. Einstein's brain was no larger or smaller than average: although some parts were bigger than the norm, others were smaller (or even missing). What's more, where Einstein's brain differed from the average, the differences were not so extreme that they wouldn't be shared by millions of people around the world. Asked about his genius, the man himself once said: "I have no particular talent. I am merely inquisitive."

68	25% of this	Multiply by thirteen	-102	+92	-119	Add sixty-eight	1/2 of this	÷2	RESULT

5

1

17	13	3	15	14
18	10	7	12	11
16	21	6	19	20
2	23	9	22	1
25	4	8	5	24

Study this arrangement of the numbers 1 to 25 for no more than two minutes. When time is up, cover it over and try to redraw it on the blank grid. Look out for patterns that may help you remember!

2

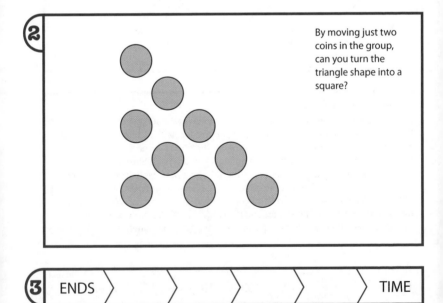

By moving just two coins in the group, can you turn the triangle shape into a square?

3 ENDS ⟩ ⟩ ⟩ ⟩ TIME

In this Kakuro puzzle, fill in each white square with a digit from 1 to 9, such that each horizontal run of consecutive blank squares adds up to the total to the left of that run, and each vertical run of consecutive white squares adds up to the total directly above that run. **No number can be used more than once in any run.**

4

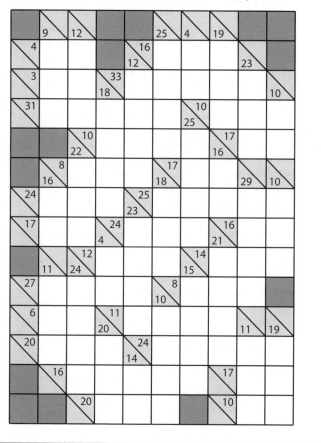

71 ⟩ -27 ⟩ 75% of this ⟩ ×2 ⟩ Divide by three ⟩ Add two hundred ⟩ 2/3 of this ⟩ 25% of this ⟩ +116 ⟩ **RESULT** **5**

Our future brains

In lots of ways, your brain already lives in a future for which it was not prepared. The early humans, hundreds of thousands of years ago, lived in small groups, visited a small number of places, used a small number of tools and had a small range of options for daily living open to them. The brains that they evolved to solve their problems are the same ones that we use to live in cities, travel the world, learning to use and then discarding hundreds of gadgets, for everything from nose-hair trimmers to church organs. If you stand at rush hour in Liverpool Street Station in London for five minutes, you will see more different people than an early human would have seen in their entire lives.

Given all this, it is amazing that modern humans are as sane and capable as we are. The secret of our brains' success is the same one that makes brain training an exciting idea: our brains are designed to adapt to what is required of them, not to have fixed and limited capacities. Technology such as cochlear implants already depends on this fact. An artificial cochlear can be used by those without hearing, transmitting electrical signals into the au-ditory nerve in response to sounds. Over time their brains learn to interpret these signals just as those with normal hearing have learnt to interpret the electrical signals from their natural cochlear. The precision engineering is astounding, but the real magic lies in the brain that can learn to interpret the signals generated by an external machine.

Future brain prostheses will rely on the same brain capacity. Artificial limbs and computer interfaces can be made to respond to the firing of different muscles, or groups of brain cells, and provide feedback either directly to the brain or via sensative parts of the skin, and with practice users' brains will al-low them to learn to treat these external devices as part of their own bodies. As early as the 1960s it was demonstrated that an electrical pad delivering precise vibrations to points on the skin according to a light sensor could give blind people an experience of artificial vision.

Using tools seems to come naturally to all humans, in a way that it does not for any other species. Neuroscientists have shown that when we pick up a tool such as a rake our brain cells adjust to build the end of the rake into our body map. This explains why we hold in our breath when we try to squeeze our cars through a narrow gap, and why we don't have to think which muscles to use when we want to move the mouse cursor around our computer screen. Our adaptable brains are designed to cope with unexpected shapes and changes in our bodies during our lifetimes, and any tool with a fluid interface can also be temporarily incorporated into the body map.

There's no reason for body and brain augmentation to stop at replacements for natural capacities. Virtual reality pioneer Jaron Lanier of MIT has described an experience he had with a computer-generated simulation in which he was given the control of eight legs at the same time. Although weird at first, over time his brain adjusted and he had the experience of a profoundly different body shape than any of the rest of us have experienced.

A more everyday experience is that of reading and writing. Although language is a universal instinct, written language is an invention and one that takes years of our lives to master. Once we have, though, it profoundly affects not just what we can do, like reading this book, but the whole style of our thinking, enabling more abstract, analytical and less memory-reliant kinds of intelligence.

The last hundred years are exciting in that they have seen a host of new cognitive technologies that also promise to alter and extend the way we think. Most of us have an email address, a mobile phone that is always on, ready access to Wikipedia, and maybe a Twitter account or other forms of social networking device. All these things allow us to do things we could never do before, as well as making certain kinds of thinking easier. The question we need to ask about the future of the brain is not "will the brain be augmented?" but "how do we want to augment the brain?"

1 Skyscraper is a Sudoku-esque logic puzzle, in which the aim is to place the numbers 1 to 6 into every row and column of the grid whilst obeying the skyscraper constraints around the edge.

Each number in the completed grid represents a building of that many storeys. Can you place the buildings in such a way that each given number outside the grid represents the number of buildings that can be seen from that point, looking only at that number's row or column?

A building with a higher value always obscures a building with a lower value, and a building with a lower value never obscures a building with a higher value.

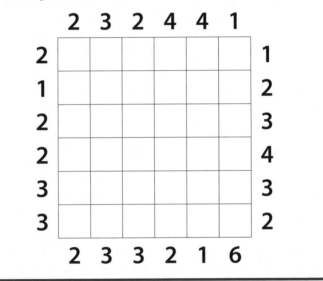

Meditation is good for you

Meditation may offset some of the effects of ageing on the brain. Some recent studies have found that people who regularly practise meditation exercises have denser brain tissue than non-meditators.

2 CUTS 〉 〉 〉 〉 TACO

3

Which of the jigsaw pieces on the left can be assembled together to make the image below? You may not overlap pieces, but they may be rotated if necessary. Shade in the pieces that are not needed.

4

Using each of the following numbers and signs only once, can you reach a total of 255?

4	4	5	6	8	75
+	+	×	×	÷	

You can use as many brackets as you like – for example, given 1, 2, 2, 3, + and ×, you could have (2+2) × (1+3) for a total of 16.

5

62 〉 -44 〉 ×11 〉 ÷3 〉 Subtract thirty-eight 〉 ×4 〉 +10 〉 One half of this 〉 +9 〉 **RESULT**

1 Three of the "shape nets" below fold up into identical cubes, while one of them is slightly different. Which shape net is the odd one out?

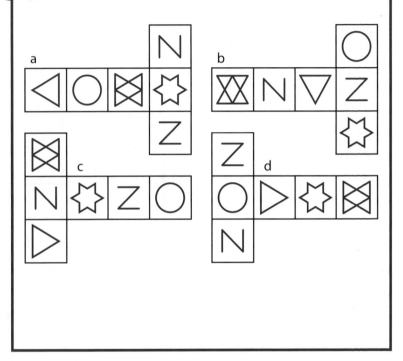

A question of willpower

We may think of willpower as a personality trait, but some research suggests that it is more like a muscle which can be improved with practice. If you've got a self-discipline problem, start training on the equivalent of light weights: break your tasks into small, manageable, daily chunks.

3

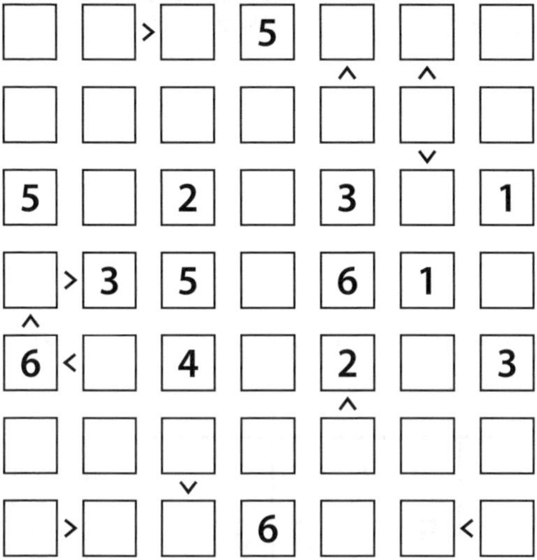

In this 7x7 Futoshiki puzzle, place all of the digits 1 to 7 into each row and column. You must place these digits so that the less-than and greater-than signs ("<" and ">") are obeyed.

4

How good are you at remembering related words? Study this set of words for no more than two minutes, then cover it over and see how many you can recall correctly.

Railway	Track	Carriage	Wagon
Train	Locomotive	Express	Coach
Electricity	Steam	Points	Guard

RESULT

98 〉 1/2 of this 〉 +51 〉 20% of this 〉 ×11 〉 ÷10 〉 +50% 〉 +134 〉 -81 〉 **5**

1 Can you match each of the following words with one other in order to form a pair of synonyms? Each word must be used in precisely one pair.

rapid	intelligent	clear	overcast
smart	bright	dull	fast
easy	clever	sting	transparent
speedy	shiny	secure	simple

2

				7				
		7	5		3	2		
	8	3				6	4	
9								4
			3		9			
2								6
	9	2				5	3	
		5	6		1	9		
				9				

The rules of Sudoku are very simple: place the numbers 1 to 9 into each row, column and bold-lined 3x3 box. Each number must appear only once in any row, column or box.

3 PICK 〉 〉 〉 〉 GUMS

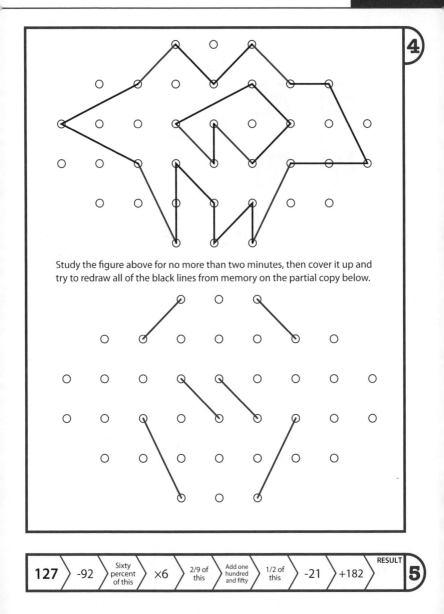

④

Study the figure above for no more than two minutes, then cover it up and try to redraw all of the black lines from memory on the partial copy below.

| 127 | -92 | Sixty percent of this | ×6 | 2/9 of this | Add one hundred and fifty | 1/2 of this | -21 | +182 | RESULT ⑤ |

1

	×		+		=	8
+		×		×		
	×		×		=	48
+		+		×		
	+		+		=	24
=		=		=		
14		20		90		

Place the numbers 1 to 9 once each into the empty boxes so that all of the sums reading both across and down are correct.

2 Can you find an anagram of each of the CAPITALIZED words in order to complete each sentence?

» On election I will INTRODUCE a _____ in red tape.

» True GREATNESS _____ many.

» The HAPPIEST life earns many _____.

» The SQUATTER listened to the _____.

3 THIN 〉 〉 〉 〉 FEET

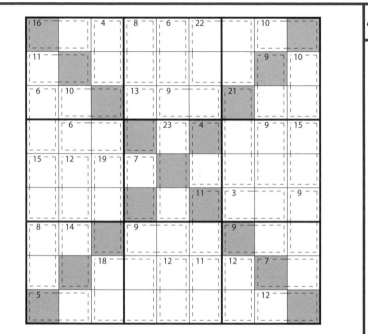

④

Here's another Killer Sudoku-X. For instructions, see **Day 56**.

Cardinal Giuseppe Mezzofanti

Giuseppe Mezzofanti was a nineteenth-century cardinal who was famous for the number of languages he spoke. He was reportedly fluent in 38 different languages, and an additional 40 dialects. Around the Vatican he was known as the "confessor of foreigners" because he could communicate with so many different pilgrims in their native language.

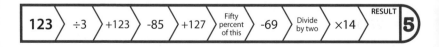

123 〉 ÷3 〉 +123 〉 -85 〉 +127 〉 Fifty percent of this 〉 -69 〉 Divide by two 〉 ×14 〉 **RESULT** 5

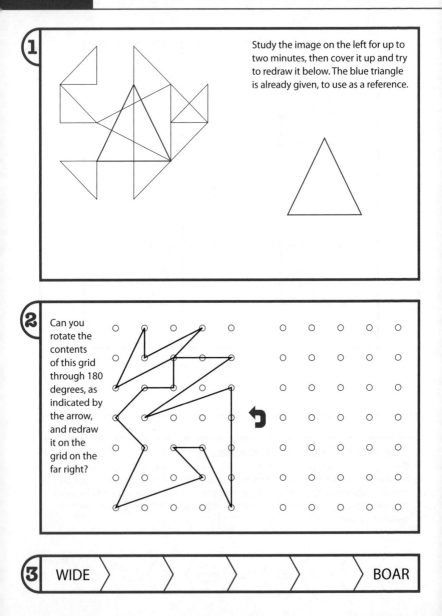

1 Study the image on the left for up to two minutes, then cover it up and try to redraw it below. The blue triangle is already given, to use as a reference.

2 Can you rotate the contents of this grid through 180 degrees, as indicated by the arrow, and redraw it on the grid on the far right?

3 WIDE 〉 〉 〉 〉 BOAR

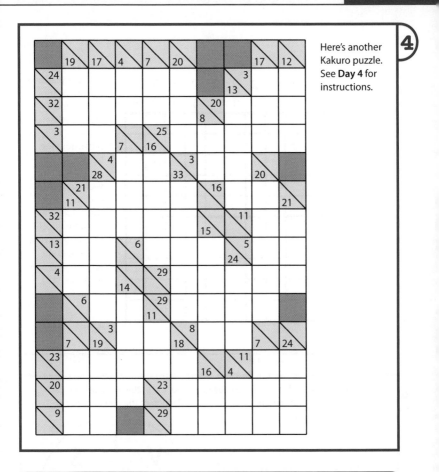

Here's another Kakuro puzzle. See **Day 4** for instructions.

Fact: Only half the cells in your brain are neurons (what we normally call brain cells). The rest are so-called glial cells, which provide a support environment for their more celebrated cousins.

| 78 | ÷2 | 7/13 of this | ×8 | 7/8 of this | -60 | ÷3 | +21 | 70% of this | **RESULT** |

1

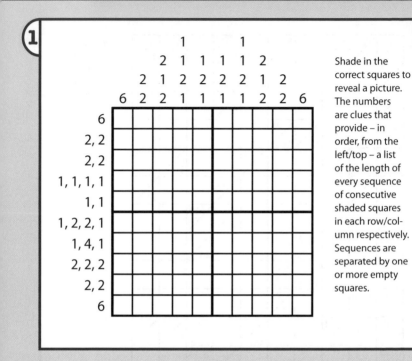

Shade in the correct squares to reveal a picture. The numbers are clues that provide – in order, from the left/top – a list of the length of every sequence of consecutive shaded squares in each row/column respectively. Sequences are separated by one or more empty squares.

2 How many words of three or more letters can you find in this word wheel? Each word must contain the centre letter, plus any selection of the other letters no more than once each.

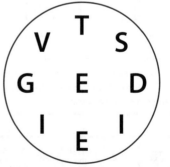

3

10 × 2 = ☐   55 + 17 = ☐   28 − 21 = ☐

14 × 8 = ☐   8 × 3 = ☐   17 × 3 = ☐

44 + 15 = ☐   57 − 7 = ☐   27 + 49 = ☐

1:55a.m. to 8:45p.m. = ☐ : ☐   3:15a.m. to 6:40p.m. = ☐ : ☐

12:00a.m. to 4:00p.m. = ☐ : ☐   7:45a.m. to 5:35p.m. = ☐ : ☐

10:30a.m. to 10:50a.m. = ☐ : ☐   5:55a.m. to 10:35a.m. = ☐ : ☐

£260 − £4.37 = ☐   £20300 + £12.80 = ☐

£383 − £31.20 = ☐   £36800 − £1 = ☐

£40500 − £2.27 = ☐   £153 + £39 = ☐

4

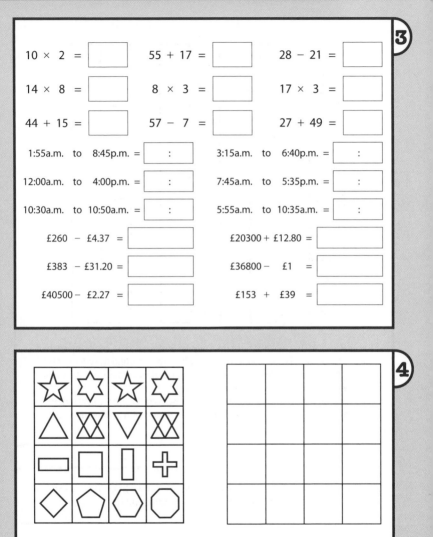

Spend no more than two minutes studying this grid of shapes, then cover it and redraw it as accurately as you can in the empty grid to the right.

1

2				3				7
4				8				1
3								8
	1						5	
7								6
6				2				3
5				1				2

Toroidal Sudoku is a devious twist on a regular Sudoku puzzle, replacing each of the 3x3 boxes with jigsaw-shaped regions which wrap around the edges of the puzzle. Where a region flows off the side of the puzzle it continues in the square directly opposite in the same row or column.

Can you place the numbers 1 to 9 into each row, column and toroidal region? You may find it helpful to start by shading each region with a different colour.

Fact: Nerves from the body cross sides as they enter the brain. This means that the left-hand side of your brain controls your right hand, and vice versa.

2   HOST 〉 〉 〉 〉 NEAR

3

If you were to lay these two images one on top of the other, how many black triangles would be formed? Count up all the possible black triangles – including those formed by the overlap of two larger triangles.

4

In each of the three rows below, delete one letter from each pair of letters in order to reveal a word. For example, deleting B and C from "AB CT" would give the word "AT".

FP	EI	EN	RA	EL	RE				_____
TC	RL	IO	DM	AO	XR				_____
CD	EU	LM	LM	EI	MN	AE	ST	ED	_____

Brain landmarks: the occipital lobes

The occipital lobes, part of the cortex at the rear of the brain, process visual information. But they are far more than a TV screen in your head: they turn sensory data into a meaningful description of the world and they are involved in managing your imagination and your memory for images.

5

111	2/3 of this	÷2	+94	-28	+104	-87	65% of this	÷3	RESULT

1

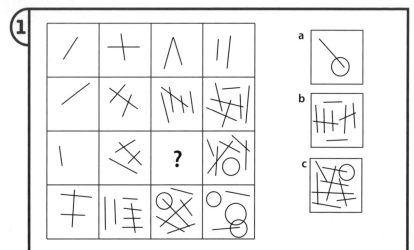

This grid of shapes is constructed by following a simple rule. Can you work out what this rule is and therefore deduce which of the three options should replace the question mark in the grid?

2

21	22	14	7	8
9	1	17	3	15
18	13	10	23	16
25	5	19	6	11
20	4	12	24	2

Study this arrangement of the numbers 1 to 25 for no more than two minutes. Then cover it up and try to redraw it on the blank grid.

3

HELD ⟩ ⟩ ⟩ ⟩ CAKE

④

The aim of Masyu is to draw a single loop that passes through the centre of every circle. At shaded circles the loop must turn through a right angle and then continue straight for at least one square each side. At white circles the loop must pass straight through without turning but then must turn through a right angle on either one or both of the adjacent squares. The loop cannot enter any square more than once, and it may only consist of horizontal and vertical lines.

"It's on the tip of my tongue..."

Everybody experiences the "tip of the tongue" phenomenon, whereby they know they know something, but can't recall it. Often, concentrating on one or two facts about something inhibits successful recall. A better strategy is to freely bring to mind everything you know that is related to the thing you want to remember.

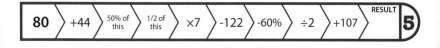

| 80 | +44 | 50% of this | 1/2 of this | ×7 | -122 | -60% | ÷2 | +107 | RESULT ⑤ |

1 Three restaurants are offering different dinner-time specials today. Can you work out what each restaurant's special item is, and what time they open their doors? Try to do so without making notes.

» The Dog & Bucket opens its doors three hours before Les Français.

» The restaurant with the chicken special opens before the fish restaurant.

» TexyMexy's opening time of 5:30pm is halfway between the opening hours of the other two places.

» The steak special will be available for purchase before either of the other two.

2

4								5
			6	1	2			
		2				8		
	9			2			8	
			7	6	4			
	5			3			1	
		6				2		
			9	5	1			
5								4

The rules of Sudoku are very simple: place the numbers 1 to 9 into each row, column and bold-lined 3x3 box. Each number must appear only once in any row, column or box.

3 SUNK 〉 〉 〉 〉 NAVY

④

By cracking the code, can you complete this crossword grid? Each of the 26 letters of the alphabet has a different numerical value, which you can write down in the box at the bottom once you've worked it out. Start by examining the "U", "Z" and "D". As you allocate each letter to a number, cross the letter off the list running down the sides of the grid.

RESULT

⑤

122 > +17 > Subtract sixty-eight > +69 > -82 > 50% of this > ×8 > Seventy-five percent of this > Divide by two >

1

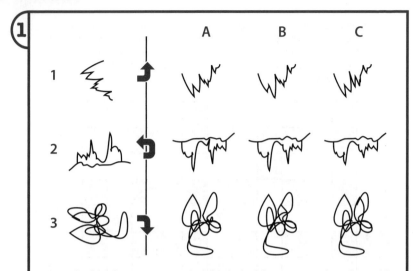

For each of the three pictures on the left, which of the images on the right would result from rotating the picture in the way shown by the arrow – 90 degrees anti-clockwise, 180 degrees and 90 degrees clockwise respectively?

2

Cover over the bottom list of words, and then study the upper list for no more than two minutes. When your time is up, uncover the lower list and cover the upper one instead. Can you write numbers next to the words to rearrange them back into their original order?

illumination, library, crisps, chair, book, tree, floodlight, window, cable, camera, spectacles, paper

book, cable, camera, chair, crisps, floodlight, illumination, library, paper, spectacles, tree, window

3 HARD 〉 〉 〉 〉 BOOK

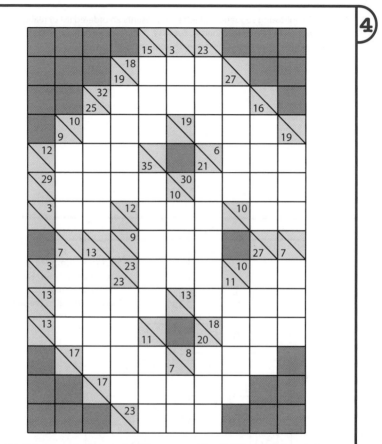

In this Kakuro puzzle, fill in each white square with a digit from 1 to 9, such that each horizontal run of consecutive blank squares adds up to the total to the left of that run, and each vertical run of consecutive white squares adds up to the total directly above that run. **No number can be used more than once in any run.**

59 ⟩ ×4 ⟩ -76 ⟩ Divide by two ⟩ Subtract thirty-five percent ⟩ 9/13 of this ⟩ ×5 ⟩ Ten percent of this ⟩ +137 ⟩ **RESULT 5**

1 Each of the following sequences of letters represents an ordered list of real-world initials, such as M T W T F for Monday, Tuesday, Wednesday, Thursday, Friday. Can you work out which letter comes next in each sequence, and why?

M	V	E	M	J	_____
F	S	T	F	F	_____
B	C	D	G	J	_____
H	H	L	B	B	_____
J	M	M	J	A	_____

2 Can you complete this number pyramid? Each brick in the pyramid should contain a value equal to the sum of the two blocks directly below it.

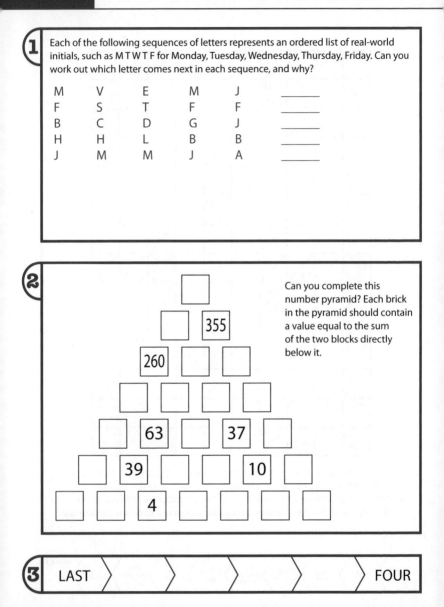

355

260

63   37

39   10

4

3 LAST ⟩ ⟩ ⟩ ⟩ FOUR

4

4	20	8		6		15		7
		14		7		12		
14	14		13				17	
13		6		13		6		
15	13	26						
	3		17		16	13		
4	17					3		
12	14		11		16		12	
6		7		11				

Here is another Killer Sudoku-X for you to try. See **Day 56** for instructions.

Thinking with your stomach

"Gut feelings" may be more than just a metaphor. Your gut contains a diverse and richly connected set of neurons, which control digestion and which send and receive information to and from the brain.

| 63 | +1 | 25% of this | ×15 | ÷4 | 2/3 of this | 60% of this | +30 | -10 | RESULT **5** |

Getting enough sleep

Everybody knows that good sleep is essential for optimal mental performance, but nearly everybody complains that they don't get enough sleep.
Whether it is work, kids or noisy neighbours, we all sometimes have to cope
with a broken night's sleep or not quite as many hours of kip as we'd like. Well,
fortunately the science of sleep has provided some important insights into
how to cope without as much sleep as you think you need.

We generally want to get to sleep as quickly as possible. Unfortunately,
worrying about getting to sleep is a sure way to stop you dropping off right
away. A good way to encourage rapidly falling asleep, and to help avoid worrying about falling asleep, is to create a routine around going to bed, maintaining a clean distinction between sleeping time and waking time.

This means not spending time in bed when you should be asleep, or time
awake in your pyjamas. Rituals you do before sleeping, such as brushing your
teeth, should be done immediately before sleeping, not hours before. You
don't need to have a long routine, just something to announce to your body
that you'll be falling asleep soon.

Of course, once you're in bed you can't really control whether you are sleeping or not. However, it is important to know that our perception of time is
distorted while we're slipping in and out of sleep. This means that sometimes
you think you haven't slept, or have only slept for a few minutes, when in fact
you have had hours of shut-eye.

Professor Alison Harvey, now of the University of California, Berkeley, measured the actual sleep time of insomniacs and then asked them how long they
thought they'd slept for. She found that while the insomniacs reported that
they hadn't slept at all, or had only slept for a few hours, they had in fact been
asleep for an average of 7 hours – only about 30 minutes less than the average person.

A second important thing to know is revealed by what Prof Harvey did
next. In an experiment on how people's perceptions affects their feelings, she

told one group of insomniacs that they had, in fact, had enough sleep and measured their mood.

This group felt happier, were less anxious and subsequently more accurate in gauging their time to get to sleep than a group who had had the same amount of sleep but, like typical insomniacs, mistakenly believed they'd been asleep for less time than they really had. The lesson here is that not worrying too much about how much sleep you've had is just as important as getting to sleep.

This is supported by another classic experiment in which insomniacs were given inert placebo pills but told that they were stimulants that would stop them sleeping. Normally a placebo pill has an effect matching people's beliefs about them, but in this case the group given the placebo stimulants fell asleep faster than the group given placebo sleeping pills.

The explanation is that worrying about getting to sleep plays a major role in insomnia. On a normal night, or if given a sleeping pill, the insomniacs pay lots of attention to whether they are asleep or not, and this stops them actually getting to sleep. The group with the placebo stimulant believed that they wouldn't get to sleep, so they stopped worrying about it and, paradoxically, fell asleep.

Years of sleep research have failed to show that there's any difference between continuous sleep and fragmented sleep in terms of subsequent daytime performance. This means that it is as good to get two sessions of four hours' sleep as eight hours of straight sleep. The sole reason continuous sleep is better is because people often have trouble getting back to sleep once they've woken up. Again, this may be because of the frustration and worry of being awake in the middle of the night when you know you have to get up in a few hours.

But now you know that having interrupted sleep doesn't seem to matter you can worry less if you are woken up in the middle of the night, and this will help you get back to sleep. Sleep is essential, but the best thing to do if you miss a few hours is to not worry about it and get on with things.

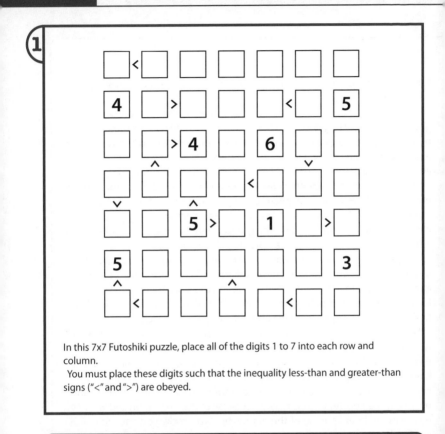

In this 7x7 Futoshiki puzzle, place all of the digits 1 to 7 into each row and column.

You must place these digits such that the inequality less-than and greater-than signs ("<" and ">") are obeyed.

Brains and pains

There are no pain sensors in the brain. This means that brain surgery can be performed on wide-awake patients. In fact, most brain surgery has to be performed on awake patients so that the surgeons can tell immediately if the operation is having a negative effect on the patient's mental function.

2 WRONG 〉 〉 〉 〉 POISE

3

A clothes store recently saw three particularly colourful clothing purchases. In each case two items were bought. Can you work out which pairs of item were bought together, and what colour each item was? Try to do so without making notes.

» Neither the shorts nor the shoes were orange or green.

» The pink T-shirt was not paired with the jacket, which wasn't orange.

» The yellow socks were bought with the trousers.

» The shoes, which were not red, were not bought with the T-shirt.

4

How good is your memory for detail? Spend no more than two minutes studying these two unusual sentences, then cover them up and see how accurately you can recall them – word for word, punctuation mark for punctuation mark.

» Catalogued under numerous, seemingly unrelated headings, a full description of the behaviour of this strange entity escaped even the finest of the University's xenologists – let alone the first semblance of an explanation.

» Even on the edge of the abyss, staring down the face of Creation, I could not stop the unwitting recall of the key moments in the sequence of events that formed the twisted and torturous story of my life so far.

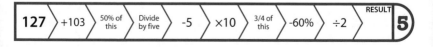

127 〉 +103 〉 50% of this 〉 Divide by five 〉 -5 〉 ×10 〉 3/4 of this 〉 -60% 〉 ÷2 〉 **RESULT 5**

1

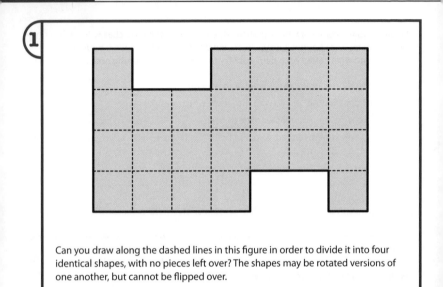

Can you draw along the dashed lines in this figure in order to divide it into four identical shapes, with no pieces left over? The shapes may be rotated versions of one another, but cannot be flipped over.

2 Cover up the set of words on the right (in blue). Then spend no more than two minutes looking at the list of word-pairs on the left. Once the time is up, cover the word-pairs instead. See if you can recall each pair when given just one of the two words.

Airline	Transit	Obstruction
Temperature	Fever	Ceasing
Ceasing	Possessing	Fever
Parallelogram	Shape	Millionth
Verbose	Sesquipedalian	Vacuum
Millionth	Fractional	Airline
Wall	Obstruction	Shape
Suck	Vacuum	Sofa
Space	Emptiness	Emptiness
Sofa	Relaxation	Sesquipedalian

3 READY 〉   〉   〉   〉 STEPS

4

			B	C	6	A					
		5	6					3	2		
	4	B							7	C	
B	6		9		8	7		A		1	5
	8		A					C		2	
					9	1					
					3	5					
	3		2					4		7	
7	5		C		A	2		1		8	B
	B	8							C	4	
		1	5					9	6		
				6	1	3	2				

In this Sudoku 12x12 you must place the numbers 1 to 9 and the letters A to C in each row, column and bold-lined 4x3 box. Each number and letter must appear only once in any row column or box.

Easy as pi

The world record for reciting the number pi from memory is held by Chao Lu, of China. On 20 November 2005, he recited the number to 67,890 decimal places.

122 ⟩ ÷2 ⟩ +169 ⟩ -10% ⟩ Divide by nine ⟩ +64 ⟩ 1/3 of this ⟩ ×4 ⟩ -8 ⟩ **RESULT** **5**

1 Try to decode this quotation by replacing each letter with another one a fixed number of places forwards/backwards in the alphabet. (Wrap around from Z to A or from A to Z when counting.)

Hmpsz jt gmffujoh, cvu pctdvsjuz jt gpsfwfs.

Obqpmfpo Cpobqbsuf

2

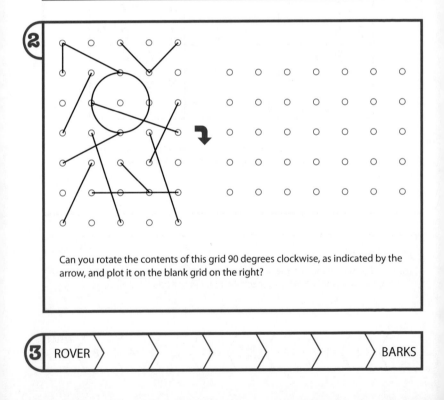

Can you rotate the contents of this grid 90 degrees clockwise, as indicated by the arrow, and plot it on the blank grid on the right?

3 ROVER 〉 〉 〉 〉 〉 BARKS

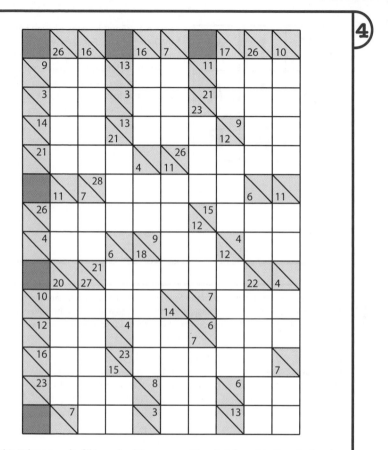

In this Kakuro puzzle, fill in each white square with a digit from 1 to 9, so that each horizontal run of blank squares adds up to the total to the left of that run, and each vertical run of white squares adds up to the total directly above that run. **No number can be used more than once in any run.**

116 〉 1/2 of this 〉 +116 〉 50% of this 〉 -19 〉 75% of this 〉 Divide by three 〉 ×11 〉 -150 〉 **RESULT** 5

1

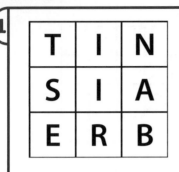

How many English words can you find in this word square? For each word, start on any square and move only to adjacent squares – including diagonals – but without visiting any square more than once. There are at least 54 words to be found, including a nine-letter one.

2 Can you put the results of each of the following rows of sums in ascending order? You will almost certainly find it easiest to estimate the majority of the values, rather than calculate them all. The first one has been done for you, as an example.

a	b	c	d	e	
1+3	2+1	3+4	7+2	1+1	ebacd
10,000 x 100	9785 x 95	15,000 x 101	14,806 x 99	20,394 x 51	_____
1783 + 395	2035 + 470	3547 + 580	1987 + 1750	1997 + 3040	_____
295 x 105	195 x 205	395 x 405	395 x 305	295 x 395	_____

3 MOUSE > > > > > PESTS

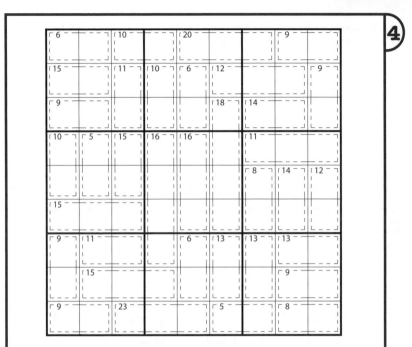

In Killer Sudoku, as in regular Sudoku, the aim is to place the digits 1 to 9 into each row, column and bold-lined 3x3 box.

Additionally, place digits so that the total of each dashed-line cage is the value given at the top-left of that cage. Digits may *not* be repeated within a cage.

Are kids getting cleverer?

Scores on IQ tests seem to be increasing every generation, a phenomenon known as the Flynn Effect. Whether this means people are getting better at the tests or more intelligent generally is hotly debated.

| 136 | One eighth of this | ×14 | ÷2 | -16 | +114 | Divide by seven | +82 | ×2 | RESULT 5 |

1 How good are you at remembering related words? Study this set of words for no more than two minutes, then cover it over and see how many you can recall correctly.

Chalk	Clay	Limestone	Shale
Gypsum	Anthracite	Dolomite	Basalt
Flint	Granite	Marble	Obsidian

2 These three boxes follow a visual progression. Which of the three lettered options below should come fourth in the sequence?

 ⇨ ⇨ ⇨ **?**

a   **b**   **c**

3 STICK ⟩ ⟩ ⟩ ⟩ ⟩ CRANE

④

	9						1	
			1	6	8			
		3				5		
1								9
3								8
		4				8		
			6	3	5			
	7						3	

Sudoku-X adds one extra rule to a traditional Sudoku puzzle: you must place the numbers 1 to 9 not only into each row, column and bold-lined 3x3 box, but also into each of the two main diagonals (shaded on the puzzle).

83 〉 +103 〉 ÷2 〉 +87 〉 9/10 of this 〉 50% of this 〉 ÷3 〉 ×9 〉 Eight ninths of this 〉 **RESULT** 5

1

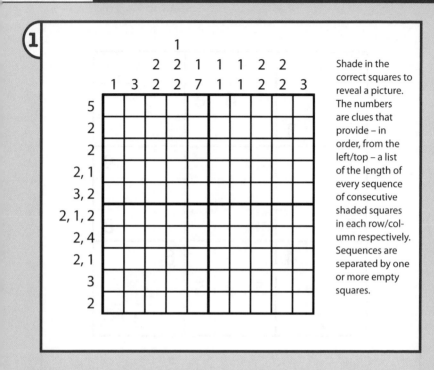

Shade in the correct squares to reveal a picture. The numbers are clues that provide – in order, from the left/top – a list of the length of every sequence of consecutive shaded squares in each row/column respectively. Sequences are separated by one or more empty squares.

2 How many words of three or more letters can you find in this word wheel? Each word must contain the centre letter, plus any selection of the other letters no more than once each.

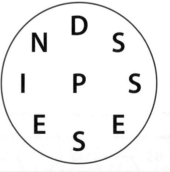

3

13 × 9 = ☐   77 − 21 = ☐   27 + 96 = ☐

8 + 83 = ☐   7 × 7 = ☐   52 + 13 = ☐

70 − 22 = ☐   73 − 25 = ☐   89 − 6 = ☐

1:50a.m. to 5:00p.m. = ☐ : ☐   2:05a.m. to 6:10a.m. = ☐ : ☐

6:50a.m. to 4:50p.m. = ☐ : ☐   5:30a.m. to 4:45p.m. = ☐ : ☐

2:50a.m. to 4:15p.m. = ☐ : ☐   2:30a.m. to 5:40p.m. = ☐ : ☐

£7700 − £1.21 = ☐   £2050 + £42.70 = ☐

£23600 − £246 = ☐   £401 + £29600 = ☐

£5000 + £3.56 = ☐   £2200 − 69p = ☐

4

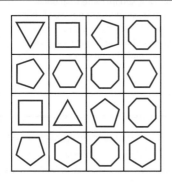

Spend no more than two minutes studying this grid of shapes, then cover it and redraw it as accurately as you can in the empty grid to the right.

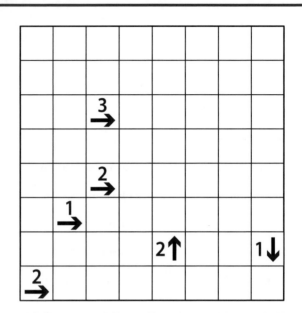

The aim of Yajilin is to draw a single loop using only horizontal and vertical lines such that the loop does not pass through any square more than once. Any squares which the loop does not visit must be shaded, but no two of these shaded squares can touch in either a horizontal or vertical direction.

Numbers with arrows indicate the exact number of shaded squares in a given direction in a specific row or column, but not all shaded squares are necessarily identified with arrows.

Fact: Your brain weighs about 1.4kg and has the consistency of warm butter. All your hopes, fears, thoughts and feelings happen there.

3

All of the vowels have been eliminated from each of the following four words. Can you work out what the original set of words was?

mlg

rtstc

rtk

rdynmc

4

Study these pictures of different houses for up to two minutes, then cover them over and try to redraw them on the empty squares below as precisely as possible.

| 350 | ÷7 | ×14 | 4/5 of this | ÷14 | ×10 | One half of this | 52% of this | +352 | **RESULT** **5** |

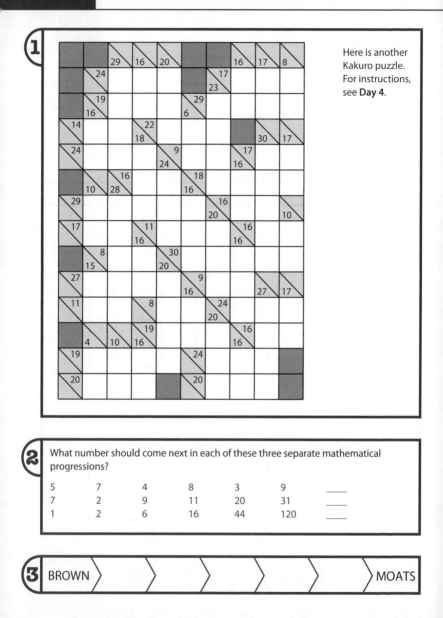

1 Here is another Kakuro puzzle. For instructions, see **Day 4**.

2 What number should come next in each of these three separate mathematical progressions?

5	7	4	8	3	9	____
7	2	9	11	20	31	____
1	2	6	16	44	120	____

3 BROWN 〉 〉 〉 〉 MOATS

④

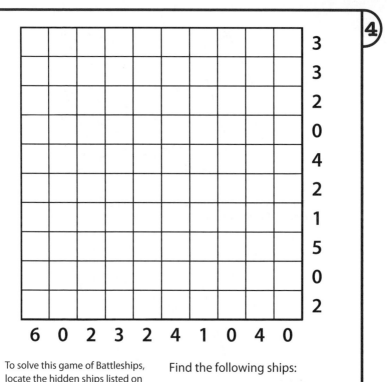

											3
											3

Row clues (top to bottom): 3, 3, 2, 0, 4, 2, 1, 5, 0, 2

Column clues (left to right): 6, 0, 2, 3, 2, 4, 1, 0, 4, 0

To solve this game of Battleships, locate the hidden ships listed on the right in the grid. Each ship can be placed horizontally or vertically only, and cannot touch another ship in any direction. Numbers next to each row and column indicate the number of shaded ship segments in that row or column.

Find the following ships:

1 x Aircraft carrier

1 x Battleship

2 x Cruiser

2 x Destroyer

3 x Submarine

Ships cannot touch (including diagonally)

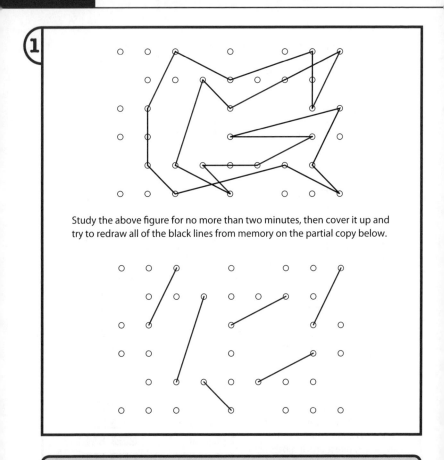

Study the above figure for no more than two minutes, then cover it up and try to redraw all of the black lines from memory on the partial copy below.

A brain of two halves

The brain is built like the body: two of everything down the side and one of everything down the middle. This means that nearly all parts of the brain you hear mentioned come in pairs.

2 THICK 〉 〉 〉 〉 〉 CREAM

3

	3	8			C	9			B	1	
4				6	2	B	3				9
1	9		A					3		2	4
7	C			5			9			A	8
				6	4						
				4	1						
8	5			A			B			6	2
A	4		2					1		5	7
3				1	8	6	2				5
	6	4			B	5			1	C	

Here is another Sudoku 12x12 for you to try. For instructions, see **Day 77**.

4

Cover over the bottom three rows of words and then spend no more than two minutes looking at the first three rows. When time's up, uncover the lower rows and cover the upper ones instead. Can you spot which word is missing from each of the rows?

Gondola	Punt	Dinghy	Kayak	Canoe	Skiff
Bicycle	Helmet	Handlebars	Pedal	Crank	Chain
Manager	Boss	Chief	Director	Owner	Chairman

Kayak	Canoe	Punt	Gondola	Skiff
Helmet	Handlebars	Chain	Pedal	Bicycle
Director	Owner	Manager	Chairman	Chief

5

| 121 | Ten elevenths of this | ×6 | −255 | Subtract sixty percent | 50% of this | Add two hundred and forty | 2/3 of this | ×2 | RESULT |

1

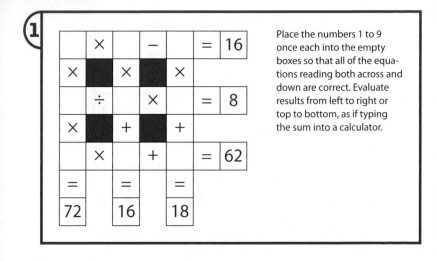

Place the numbers 1 to 9 once each into the empty boxes so that all of the equations reading both across and down are correct. Evaluate results from left to right or top to bottom, as if typing the sum into a calculator.

2

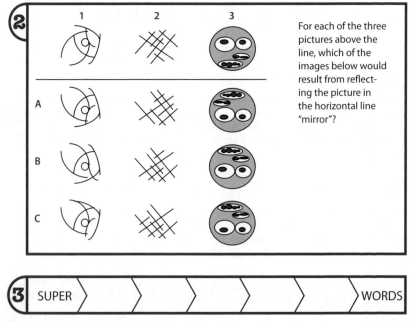

For each of the three pictures above the line, which of the images below would result from reflecting the picture in the horizontal line "mirror"?

3   SUPER ⟩   ⟩   ⟩   ⟩   ⟩ WORDS

4

		5				
2			3		6	4
	3	6				
2					8	
				2		
	8			6		2
						2
3					2	

Sikaku is a Japanese shape-placing number puzzle with just one simple aim: draw rectangles on the existing grid lines so that each square in the grid ends up in exactly one rectangle, and so that each rectangle contains precisely one number. The number inside each rectangle must be equal to the number of grid squares inside that rectangle.

Joined-up thinking

Synaesthesia (from the Greek for "joined senses") is the condition in which experiences in one modality, such as hearing, create sensations in another modality, like seeing. Some individuals see colours when they hear musical notes, for example, while some taste flavours when they see certain words. The most common kind of synaesthesia is between word-shapes and colours. Many people report associations between letters, numbers or days of the week and different colours ("Tuesday is red", for example). Although this is different from actually seeing colours when you are shown letters – true synaesthesia – it suggests that a degree of "cross-wiring" is actually normal in the brain. Synaesthesia has been suggested as the secret of some unusually strong calculating and memory abilities. A way you can use this for yourself is to practise visualizing things, or, when you have a list of items to remember, use the natural associations you have for smells, colours, sounds and shapes to make the list become more "alive" with character. This will make it easier to recall later.

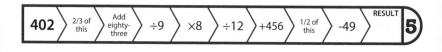

| 402 | 2/3 of this | Add eighty-three | ÷9 | ×8 | ÷12 | +456 | 1/2 of this | -49 | **RESULT** **5** |

1 How good are you at remembering related words? Study this set of words for no more than two minutes, then cover it over and see how many you can recall correctly.

Sandpaper	Chisel	Hammer	Pliers	Stapler
Screwdrivers	Wrench	Knife	Jigsaw	Mallet
Measure	Clamp	Bench	Roller	Flashlight

2

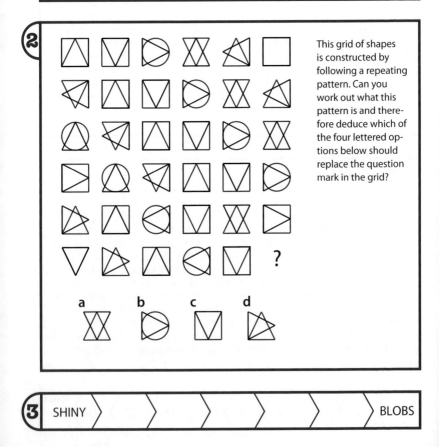

This grid of shapes is constructed by following a repeating pattern. Can you work out what this pattern is and therefore deduce which of the four lettered options below should replace the question mark in the grid?

3 SHINY 〉 〉 〉 〉 BLOBS

4

```
| 7 |   |   | > |   |   |   | 4 |
                                  v
|   |   |   |   |   |   | < |   |
| 1 |   | < |   |   |   | > |   | 6 |
      ^       ^               v
|   | > |   |   |   | > |   | < |   |
| 3 |   | < |   | < |   |   |   | 7 |
                      v
|   |   | > |   |   |   |   | > |   |
              ^
| 5 |   |   | < |   | < |   |   | 1 |
```

In this 7x7 Futoshiki puzzle, place all of the digits 1 to 7 into each row and column. You must place these digits such that the inequality less-than and greater-than signs ("<" and ">") are obeyed.

Brain landmarks: the corpus callosum

The corpus callosum is a bundle of fibres which connects the two hemispheres of the cortex. Some studies have claimed that women have a thicker corpus callosum than men, which would result in a tighter linking between the two hemispheres.

| 460 | -20% | ÷8 | 1/2 of this | +296 | ÷11 | ×18 | +100 | -70 | RESULT **5** |

The art of memory

Memories are associations. There are lots of memory techniques and systems, but they all work in the same way: increasing the strength or number of associations for the things that you want to remember. The oldest memory technique is so obvious that it hardly seems like a technique: practice. Every repetition strengthens the association among a list of items, or between a question and an answer. Repetition is probably how you learnt the letters of the alphabet. But could you immediately name the tenth letter? Most people have to count through from A. This illustrates the weakness of simple practice – that we tend to learn things exactly as we practise them. This is fine if you want to be able to recite the alphabet from start to finish, and have time to do it, but it's not ideal if you want to have access to each individual item immediately.

Research has shown that repetitive learning with breaks is more effective than continuous repetition. In other words, five hours of study is better spent as five hour-long sessions, rather than one five-hour monster session. A very straightforward way to maximize the efficiency of your time studying is make sure you space out your practice, rather than try and fit it all into one session (the evening before the exam, for example).

Also, you should make sure that after you feel you have got to grips with something you review it several times at increasing intervals. Of course, the problem with this method is that it requires some forward planning and self-discipline. There are various tools available for computers and mobile phones that will automate optimally spaced repetition for material that you want to learn: try googling "supermemo" or "mnemosyne".

Repetition strengthens associations, but it is also possible to improve your recall by building a richer web of associations around things you want to learn. Psychologists call this "depth of processing" and it is the key to the most powerful memory techniques, as well as being a good guide to effective learning in most situations. The basic principle is straightforward: the more involved you are in something, the better you will remember it. It is better to try something yourself rather than watch someone else do it; it is better to practise writing out the things you want to remember rather than just practising recognizing these items in a list.

The most powerful associations come when you integrate new material into a set of associations that you already have well established in memory. This is why mnemomics such as "Richard Of York Gave Battle In Vain" are so powerful. Without the structure of the sentence, the first letters would just be an arbitrary list. In the sentence we can connect them with our knowledge both of the associations common in English grammar and of British history. Songs and rhymes can be easy to remember for the same reason: they have a structure or rhythm and rhyme which makes the words seem obvious. Psychologists call these kinds of structures in memory "schema" and have shown how important they are for organizing and making sense of our memories. If you want to remember something, a powerful technique is to find some way to organize the information. Not only does this encourage depth of processing, but organized information is far easier to recall than disorganized information.

There are also a number of special memory techniques that "memory magicians" use to perform amazing feats, such as remembering all the cards in order from a shuffled deck, or even three shuffled decks. These techniques generally rely on some existing structure, such as the idea of a hotel with a number of sequential rooms, which is then filled in with vivid mental images created by the memory magician. The creation of mental images for each item you want to remember encourages depth of processing and also means that each item is embedded in a set of associations that makes it easier to recall. Our species seems to favour vision over the other senses, so mental images are a particularly strong kind of association for most people.

A famous, old and effective memory trick is called the Method of Loci – as used by the ancient Greek rhetoricians. It can be used to remember arbitrary lists of things. You start by choosing a journey you know well, such as from home to work, and you imagine taking that journey, placing the items you need to remember along the way. It helps if you imagine the items in an unusual or striking way.

So, for example, if you wanted to remember the order of the colours of the rainbow, you might imagine your day like this: you wake up in a bed of roses (red), stumble to the bathroom, where you have to take a shower because the bath is full of a giant orange (orange, of course). Next you have breakfast, served by your butler, a chicken (yellow) and who passes you a banana for your muesli (also yellow) – just to make sure. And so on. To remember the list of items, you just run through your normal journey to work and your visual memory will provide the items that you previously imagined there.

1

	9						6	
				4				
	8		6		1		2	
				8				
				6				
	1		3		9		7	
				2				
	2						4	

Sudoku Extra Regions adds, as its name suggests, extra regions to a traditional Sudoku puzzle. You must place the numbers 1 to 9 not only into each row, column and bold-lined 3x3 box, but also into each of the four shaded areas.

It's never too late for some new neurons

Once scientists believed that it was impossible for the brain to grow new neurons, but we now know that this isn't true. New neurons can be generated during adulthood. Not surprisingly, this happens in the areas of the brain associated with learning and memory.

2 PHONY 〉 〉 〉 〉 SMILE

3

Using each of the following numbers and signs only once, can you reach a total of 635?

2	3	5	9	10	75
+	-	-	×	×	

You can use as many brackets as you like – for example given 1, 2, 2, 3, + and × you could have (2+2) × (1+3) for a total of 16.

The speed of thought

Signals travel down the wires between brain cells at up to 200 mph. This might seem surprisingly fast, but it is in fact over two million times slower than the transmission speed of a fibre optic cable.

Or, to put it another way, if you were using neurons to have a phone conversation across the Atlantic, there would be a lag of about two days between you saying hello and hearing a reply.

4

How many pairs of anagrams can you find among the following words?

COBBLERS	MARCHING	SILKIEST	SHAMBLES
APPRAISE	BOTHERED	SIMPERED	REBATING
OLDENING	IMMORTAL	DIRECTED	PREMISED
BERATING	CHARMING	CREDITED	CLOBBERS

5

301 ⟩ 6/7 of this ⟩ ÷2 ⟩ +208 ⟩ -112 ⟩ ÷3 ⟩ 3/5 of this ⟩ 60% of this ⟩ +96 ⟩ **RESULT**

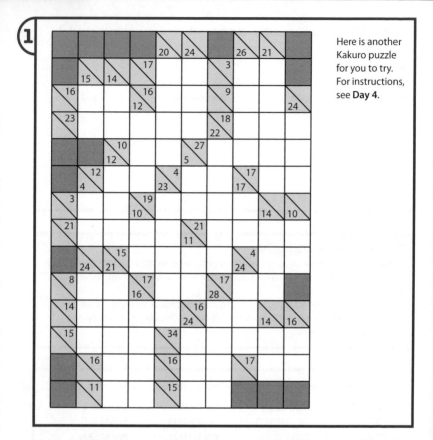

Here is another Kakuro puzzle for you to try. For instructions, see **Day 4**.

Windows for learning

Some skills have "critical periods" – windows of time early in life during which they are far easier to learn. Learning the sounds particular to a language, so you can speak it without an accent, is a good example of such a skill.

② CRAZY 〉 〉 〉 〉 〉 GLOBE

3

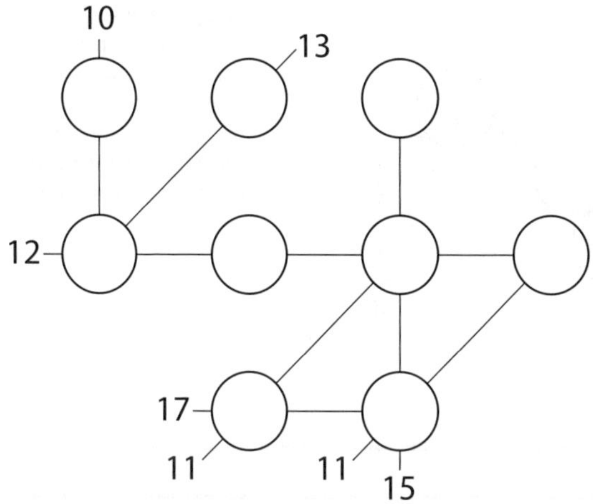

Can you place each of the digits 1 to 9 into the empty circles so that the total along each line adds up to the number given at its end?

10
13
12
17
11
11
15

4

Cover up the set of words on the right (in blue). Then spend no more than two minutes looking at the list of word-pairs on the left. Once the time is up, cover the word-pairs instead. See if you can recall each pair when given just one of the two words.

Headphones	Listening	Magnificence
Holder	Containing	Confluence
Railing	Complaint	Promotion
Brick	Destroy	Containing
Alien	Inadmissible	Sophistic
Plummet	Rise	Listening
Sophistic	Dissimilate	Destroy
Splendid	Magnificence	Melody
Interstitial	Promotion	Railing
Melody	Harmony	Alien
Confluence	Meeting	Rise

5

| 380 | -277 | +203 | 1/3 of this | ÷2 | ×8 | -236 | 3/4 of this | Add three hundred and thirty-five | RESULT |

1

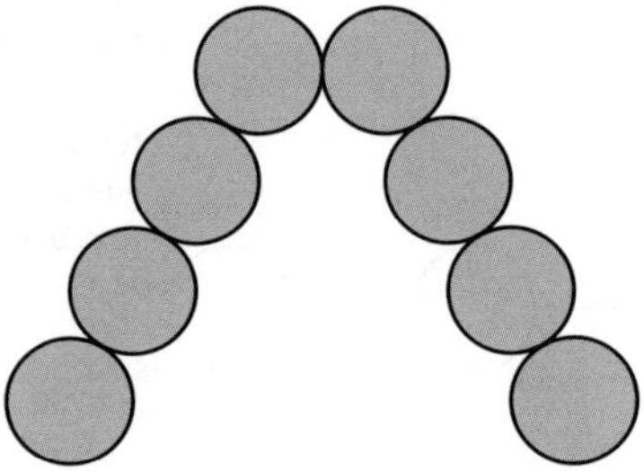

Imagine that each of these circles represent a coin. How could you rearrange these eight coins so that there is one coin that touches all of the the other coins simultaneously?

2

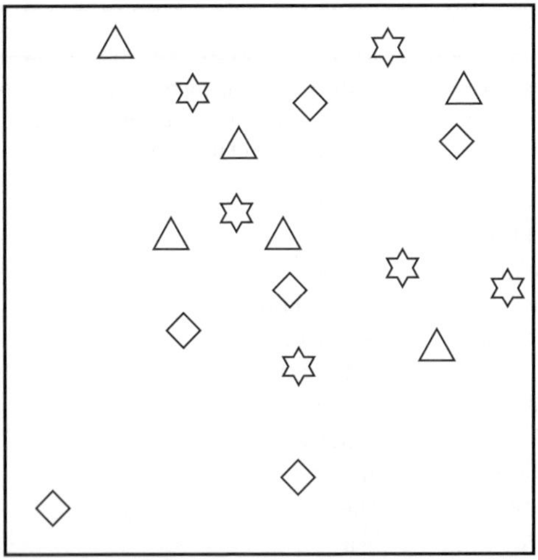

Can you draw three perfect circles in order to divide this box into separate regions, each containing exactly one of each type of shape?

3 NOISY 〉 〉 〉 〉 DRONE

(4)

13	12	9	11
5	12	5	23	13	15
7	13	7		5
11	8		22	10	9
	8	21		7	12
12		11	10	
16	9	5	7
10		10	12
8	15	10	12

In Killer Sudoku, as in regular Sudoku, the aim is to place the digits 1 to 9 into each row, column and bold-lined 3x3 box. Additionally, place digits so that the total of each dashed-line cage is the value given at the top-left of that cage. Digits may *not* be repeated within a cage.

Brain landmarks: the parietal lobes

The parietal lobes, a centrally positioned part of the cortex, are thought to be responsible for attention and visuospatial tasks, such as mental rotation.

| 368 | -203 | ÷3 | Eighty percent of this | +461 | -80% | +191 | ÷4 | ×5 | RESULT **5** |

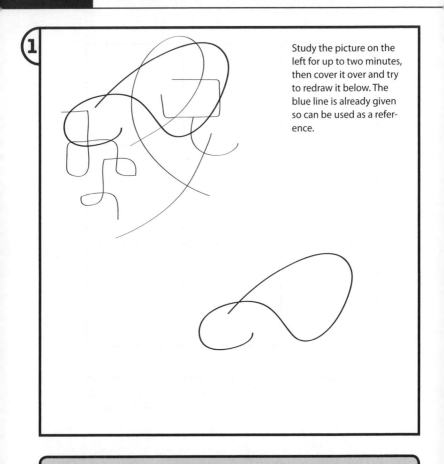

Study the picture on the left for up to two minutes, then cover it over and try to redraw it below. The blue line is already given so can be used as a reference.

Test yourself ... and then test yourself again

When trying to learn a set of answers for a test, try to recall each item and then check if you are right. This is more effective then merely re-studying the items without testing yourself properly.

SHARK 〉 〉 〉 〉 〉 ROCKS

3

				9	4						
		1	8		C	B		3	2		
	6		9	7			5	C		B	
			6				1				
C											4
5	3			6			7			8	A
B	5			1			9			4	6
8											5
			1					A			
	B		4	5			C	2		A	
		3	5		4	A		B	6		
					1	8					

Here is another Sudoku 12x12. See **Day 77** if you need a reminder of the instructions.

4

» On a flat piece of land, there is a post which I know to be exactly 4.5m in height. If I glue one end of a 5m-long rope to the top of the post, what is the furthest distance from the base of the post that I can stand while still holding on to the other end of the rope? I can raise my hands no higher than 1.5m above the ground, and the rope cannot stretch.

» I have a pack of 52 playing cards, consisting of 4 suits each containing 13 different cards. If I pick two cards entirely at random out of the full pack, what is the likelihood that I end up with two cards from the same suit?

| 64 | +50% | ×5 | 50% of this | +301 | -183 | One half of this | +35 | Subtract forty | **RESULT** **5** |

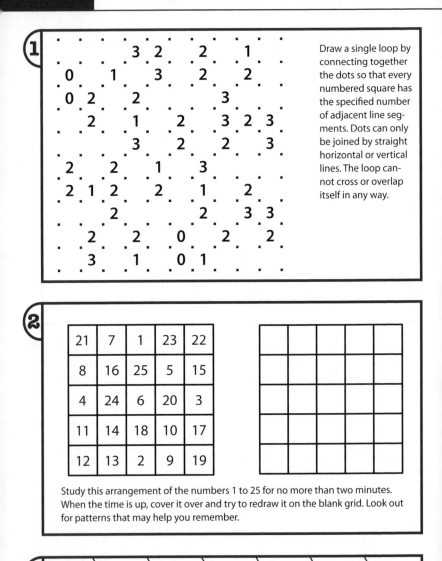

1 Draw a single loop by connecting together the dots so that every numbered square has the specified number of adjacent line segments. Dots can only be joined by straight horizontal or vertical lines. The loop cannot cross or overlap itself in any way.

2

21	7	1	23	22
8	16	25	5	15
4	24	6	20	3
11	14	18	10	17
12	13	2	9	19

Study this arrangement of the numbers 1 to 25 for no more than two minutes. When the time is up, cover it over and try to redraw it on the blank grid. Look out for patterns that may help you remember.

3 QUITS ⟩ ⟩ ⟩ ⟩ ⟩ PLACE

Can you reflect all of the lines in this grid in the dashed-line "mirror"?

④

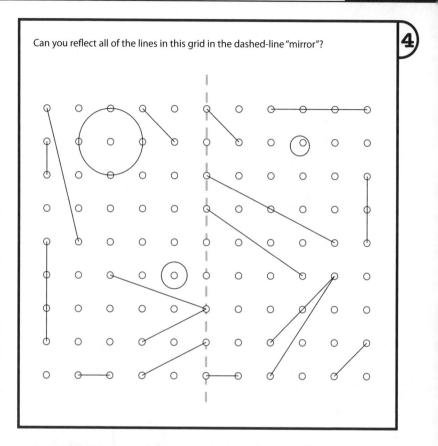

A race of tool-users

Flexible tool use is rare in nature. Only some of the primates, and some bird species, have been shown to be capable of it. The way our brains can adapt to different tools is key to our exceptional intelligence as a species.

| 140 | +244 | Divide by four | 2/3 of this | Fifty percent of this | +34 | -44 | Multiply by eleven | 1/2 of this | RESULT ⑤ |

1

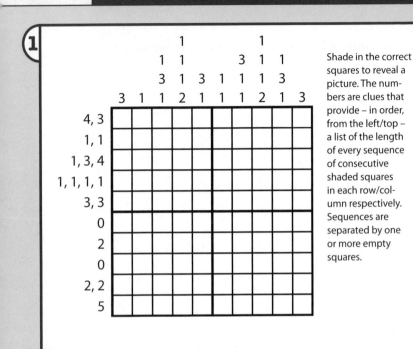

Shade in the correct squares to reveal a picture. The numbers are clues that provide – in order, from the left/top – a list of the length of every sequence of consecutive shaded squares in each row/column respectively. Sequences are separated by one or more empty squares.

2 How many words of three or more letters can you find in this word wheel? Each word must contain the centre letter, plus any selection of the other letters no more than once each.

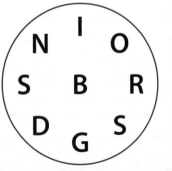

3

2 × 6 = ☐   46 − 22 = ☐   25 − 10 = ☐

10 × 7 = ☐   37 − 21 = ☐   2 × 11 = ☐

57 + 10 = ☐   40 + 22 = ☐   34 − 16 = ☐

5:05a.m. to 9:45a.m. = ☐ : ☐   5:40a.m. to 4:50p.m. = ☐ : ☐

1:05a.m. to 10:40p.m. = ☐ : ☐   12:10a.m. to 10:40a.m. = ☐ : ☐

10:50a.m. to 11:05p.m. = ☐ : ☐   12:30a.m. to 8:35a.m. = ☐ : ☐

£125 − £1.67 = ☐   £8.40 + £286 = ☐

£3180 + £3290 = ☐   £22300 − £3270 = ☐

£80 + £433 = ☐   £3440 − £14 = ☐

4

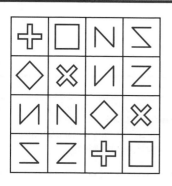

Spend no more than two minutes studying this grid of shapes, then cover it and redraw it as accurately as you can in the empty grid to the right.

1

			7		8			
	8		5		7		2	
9								8
	3						6	
	6						4	
1								7
	2		4		9		1	
			1		2			

This 9x9 Jigsaw Sudoku puzzle is solved just like a regular Sudoku puzzle, except that instead of 3x3 boxes you must now place 1 to 9 into each row, column and bold-lined jigsaw region.

Power naps of the aquatic mammals

Dolphins can sleep with half their brains at a time. Like all aquatic mammals they need to stay half awake while in the water to control their breathing.

2 LEAVE 〉 〉 〉 〉 〉 PORCH

3

What number should come next in each of these three separate mathematical progressions?

1	3	7	15	31	63	___
4	4	6	12	30	90	___
3	5	10	12	24	26	___

Doin' the knowledge improves the IQ

All London taxi cab drivers have to pass an exam known as "the knowledge", that tests their familiarity with London's road network. Brain scans have shown that London cab drivers have an enlarged hippocampus – a part of the brain associated with navigating. The longer-serving drivers had even more enlargement, seeming to prove that their job has an effect on the structure of their brain.

4

Cover over the bottom list of words, and then study the upper list for no more than two minutes. When the time is up, uncover the lower list and cover the upper one instead. Can you write numbers next to the words in order to rearrange them into their original order?

pencil, travel, reading, fork, time, greenery,
video, clothes, painting, memory, cloud, socket

clothes, cloud, fork, greenery, memory, painting,
pencil, reading, socket, time, travel, video

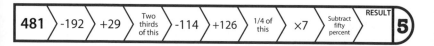

481 ⟩ -192 ⟩ +29 ⟩ Two thirds of this ⟩ -114 ⟩ +126 ⟩ 1/4 of this ⟩ ×7 ⟩ Subtract fifty percent ⟩ RESULT **5**

1 Here is another Kakuro puzzle. For instructions, see **Day 4**.

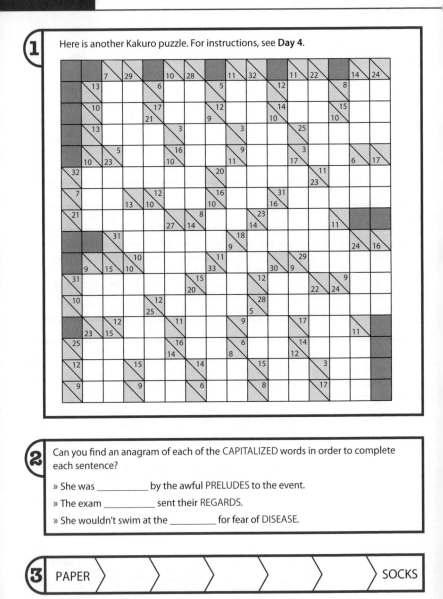

2 Can you find an anagram of each of the CAPITALIZED words in order to complete each sentence?

» She was _____ by the awful PRELUDES to the event.

» The exam _____ sent their REGARDS.

» She wouldn't swim at the _____ for fear of DISEASE.

3 PAPER > > > > > SOCKS

Four items have been hidden at different grid co-ordinates in a village fair's treasure hunt competition. By reference to the empty map and the clues below, can you work out where the items are, and which villager placed each item?

4

» No two gifts were hidden in the same row or column.

» Jimmy's item in column C was both the furthest north and the furthest west.

» Marianne placed her item in an adjacent row to David's item, but both columns on either side of her item were entirely empty.

» Laura's item, in row 3, was one block south and east of Jim's.

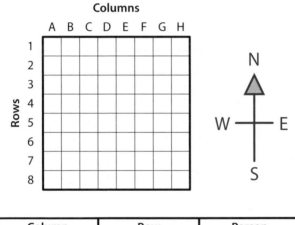

Column	Row	Person

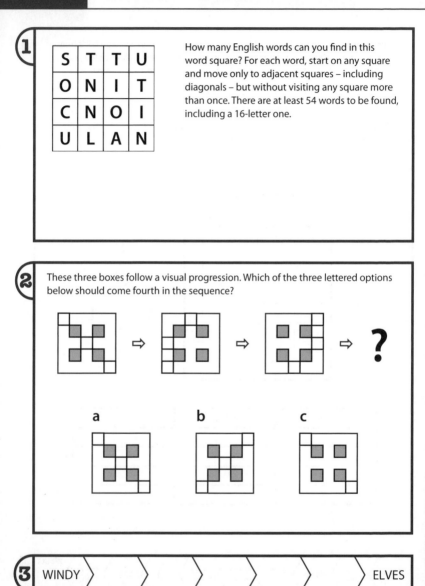

1

S	T	T	U
O	N	I	T
C	N	O	I
U	L	A	N

How many English words can you find in this word square? For each word, start on any square and move only to adjacent squares – including diagonals – but without visiting any square more than once. There are at least 54 words to be found, including a 16-letter one.

2 These three boxes follow a visual progression. Which of the three lettered options below should come fourth in the sequence?

a   b   c

3 WINDY 〉 〉 〉 〉 〉 ELVES

4

			6	9			4	3			
		4		2			1		8		
A		5							6		4
		C	1	9	5	A	B				
6											8
9					2	B					C
7					8	6					B
8											A
			2	7	4	C	9	6			
3		1							C		9
		7		8			B		A		
			4	3			5	2			

Here's another Sudoku 12x12 for you to try. To remind yourself of the instructions, see **Day 77**.

Brain landmarks: dorsolateral prefrontal cortex

At the front and sides of the cortex lies a key structure in flexible thinking. It appears to be responsible for updating what we're consciously holding in mind, such as what we're planning to say next or what our current task is – what is known as "working memory" by psychologists.

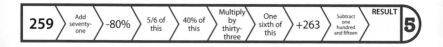

259 → Add seventy-one → -80% → 5/6 of this → 40% of this → Multiply by thirty-three → One sixth of this → +263 → Subtract one hundred and fifteen → **RESULT** **5**

1 Three of the "shape nets" below fold up into identical cubes, but one of the four is slightly different. Which shape net is the odd one out?

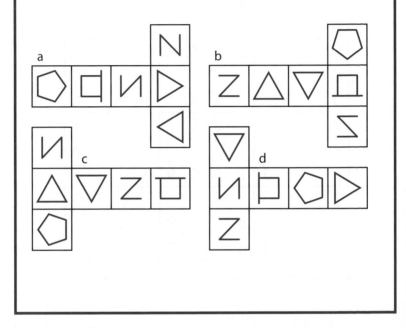

Muscle memory

Some people use the phrase "muscle memory" to refer to the techniques we retain for physical tasks such as riding a bike – skills which we might not consciously understand or even remember that we have. Like all memories, these are actually stored in the brain – not literally in our muscles – but in a different part of the brain from our conscious memories.

2 LOVES 〉 〉 〉 〉 JELLY

3

To solve this Nurikabe, shade in certain squares so that every given number in the puzzle remains as part of a continuous unshaded area of the stated number of squares. There can be only one number per unshaded area. Shaded squares cannot form any solid 2x2 (or larger) areas, and together all the shaded squares must form one single continuous area. White areas cannot touch each other in either a horizontal or vertical direction.

				3		
	1				5	
3						
	5		7			
					2	

4

How good is your memory for detail? Spend no more than two minutes studying these two unusual sentences, then cover them over and see how accurately you can recall them – word for word, punctuation mark for punctuation mark.

» How strange must be the truth for mere fiction to pale into a distant, improbable illusion; in a moment my viewpoint had been transformed in all dimensions but one: compassion.

» If broccoli be the distaste of a president, and sprouts the dislike of an army, then where now the green revolution that stood so proud on the youthful plates of former policy?

407 〉 -110 〉 +67 〉 ÷2 〉 50% of this 〉 Three thirteenths of this 〉 ×6 〉 2/3 of this 〉 +21 〉 RESULT

5

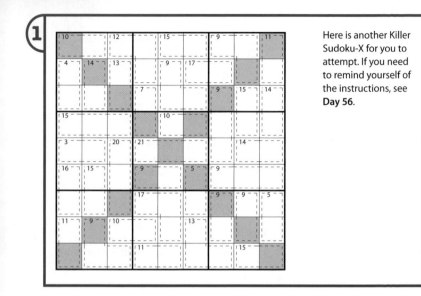

1 Here is another Killer Sudoku-X for you to attempt. If you need to remind yourself of the instructions, see **Day 56**.

2 By choosing exactly one number from each ring of this dartboard, can you find three segments with values that add up to a total of 141? Can you then do the same thing for a total of 171?

For example, to reach a total of 101 you would take 21 from the outer ring, 47 from the middle ring and 33 from the inner ring.

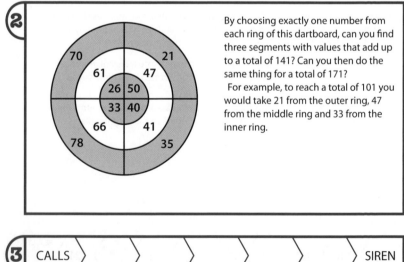

3 CALLS 〉 〉 〉 〉 〉 SIREN

By cracking the code, can you complete this crossword grid? Each of the 26 letters of the alphabet has a different numerical value, which you can write down in the box at the bottom once you've worked it out. Start by examining the "H", "V" and "S". As you allocate each letter to a number, cross the letter off the list running down the sides of the grid.

1	2	3	4	5	6	7	8	9	10	11	12	13
14	15	16	17	18	19	20	21	22	23	24	25	26

| 75 | ×5 | Four fifteenths of this | Thirty percent of this | Add four hundred and ninety-seven | ÷17 | ×22 | ÷11 | +78 | RESULT **5** |

1

	7					5	
	4	3		8		1	
4							5
7							3
	5	2		7		8	
	6					3	

Sudoku Extra Regions adds, as its name suggests, extra regions to a traditional Sudoku puzzle. You must not only place the numbers 1 to 9 into each row, column and bold-lined 3x3 box, but also into each of the four shaded areas.

2 Can you put the results of each of the following rows of sums in ascending order? You will almost certainly find it easiest to estimate the values, rather than calculate them. The first one has been done for you, as an example. (You'll need to think about the relationship between the numbers in the second row.)

a	b	c	d	e
15030 x 998	35040 x 1587	5780 x 9959	154330 x 1987	39499 x 41304
4783	73^2	35^3	24^4	15^5
77.7 x 55.5	22.2 x 33.3	44.4 x 88.8	11.1 x 99.9	66.6 x 22.2

3 MAYOR ⟩ ⟩ ⟩ ⟩ ⟩ FIRED

④

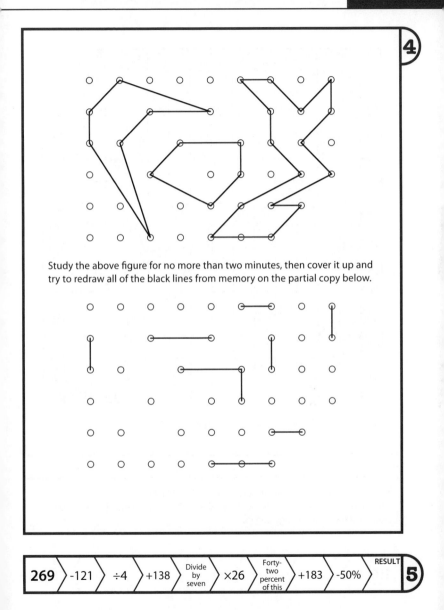

Study the above figure for no more than two minutes, then cover it up and try to redraw all of the black lines from memory on the partial copy below.

RESULT

| 269 | -121 | ÷4 | +138 | Divide by seven | ×26 | Forty-two percent of this | +183 | -50% | ⑤ |

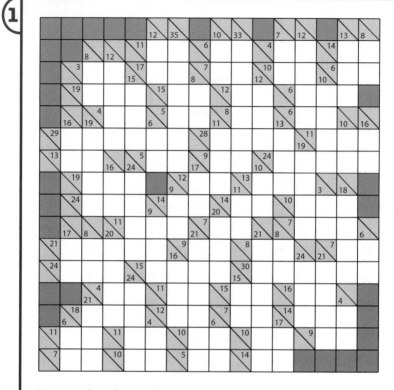

Here is another Kakuro puzzle. For instructions, see **Day 4**.

Fact: The first brain scanners (using the PET and MRI techniques) were developed in the 1970s. But it wasn't until the mid-1990s that the explosion of discoveries made using the technology began.

STOPS ⟩ ⟩ ⟩ ⟩ CRASH

3

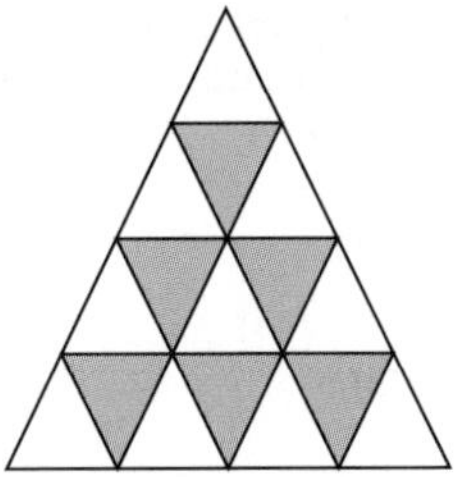

Which of the jigsaw pieces below can be assembled together to make the image at the top? You may not overlap pieces, but they may be rotated if necessary.

4

» I place five cubes on a table so that they make a symmetric capital letter "T", with no gaps within the shape of the "T". If each of the cubes has all sides of length 1cm, then what is the total surface area of my 3D letter "T"?

» A train travels through a tunnel at a constant speed of 225kph. The tunnel is 2km in length, and the train consists of five carriages, each 50m long. For how many seconds is any part of the train in the tunnel?

| 275 | ÷5 | Four fifths of this | ×15 | +45 | 60% of this | -386 | ×2 | Add four hundred and eighty-one | RESULT **5** |

1 Can you match each of the following words with one other in order to form a synonym pair? Each word must be used in precisely one pair.

sad	tolerant	open	extant
enlightened	liable	green	blue
ready	clear	naïve	done
patient	aware	alive	prone

2 Cover up the set of words on the right (in blue). Then spend no more than two minutes looking at the list of word-pairs on the left. Once the time is up, cover the word pairs instead. See if you can recall each pair when given just one of the two words.

Tonal	Discordant	Modernity
Usurp	Overthrow	Table
Anachronism	Modernity	Chair
Transit	Car	Pushchair
Perambulator	Pushchair	Stethoscope
Maternity	Familial	Overthrow
Hysterical	Tickling	Transit
Reporting	Telling	Discordant
Stethoscope	Hearty	Cessation
Table	Desk	Telling
Chair	Govern	Tickling
Finality	Cessation	Maternity

3 CRIES 〉 〉 〉 〉 TEARY

The crowd within

A simple way to improve your estimation ability is to make two estimates and take the average. For the full effect, you should pause after the first guess and assume it is wrong while considering why this might be. Psychologists have described this as "unleashing the crowd within".

4

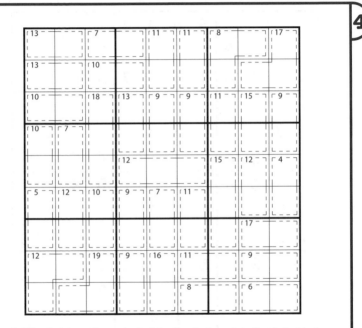

In Killer Sudoku, as in regular Sudoku, the aim is to place the digits 1 to 9 into each row, column and bold-lined 3x3 rectangle. Additionally, place digits so that the total of each dashed-line cage is the value given at the top-left of that cage. Digits may *not* be repeated within a cage.

| 242 | -3 | +434 | -89 | ÷2 | One half of this | +398 | -50% | 50% of this | RESULT **5** |

Aristotle's brain

It has not always been obvious what the brain is for. Aristotle believed that thinking was done with the heart and that the brain's function was to cool the blood.

1

				5	6	A	4				
			B					7			
		2	4	1			7	A	8		
6	3									2	7
	8				5	B				C	
		B	A						4	5	
		5	6						B	3	
	B				4	7				A	
3	C									7	8
		8	1	6			C	5	2		
			7					9			
				3	1	4	8				

In this Sudoku 12x12 you must place the numbers 1 to 9 and the letters A to C in each row, column and bold-lined 4x3 box. Each number and letter must appear only once in any row column or box.

2   NEARS ⟩ ⟩ ⟩ ⟩ ⟩ DAILY

3

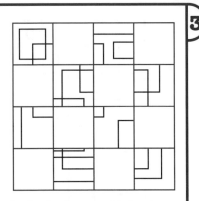

If you were to lay these two images on top of each other, how many black rectangles would be formed? Count all possible black rectangles, including those formed by the overlap of larger rectangles.

4

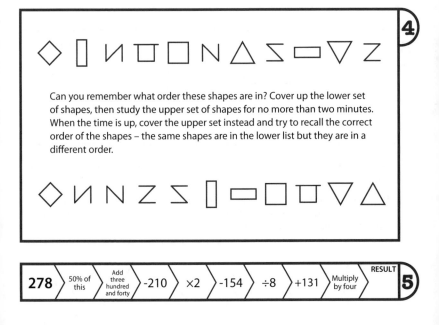

Can you remember what order these shapes are in? Cover up the lower set of shapes, then study the upper set of shapes for no more than two minutes. When the time is up, cover the upper set instead and try to recall the correct order of the shapes – the same shapes are in the lower list but they are in a different order.

| 278 | 50% of this | Add three hundred and forty | -210 | ×2 | -154 | ÷8 | +131 | Multiply by four | **RESULT** **5** |

1

		2			9			
5		7	1	6	3			
				5				
				9				
		3	2	7	9		8	
		5			6			

Here is another Toroidal Sudoku.

Where a region flows off the side of the puzzle it continues in the square directly opposite in the same row or column.

Can you place the numbers 1 to 9 into each row, column and toroidal region? You may find it helpful to start by shading each region with a different colour.

2

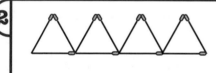

This picture shows 12 matches arranged to form 4 triangles. By moving precisely 6 matches can you change the picture to show 14 triangles?

Kids acting up

Brain training can take all sorts of forms. Some recent provisional research has suggested that teaching drama to children can improve their planning, attention and ability to control their own behaviour.

3 SUPER 〉 〉 〉 〉 FINIS

④

		Instrument				Seat				Composer			
		Violin 1	Violin 2	Viola	Cello	A	B	C	D	Bach	Beethoven	Liszt	Mozart
Person	Eliza												
	Kevin												
	Lindsay												
	Simon												
Composer	Bach												
	Beethoven												
	Liszt												
	Mozart												
Seat	A												
	B												
	C												
	D												

A string quartet sit down to perform, with their seats A, B, C and D arranged as shown in the diagram. Using the information below, can you work out who plays what part, where they sat and who their favourite composer is?

People: Eliza, Kevin, Lindsay, Simon

Instrument: Violin 1, Violin 2, Viola, Cello

Seat: A, B, C, D (see diagram for arrangement)

Favourite Composer: Bach, Beethoven, Liszt, Mozart

Person	Instrument	Seat	Composer

» The violin players, who were of opposite genders, sat next to one another.

» The viola player in seat B was not Eliza.

» Lindsay's favourite composer was Liszt; she did not play the cello.

» Simon did not sit in seat D; neither did he play the cello.

» The player on Violin 1 favoured Mozart, but did not sit next to a player who most liked Bach or Liszt.

| 367 | -173 | +295 | -433 | 1/2 of this | ×18 | ÷8 | ×2 | +264 | RESULT **5** |

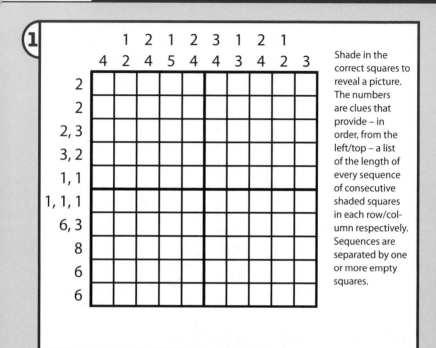

1 Shade in the correct squares to reveal a picture. The numbers are clues that provide – in order, from the left/top – a list of the length of every sequence of consecutive shaded squares in each row/column respectively. Sequences are separated by one or more empty squares.

Column clues (top):
1 2 1 2 3 1 2 1
4 2 4 5 4 4 3 4 2 3

Row clues (left):
2
2
2, 3
3, 2
1, 1
1, 1, 1
6, 3
8
6
6

2 How many words of three or more letters can you find in this word wheel? Each word must contain the centre letter, plus any selection of the other letters no more than once each.

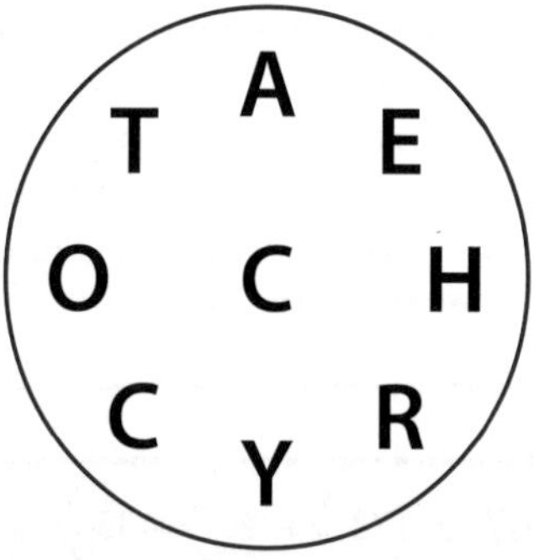

Word wheel letters: T, A, E, O, C (centre), H, C, Y, R

3

36 ÷ 6 = ☐   11 × 7 = ☐   87 − 19 = ☐

56 ÷ 8 = ☐   126 ÷ 9 = ☐   6 × 17 = ☐

26 − 21 = ☐   94 + 11 = ☐   51 − 23 = ☐

8:15a.m. to 1:25p.m. = ☐ : ☐   7:25a.m. to 9:40a.m. = ☐ : ☐

6:30a.m. to 3:10p.m. = ☐ : ☐   8:00a.m. to 9:40a.m. = ☐ : ☐

4:40a.m. to 9:45a.m. = ☐ : ☐   9:35a.m. to 5:00p.m. = ☐ : ☐

£10 + £47700 = ☐   £37000 − £3.93 = ☐

£1690 − £47 = ☐   £480 + £301 = ☐

£3810 − £16.70 = ☐   £43.90 + £4.92 = ☐

4

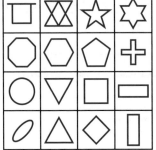

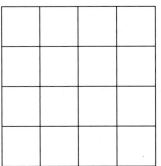

Spend no more than two minutes studying this grid of shapes, then cover it and redraw it as accurately as you can in the empty grid to the right.

SOLUTIONS

Day 1

1.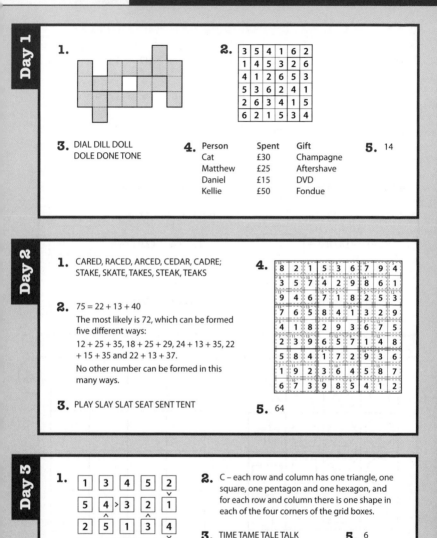

2.

3	5	4	1	6	2
1	4	5	3	2	6
4	1	2	6	5	3
5	3	6	2	4	1
2	6	3	4	1	5
6	2	1	5	3	4

3. DIAL DILL DOLL DOLE DONE TONE

4.

Person	Spent	Gift
Cat	£30	Champagne
Matthew	£25	Aftershave
Daniel	£15	DVD
Kellie	£50	Fondue

5. 14

Day 2

1. CARED, RACED, ARCED, CEDAR, CADRE; STAKE, SKATE, TAKES, STEAK, TEAKS

2. 75 = 22 + 13 + 40

The most likely is 72, which can be formed five different ways:

12 + 25 + 35, 18 + 25 + 29, 24 + 13 + 35, 22 + 15 + 35 and 22 + 13 + 37.

No other number can be formed in this many ways.

3. PLAY SLAY SLAT SEAT SENT TENT

4.

8	2	1	5	3	6	7	9	4
3	5	7	4	2	9	8	6	1
9	4	6	7	1	8	2	5	3
7	6	5	8	4	1	3	2	9
4	1	8	2	9	3	6	7	5
2	3	9	6	5	7	1	4	8
5	8	4	1	7	2	9	3	6
1	9	2	3	6	4	5	8	7
6	7	3	9	8	5	4	1	2

5. 64

Day 3

1.

1	3	4	5	2
5	4 > 3	2	1
2	5	1	3	4
4	2	5	1 < 3
3	1	2	4	5

2. C – each row and column has one triangle, one square, one pentagon and one hexagon, and for each row and column there is one shape in each of the four corners of the grid boxes.

3. TIME TAME TALE TALK TANK BANK

5. 6

Day 4

1.

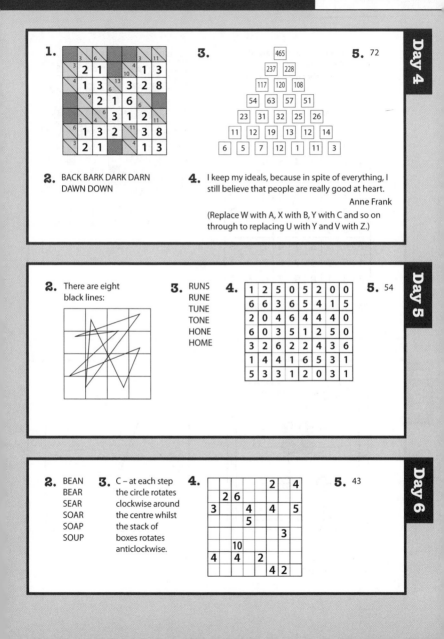

2. BACK BARK DARK DARN DAWN DOWN

3.

465
237 228
117 120 108
54 63 57 51
23 31 32 25 26
11 12 19 13 12 14
6 5 7 12 1 11 3

4. I keep my ideals, because in spite of everything, I still believe that people are really good at heart.

Anne Frank

(Replace W with A, X with B, Y with C and so on through to replacing U with Y and V with Z.)

5. 72

Day 5

2. There are eight black lines:

3. RUNS
RUNE
TUNE
TONE
HONE
HOME

4.

1	2	5	0	5	2	0	0
6	6	3	6	5	4	1	5
2	0	4	6	4	4	4	0
6	0	3	5	1	2	5	0
3	2	6	2	2	4	3	6
1	4	4	1	6	5	3	1
5	3	3	1	2	0	3	1

5. 54

Day 6

2. BEAN
BEAR
SEAR
SOAR
SOAP
SOUP

3. C – at each step the circle rotates clockwise around the centre whilst the stack of boxes rotates anticlockwise.

4.

				2		4
	2	6				
3			4	4		5
			5			
					3	
	10					
4		4	2			
				4	2	

5. 43

SOLUTIONS

Day 7

1. 70 – each number is 13 greater than the preceding number.

20 – each number is 9 less than the preceding number.

96 – each number is twice the preceding number.

2.

9	5	2	6	3	1	8	4	7
3	7	8	2	4	5	9	1	6
1	4	6	9	7	8	5	2	3
8	1	4	7	5	2	3	6	9
5	9	7	4	6	3	1	8	2
6	2	3	1	8	9	4	7	5
7	6	5	3	1	4	2	9	8
4	8	9	5	2	6	7	3	1
2	3	1	8	9	7	6	5	4

3. DAYS WAYS WARS WARY WIRY AIRY

4.

J	O	U	R	N	A	L	S		C	A	V	E
	U		A		Z		W		A		E	
S	T	A	D	I	A		E	N	R	A	G	E
	B		A		L	E	A		I		A	
P	A	I	R		E		R	E	B	I	N	D
	C				A				O			
S	K	I	R	T	S		H	A	U	N	T	S
			E				O				E	
M	O	S	Q	U	E		S		V	E	R	Y
	L		U		D	O	T		I		M	
F	I	X	I	N	G		I	R	O	N	I	C
	V		R		E		N		L		N	
C	E	D	E		D	O	G	M	A	T	I	C

K	L	W	P	Z	B	N	X	F	O	M	Y	Q
D	G	R	S	T	U	V	C	E	H	I	A	J

5. 9

Day 8

1.

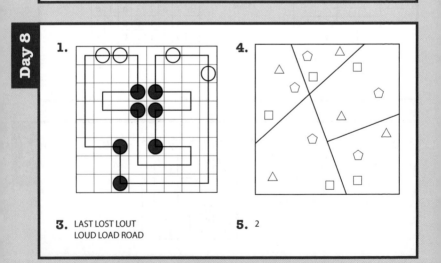

3. LAST LOST LOUT LOUD LOAD ROAD

4.

5. 2

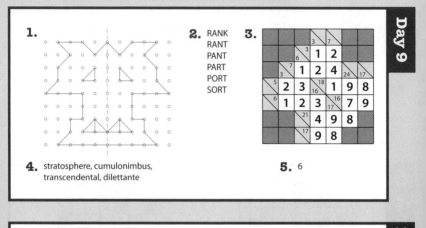

Day 9

1.

2. RANK
RANT
PANT
PART
PORT
SORT

3.

4. stratosphere, cumulonimbus, transcendental, dilettante

5. 6

Day 10

1. den, dent, dethrone, end, enthrone, enthroned, ether, hen, her, hero, heron, net, nether, none, nor, one, ore, rend, rennet, rent, rented, ten, tend, tenon, tenor, the, then, throne

2.

9	8	1	4	6	7	3	5	2
3	4	6	1	5	2	7	8	9
7	5	2	3	9	8	4	1	6
2	1	3	8	4	6	9	7	5
6	7	4	5	1	9	8	2	3
8	9	5	7	2	3	6	4	1
4	2	9	6	7	1	5	3	8
1	3	7	9	8	5	2	6	4
5	6	8	2	3	4	1	9	7

3. QUIT SUIT
SLIT SLAT
SLAY PLAY

5. 21

Day 11

2. 1. C
2. A
3. A

3. EARN
WARN
WARD
WORD
WOOD
FOOD

4.

5. 39

SOLUTIONS

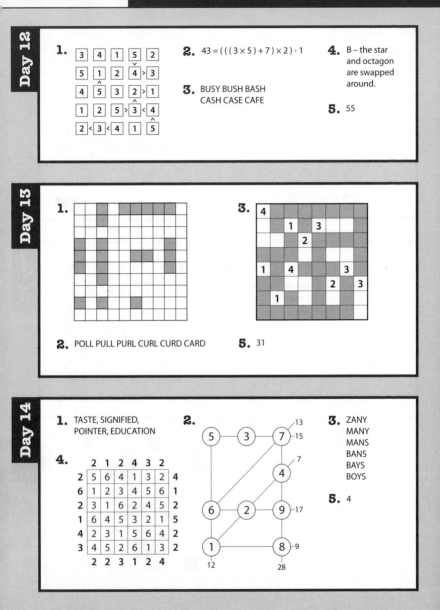

Day 12

1.

3	4	1	5	2
5	1	2	4 >	3
4	5	3	2 >	1
1	2	5 >	3 <	4
2 <	3 <	4	1	5

2. 43 = (((3 × 5) + 7) × 2) - 1

3. BUSY BUSH BASH
CASH CASE CAFE

4. B – the star and octagon are swapped around.

5. 55

Day 13

1.

3.

2. POLL PULL PURL CURL CURD CARD

5. 31

Day 14

1. TASTE, SIGNIFIED, POINTER, EDUCATION

4.

	2	1	2	4	3	2	
2	5	6	4	1	3	2	4
6	1	2	3	4	5	6	1
2	3	1	6	2	4	5	2
1	6	4	5	3	2	1	5
4	2	3	1	5	6	4	2
3	4	5	2	6	1	3	2
	2	2	3	1	2	4	

2.

3. ZANY
MANY
MANS
BANS
BAYS
BOYS

5. 4

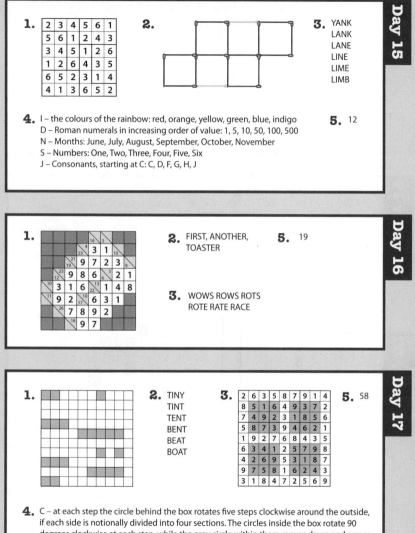

Day 15

1.

2	3	4	5	6	1
5	6	1	2	4	3
3	4	5	1	2	6
1	2	6	4	3	5
6	5	2	3	1	4
4	1	3	6	5	2

2.

3. YANK
LANK
LANE
LINE
LIME
LIMB

4. I – the colours of the rainbow: red, orange, yellow, green, blue, indigo
D – Roman numerals in increasing order of value: 1, 5, 10, 50, 100, 500
N – Months: June, July, August, September, October, November
S – Numbers: One, Two, Three, Four, Five, Six
J – Consonants, starting at C: C, D, F, G, H, J

5. 12

Day 16

1.

				^{16}	^{3}	
			$^{4}_{23}$	3	1	$_{10}$
	$^{21}_{19}$	9	7	2	3	$_{9}$
$^{23}_{12}$	9	8	6	$^{3}_{6}$	2	1
^{10} 3	1	6	$^{13}_{22}$	1	4	8
^{11} 9	2	$^{10}_{17}$	6	3	1	
	^{26}	7	8	9	2	
	^{16}	9	7			

2. FIRST, ANOTHER, TOASTER

3. WOWS ROWS ROTS ROTE RATE RACE

5. 19

Day 17

1.

2. TINY
TINT
TENT
BENT
BEAT
BOAT

3.

2	6	3	5	8	7	9	1	4
8	5	1	6	4	9	3	7	2
7	4	9	2	3	1	8	5	6
5	8	7	3	9	4	6	2	1
1	9	2	7	6	8	4	3	5
6	3	4	1	2	5	7	9	8
4	2	6	9	5	3	1	8	7
9	7	5	8	1	6	2	4	3
3	1	8	4	7	2	5	6	9

5. 58

4. C – at each step the circle behind the box rotates five steps clockwise around the outside, if each side is notionally divided into four sections. The circles inside the box rotate 90 degrees clockwise at each step, while the grey circle within them moves down and across the set of inner circles (relative to the original, unrotated, inner circle positions).

SOLUTIONS

Day 18

2. CUTE
MUTE
MUSE
MUSK
TUSK
TASK

3.

6	2	8	9	1	5	3	4	7
3	5	4	6	8	7	9	1	2
1	7	9	3	2	4	8	6	5
7	9	3	2	4	1	5	8	6
2	8	6	5	3	9	4	7	1
4	1	5	7	6	8	2	3	9
9	3	2	4	7	6	1	5	8
5	6	1	8	9	3	7	2	4
8	4	7	1	5	2	6	9	3

4. PADRES and SPARED
STEWED and TWEEDS
ROGUES and GROUSE
MALIGN and LAMING

5. 5

Day 19

1.

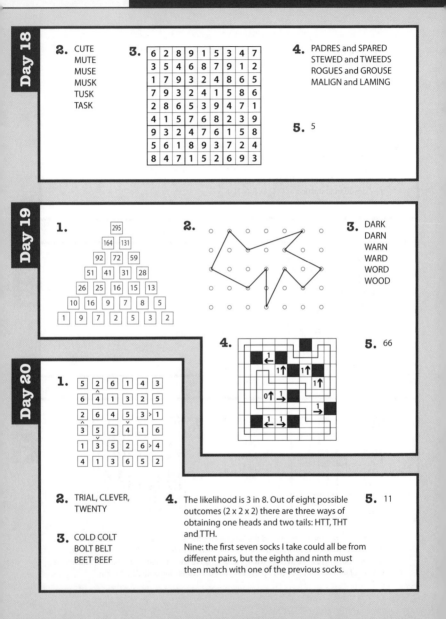

2.

3. DARK
DARN
WARN
WARD
WORD
WOOD

4.

5. 66

Day 20

1.

5	2	6	1	4	3
6	4	1	3	2	5
2	6	4	5	3	1
3	5	2	4	1	6
1	3	5	2	6	4
4	1	3	6	5	2

2. TRIAL, CLEVER,
TWENTY

3. COLD COLT
BOLT BELT
BEET BEEF

4. The likelihood is 3 in 8. Out of eight possible outcomes (2 x 2 x 2) there are three ways of obtaining one heads and two tails: HTT, THT and TTH.

Nine: the first seven socks I take could all be from different pairs, but the eighth and ninth must then match with one of the previous socks.

5. 11

Day 21

1. 1. A
2. A
3. C

3. CATS
PATS
PALS
PALL
POLL
LOLL

4.

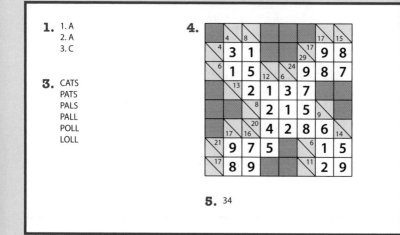

5. 34

Day 22

2.

6	1	2	4	8	5	9	7	3
4	9	3	2	1	7	5	6	8
7	5	8	6	9	3	1	2	4
3	6	7	5	4	1	2	8	9
9	2	1	3	7	8	4	5	6
5	8	4	9	6	2	3	1	7
2	4	9	7	5	6	8	3	1
1	3	6	8	2	4	7	9	5
8	7	5	1	3	9	6	4	2

3. MAIN LAIN LOIN LOAN ROAN ROAD

4. abed, able, abler, ables, ace, aced, aces, acre, acres, amber, amble, ambled, ambles, arc, arced, arcs, are, bar, bare, bared, bares, beam, bear, bed, beds, bled, cab, cable, cabled, cables, cabs, cam, camber, came, camel, camels, car, care, cared, cares, crab, crabs, cram, cream, dear, deb, debar, debs, ear, era, lea, led, mace, maced, maces, mar, mare, mares, race, raced, races, ram, ramble, rambled, rambles, ream, red, reds, scab, scar, scare, scared, scram, scramble, scrambled, scream, sea, seam, sear, sled

5. 4

SOLUTIONS

Day 23

1.

3	9	4	2	5	1	6	7	8
5	2	7	8	4	6	9	1	3
1	6	8	7	9	3	5	2	4
2	5	1	4	8	9	3	6	7
7	4	9	6	3	5	2	8	1
8	3	6	1	2	7	4	9	5
9	8	2	3	7	4	1	5	6
6	7	3	5	1	2	8	4	9
4	1	5	9	6	8	7	3	2

2. ROCK
LOCK
LACK
LACE
LAME
GAME

3.

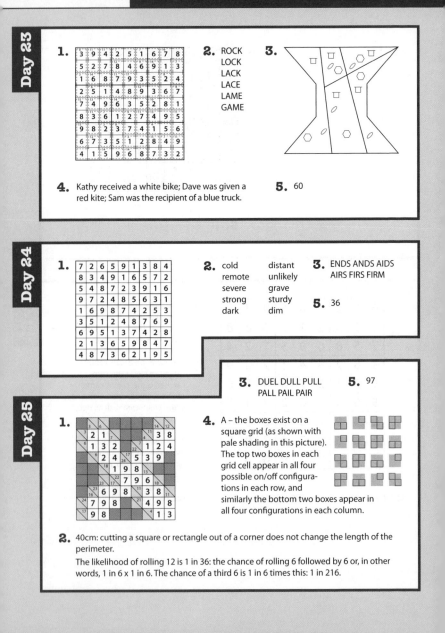

4. Kathy received a white bike; Dave was given a red kite; Sam was the recipient of a blue truck.

5. 60

Day 24

1.

7	2	6	5	9	1	3	8	4
8	3	4	9	1	6	5	7	2
5	4	8	7	2	3	9	1	6
9	7	2	4	8	5	6	3	1
1	6	9	8	7	4	2	5	3
3	5	1	2	4	8	7	6	9
6	9	5	1	3	7	4	2	8
2	1	3	6	5	9	8	4	7
4	8	7	3	6	2	1	9	5

2.
cold	distant
remote	unlikely
severe	grave
strong	sturdy
dark	dim

3. ENDS ANDS AIDS
AIRS FIRS FIRM

5. 36

Day 25

3. DUEL DULL PULL
PALL PAIL PAIR

5. 97

1.

4. A – the boxes exist on a square grid (as shown with pale shading in this picture). The top two boxes in each grid cell appear in all four possible on/off configurations in each row, and similarly the bottom two boxes appear in all four configurations in each column.

2. 40cm: cutting a square or rectangle out of a corner does not change the length of the perimeter.

The likelihood of rolling 12 is 1 in 36: the chance of rolling 6 followed by 6 or, in other words, 1 in 6 x 1 in 6. The chance of a third 6 is 1 in 6 times this: 1 in 216.

SOLUTIONS

Day 26

1.

```
                258
            131   127
         68    63   64
      36   32   31   33
   19   17   15   16   17
 10    9    8    7    9    8
4    6    3    5    2    7    1
```

2.

2	9	1	4	6	7	8	5	3
6	3	4	9	8	5	7	1	2
7	5	8	1	3	2	4	6	9
1	6	7	2	4	3	9	8	5
5	2	3	8	9	6	1	4	7
8	4	9	5	7	1	2	3	6
9	1	6	3	2	8	5	7	4
3	8	2	7	5	4	6	9	1
4	7	5	6	1	9	3	2	8

3. WALK
WALL
WELL
FELL
FELT
FEET

5. 48

Day 27

1. All truths are easy to understand once they are discovered; the point is to discover them.

Galileo

(Replace B with A, C with B, D with C and so on through to replacing Z with Y and A with Z.)

3. JUNK SUNK SANK SANE SALE MALE

5. 12

2. Jennifer — Cycling — Mon
Kate — Swimming — Tues
Vanessa — Yoga — Thurs

4.

8	7	6	2	1	3	4	5	9
5	4	3	7	6	9	1	8	2
1	2	9	4	5	8	7	3	6
3	5	2	9	4	6	8	1	7
9	6	1	5	8	7	2	4	3
4	8	7	3	2	1	9	6	5
6	3	8	1	9	2	5	7	4
7	9	4	8	3	5	6	2	1
2	1	5	6	7	4	3	9	8

Day 28

1.

```
3 3 2 2 2 3 3 3
2       2 2     2
 2      2  3 2
  3    2 3 1    3
3   1 1 3     3
  3 2   2      3
2   0 1        3
3 3 2 1 2 3 2 3
```

2. obfuscatory
youngster
happenstance
understandable

3. KING WING
WINE WIRE
WORE WORM

4. B – the two triangles rotate clockwise around the corners of the square, alternating back and forth between being filled and unfilled. The ellipse moves back and forth between the two bottom corners of the square.

5. 63

SOLUTIONS

Day 29

2.

2	4	3	6	7	5	8	1	9
5	1	6	8	3	9	2	7	4
9	7	8	4	2	1	6	5	3
6	9	2	5	1	3	7	4	8
8	3	1	7	4	2	9	6	5
7	5	4	9	6	8	3	2	1
1	2	7	3	8	4	5	9	6
3	6	5	1	9	7	4	8	2
4	8	9	2	5	6	1	3	7

3. MOON
MOOT
MOST
MUST
DUST
DUSK

4.

5. 62

Day 30

1.

2. COWS COBS LOBS LOBE LOVE LIVE

3. $117 = (((25 \times 2) + 5) \times 2) + 7$

5. 81

Day 31

1.

2. DUCK
DUNK
PUNK
PUNY
PONY
POND

3. APEX,
TESTED,
PROBED

4.

5. 39

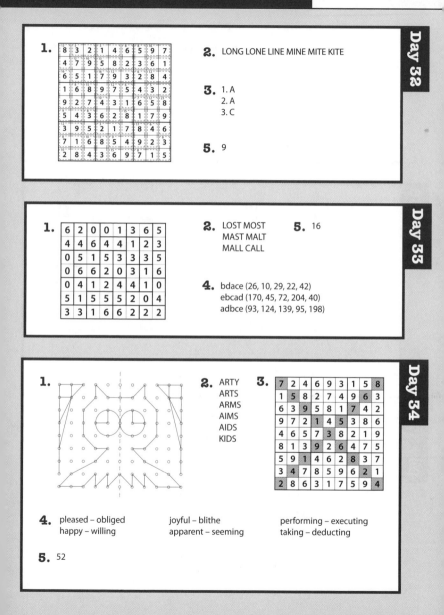

Day 32

1.

8	3	2	1	4	6	5	9	7
4	7	9	5	8	2	3	6	1
6	5	1	7	9	3	2	8	4
1	6	8	9	7	5	4	3	2
9	2	7	4	3	1	6	5	8
5	4	3	6	2	8	1	7	9
3	9	5	2	1	7	8	4	6
7	1	6	8	5	4	9	2	3
2	8	4	3	6	9	7	1	5

2. LONG LONE LINE MINE MITE KITE

3. 1. A
2. A
3. C

5. 9

Day 33

1.

6	2	0	0	1	3	6	5
4	4	6	4	4	1	2	3
0	5	1	5	3	3	3	5
0	6	6	2	0	3	1	6
0	4	1	2	4	4	1	0
5	1	5	5	5	2	0	4
3	3	1	6	6	2	2	2

2. LOST MOST
MAST MALT
MALL CALL

5. 16

4. bdace (26, 10, 29, 22, 42)
ebcad (170, 45, 72, 204, 40)
adbce (93, 124, 139, 95, 198)

Day 34

1.

2. ARTY
ARTS
ARMS
AIMS
AIDS
KIDS

3.

7	2	4	6	9	3	1	5	8
1	5	8	2	7	4	9	6	3
6	3	9	5	8	1	7	4	2
9	7	2	1	4	5	3	8	6
4	6	5	7	3	8	2	1	9
8	1	3	9	2	6	4	7	5
5	9	1	4	6	2	8	3	7
3	4	7	8	5	9	6	2	1
2	8	6	3	1	7	5	9	4

4. pleased – obliged
happy – willing

joyful – blithe
apparent – seeming

performing – executing
taking – deducting

5. 52

SOLUTIONS

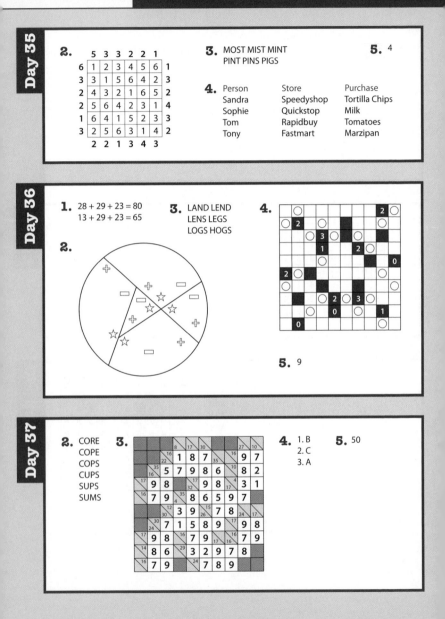

Day 35

2.

	5	3	3	2	2	1	
6	1	2	3	4	5	6	1
3	3	1	5	6	4	2	3
2	4	3	2	1	6	5	2
2	5	6	4	2	3	1	4
1	6	4	1	5	2	3	3
3	2	5	6	3	1	4	2
	2	2	1	3	4	3	

3. MOST MIST MINT
PINT PINS PIGS

5. 4

4.
Person	Store	Purchase
Sandra	Speedyshop	Tortilla Chips
Sophie	Quickstop	Milk
Tom	Rapidbuy	Tomatoes
Tony	Fastmart	Marzipan

Day 36

1. 28 + 29 + 23 = 80
13 + 29 + 23 = 65

3. LAND LEND
LENS LEGS
LOGS HOGS

2.

4.

5. 9

Day 37

2. CORE
COPE
COPS
CUPS
SUPS
SUMS

3.

4. 1. B
2. C
3. A

5. 50

1.

4	1	6	5	7	8	2	3	9
2	8	5	6	3	9	4	1	7
3	9	7	1	2	4	5	8	6
1	5	8	7	6	2	9	4	3
9	3	2	4	1	5	6	7	8
7	6	4	8	9	3	1	2	5
6	2	3	9	4	7	8	5	1
5	4	9	3	8	1	7	6	2
8	7	1	2	5	6	3	9	4

3.
FIRE
FORE
CORE
COPE
COPS
COWS

4.

A	B	S		M	U	M		M	U	F	T	I
B		E			O		O		I		N
U	R	I	C		A	D	J	U	D	G	E	D
S		Z		O		U		R		S		E
E	Q	U	I	V	A	L	E	N	T			X
	R		E		I				C		E
C	L	E	A	N	S		A	T	O	L	L	S
L		S			P		R		A			
A			C	O	V	A	R	I	A	N	C	E
N		K		P		R		P		G		V
K	A	N	G	A	R	O	O		W	E	R	E
E		E		L		L			R		R
D	U	E	T	S		E	A	R		S	H	Y

B	Q	K	G	R	Y	L	H	I	W	V	O	T
N	P	E	J	X	A	Z	D	F	S	M	C	U

5. 30

---

1. A – at each step the grey squares rotate anti-clockwise around the set of squares, and the set of four rotated squares move back and forth behind the other set of four squares.

2. The chance is 1 in 6: There are 366 days in a leap year and June and July contain a total of 61 days (30 + 31). 61 will divide exactly six times into 366.

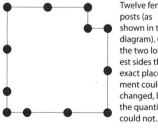

Twelve fence posts (as shown in this diagram). On the two longest sides the exact placement could be changed, but the quantity could not.

3. DOWN TOWN TORN TORE TIRE TIME

4.

8	2	1	5	7	6	3	4	9
9	5	3	1	8	4	2	6	7
7	4	6	3	9	2	5	1	8
3	8	2	7	6	5	4	9	1
5	1	7	9	4	3	8	2	6
6	9	4	8	2	1	7	3	5
2	7	9	6	3	8	1	5	4
4	6	5	2	1	7	9	8	3
1	3	8	4	5	9	6	7	2

5. 18

SOLUTIONS

Day 40

1.
Bill	Bananas	2kg
Jim	Apples	4kg
Doug	Potatoes	6kg

3. BEST
BUST
MUST
MIST
MINT
MINX

5. 38

4.
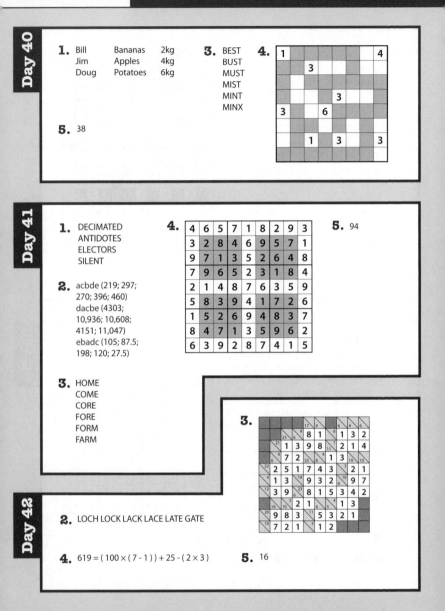

Day 41

1. DECIMATED
ANTIDOTES
ELECTORS
SILENT

2. acbde (219; 297; 270; 396; 460)
dacbe (4303; 10,936; 10,608; 4151; 11,047)
ebadc (105; 87.5; 198; 120; 27.5)

3. HOME
COME
CORE
FORE
FORM
FARM

4.
4	6	5	7	1	8	2	9	3
3	2	8	4	6	9	5	7	1
9	7	1	3	5	2	6	4	8
7	9	6	5	2	3	1	8	4
2	1	4	8	7	6	3	5	9
5	8	3	9	4	1	7	2	6
1	5	2	6	9	4	8	3	7
8	4	7	1	3	5	9	6	2
6	3	9	2	8	7	4	1	5

5. 94

Day 42

3.

2. LOCH LOCK LACK LACE LATE GATE

4. $619 = (100 \times (7 - 1)) + 25 - (2 \times 3)$

5. 16

Day 43

1. There are six pairs of anagrams: VERSATILE and RELATIVES; FLASHIEST and FAITHLESS; MEDITATES and ESTIMATED; SUCTIONED and SEDUCTION; GYRATIONS and SIGNATORY; UNALTERED and UNRELATED

2.

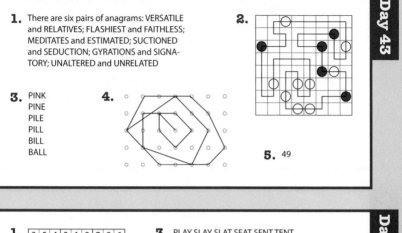

3.
PINK
PINE
PILE
PILL
BILL
BALL

4.

5. 49

Day 44

1.

2	5	4	3	1	9	7	8	6
3	9	6	7	2	8	1	5	4
8	7	1	4	6	5	3	2	9
5	3	2	9	4	1	6	7	8
7	1	9	6	8	2	5	4	3
6	4	8	5	3	7	2	9	1
1	2	7	8	9	6	4	3	5
4	8	5	1	7	3	9	6	2
9	6	3	2	5	4	8	1	7

3. PLAY SLAY SLAT SEAT SENT TENT

4. $34 + 38 + 28 = 100$
$34 + 27 + 14 = 75$

5. 57

Day 45

1. All my life I've wanted to be somebody. But I see now I should have been more specific.

Jane Wagner

(Replace W with A, X with B, Y with C and so on all the way to replacing U with Y and V with Z.)

2.

	2		4			
2	6					2
		3		3		2
		2				4
		2	4	4		
10			3			
			6	3		
					2	

3.
RAVE
GAVE
GALE
GALL
GILL
GIRL

4.

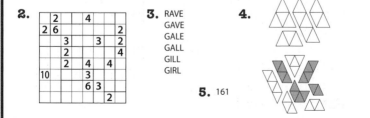

5. 161

Day 46

2. 1 – each number is a third of the preceding number.

76 – each number is 17 less than the preceding number.

256 – multiply the preceding two numbers.

3. BARE
BARK
BACK
BECK
DECK
DESK

4.

5. 102

Day 47

1.

2. incandescent
intercontinental
antidisestablishmentarianism
digestive

3. RICH RICE RIDE RODE RODS GODS

4.

9	3	5	7	2	8	6	1	4
4	1	8	3	9	6	2	5	7
7	2	6	4	5	1	3	9	8
5	7	2	9	8	3	4	6	1
1	9	4	6	7	2	5	8	3
8	6	3	1	4	5	9	7	2
2	8	9	5	3	7	1	4	6
6	4	7	2	1	9	8	3	5
3	5	1	8	6	4	7	2	9

5. 31

Day 48

1.

7	4	5	2	8	1	6	3	9
8	2	9	6	4	3	5	7	1
3	1	6	7	9	5	8	2	4
1	9	2	5	3	6	7	4	8
4	6	7	8	1	2	3	9	5
5	3	8	4	7	9	2	1	6
9	7	3	1	6	8	4	5	2
6	5	1	3	2	4	9	8	7
2	8	4	9	5	7	1	6	3

3. BLUE
GLUE
GLUT
GOUT
GOAT
MOAT

4.

5. 82

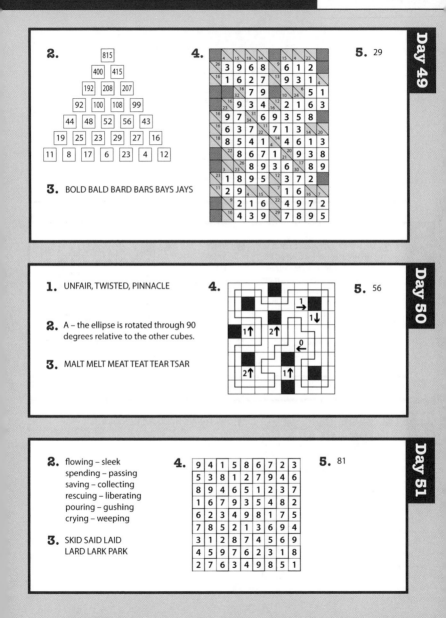

Day 49

2.

815
400 415
192 208 207
92 100 108 99
44 48 52 56 43
19 25 23 29 27 16
11 8 17 6 23 4 12

3. BOLD BALD BARD BARS BAYS JAYS

4.

5. 29

Day 50

1. UNFAIR, TWISTED, PINNACLE

2. A – the ellipse is rotated through 90 degrees relative to the other cubes.

3. MALT MELT MEAT TEAT TEAR TSAR

4.

5. 56

Day 51

2. flowing – sleek
spending – passing
saving – collecting
rescuing – liberating
pouring – gushing
crying – weeping

3. SKID SAID LAID
LARD LARK PARK

4.

9	4	1	5	8	6	7	2	3
5	3	8	1	2	7	9	4	6
8	9	4	6	5	1	2	3	7
1	6	7	9	3	5	4	8	2
6	2	3	4	9	8	1	7	5
7	8	5	2	1	3	6	9	4
3	1	2	8	7	4	5	6	9
4	5	9	7	6	2	3	1	8
2	7	6	3	4	9	8	5	1

5. 81

SOLUTIONS

2. 1. A
2. A
3. C

3. DONE
DONS
DENS
HENS
HERS
HERO

4.

5	2	1	4	3	7	8	6	9
9	8	4	5	6	2	3	1	7
3	6	7	1	9	8	5	4	2
2	1	6	7	8	4	9	3	5
8	4	9	6	5	3	2	7	1
7	3	5	9	2	1	4	8	6
4	5	2	8	1	6	7	9	3
6	7	3	2	4	9	1	5	8
1	9	8	3	7	5	6	2	4

5. 60

1. A – whichever ellipse has the small circle on it is rotated 90 degrees relative to the other ellipses. The circle is also moving anti-clockwise around the square, and isn't shown when not on an ellipse.

2. REWARDS, INFRINGE, SUN-BURNED, POSTURED

3. YAKS
YAMS
DAMS
DADS
DUDS
DUDE

5. 22

4.

3	1	9	7	6	2	5	4	8
5	2	7	4	9	8	3	6	1
4	6	8	1	5	3	7	9	2
9	7	1	6	2	5	4	8	3
8	3	5	9	4	1	6	2	7
2	4	6	3	8	7	9	1	5
6	8	2	5	7	9	1	3	4
7	9	3	2	1	4	8	5	6
1	5	4	8	3	6	2	7	9

2.

			15	4	17	15		8	23	
		22	8	3	9	2		7	1	6
	23	5	6	1	8	3	14	5	9	
11	8	2	1		23	4	9	2	8	
15	9	6	9		12	5	7	16		
	16	6	16	4	1	8	5	3		
11	21	2	9	1	15	3	2	1		
13	4	9	30	7	3	9	7	9	2	
21	7	8	6	34	2	6	1	17		
	25	4	7	9	5	9	6	3	1	
	17	15	9	8		3	2	1		
25	4	7	8	6	17	13	9	8	2	
8	2	6	33	7	9	8	5	4		
3	1	2	24	4	8	5	7			

3. WILD WIND HIND HINT HUNT AUNT

4.

Job	Person	Day	Patients
Dentist	Jane	Tues	7
Doctor	Peter	Weds	18
Optician	Susan	Mon	14

5. 26

Day 55

2.

1	4	7	8	5	3	6	9	2
7	6	4	9	2	5	3	1	8
2	9	3	6	1	8	7	4	5
8	1	2	4	6	7	9	5	3
6	5	8	7	3	9	1	2	4
9	3	5	2	4	6	8	7	1
5	8	9	1	7	4	2	3	6
4	7	1	3	8	2	5	6	9
3	2	6	5	9	1	4	8	7

3. SAME
SOME
SORE
SORT
FORT
FOOT

4.

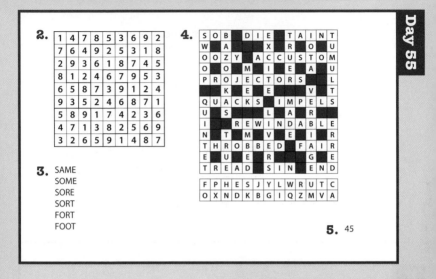

5. 45

Day 56

1.

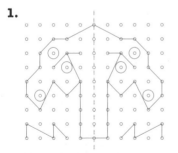

2. 34 – add the preceding two numbers.
2160 – starting from the first number, multiply by 1, then 2, then 3, then 4 and so on.
12,500,000 – multiply the preceding two numbers.

3. NEXT TEXT TENT GENT GENE GONE

4.

1	2	9	4	6	5	8	3	7
4	3	6	7	8	1	9	5	2
8	5	7	3	9	2	6	4	1
6	9	1	2	5	3	7	8	4
5	8	3	6	4	7	1	2	9
7	4	2	9	1	8	3	6	5
9	6	8	1	2	4	5	7	3
3	1	4	5	7	6	2	9	8
2	7	5	8	3	9	4	1	6

5. 156

Day 57

1.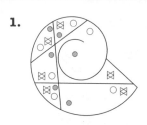

2. I was born not knowing and have had only a little time to change that here and there.

Richard Feynman

(Replace D with A, E with B, F with C and so on through to replacing B with Y and C with Z.)

3. FOOD FOND BOND
BAND BANS BAGS

4.

3	7	8	1	5	9	4	2	6
9	6	4	3	2	7	8	5	1
5	1	2	4	6	8	3	9	7
8	4	7	6	1	2	5	3	9
2	5	9	7	3	4	6	1	8
6	3	1	9	8	5	2	7	4
1	8	3	2	9	6	7	4	5
4	9	5	8	7	3	1	6	2
7	2	6	5	4	1	9	8	3

5. 24

Day 58

1. 24 + 47 + 40 = 111
24 + 12 + 30 = 66

3. WARM WART WANT
WENT WEST NEST

4.

4	1	5 <	6	2	3
6	2	1	5	3 <	4
1	4 <	6	3	5	2
3 <	5	4	2	1	6
2	6	3	1	4	5
5	3	2	4	6	1

5. 72

Day 59

1. There are six pairs of anagrams:

STILTED and SLITTED
SCENTED and DESCENT
WORDIER and WORRIED
TOUSLED and LOUDEST
BOARDER and BROADER
CANTERS and SCANTER

3. JOGS
BOGS
BAGS
BANS
BANK
BACK

5. 84

4.

3	0	5	2	6	3	4	2
3	4	5	2	1	5	5	0
4	1	0	6	2	2	6	4
3	1	4	3	5	2	5	0
1	4	0	0	0	1	4	6
6	4	0	6	3	5	2	6
1	1	3	6	1	3	2	5

Day 60

1. There are 11 circles:

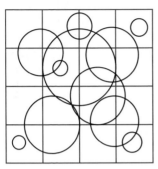

2. incongruous, teleportation, expectation, opaquer

3. CHIC CHIN COIN CORN CORE BORE

4.

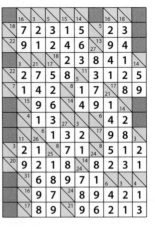

5. 118

Day 61

1.

2.

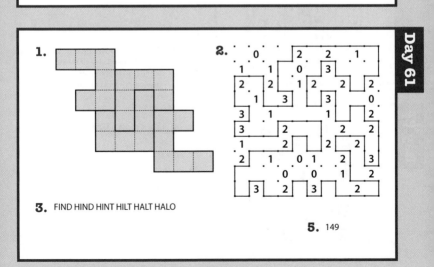

3. FIND HIND HINT HILT HALT HALO

5. 149

SOLUTIONS

Day 62

1.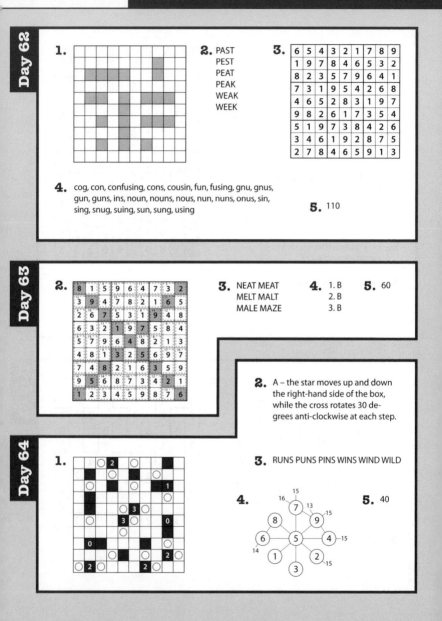

2. PAST
PEST
PEAT
PEAK
WEAK
WEEK

3.

6	5	4	3	2	1	7	8	9
1	9	7	8	4	6	5	3	2
8	2	3	5	7	9	6	4	1
7	3	1	9	5	4	2	6	8
4	6	5	2	8	3	1	9	7
9	8	2	6	1	7	3	5	4
5	1	9	7	3	8	4	2	6
3	4	6	1	9	2	8	7	5
2	7	8	4	6	5	9	1	3

4. cog, con, confusing, cons, cousin, fun, fusing, gnu, gnus, gun, guns, ins, noun, nouns, nous, nun, nuns, onus, sin, sing, snug, suing, sun, sung, using

5. 110

Day 63

2.

8	1	5	9	6	4	7	3	2
3	9	4	7	8	2	1	6	5
2	6	7	5	3	1	9	4	8
6	3	2	1	9	7	5	8	4
5	7	9	6	4	8	2	1	3
4	8	1	3	2	5	6	9	7
7	4	8	2	1	6	3	5	9
9	5	6	8	7	3	4	2	1
1	2	3	4	5	9	8	7	6

3. NEAT MEAT
MELT MALT
MALE MAZE

4. 1. B
2. B
3. B

5. 60

2. A – the star moves up and down the right-hand side of the box, while the cross rotates 30 degrees anti-clockwise at each step.

Day 64

1.

3. RUNS PUNS PINS WINS WIND WILD

4.

5. 40

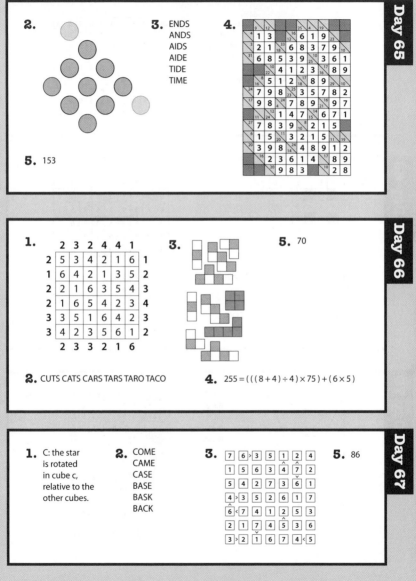

Day 65

2.

3. ENDS
ANDS
AIDS
AIDE
TIDE
TIME

4.

5. 153

Day 66

1.

	2	3	2	4	4	1	
2	5	3	4	2	1	6	1
1	6	4	2	1	3	5	2
2	2	1	6	3	5	4	3
2	1	6	5	4	2	3	4
3	3	5	1	6	4	2	3
3	4	2	3	5	6	1	2
	2	3	3	2	1	6	

3.

5. 70

2. CUTS CATS CARS TARS TARO TACO

4. $255 = (((8 + 4) \div 4) \times 75) + (6 \times 5)$

Day 67

1. C: the star is rotated in cube c, relative to the other cubes.

2. COME
CAME
CASE
BASE
BASK
BACK

3.

7	6 > 3	5	1	2	4
1	5	6	3	4	7	2
5	4	2	7	3	6	1
4 > 3	5	2	6	1	7
6 < 7	4	1	2	5	3
2	1	7	4	5	3	6
3 > 2	1	6	7	4 < 5

5. 86

SOLUTIONS

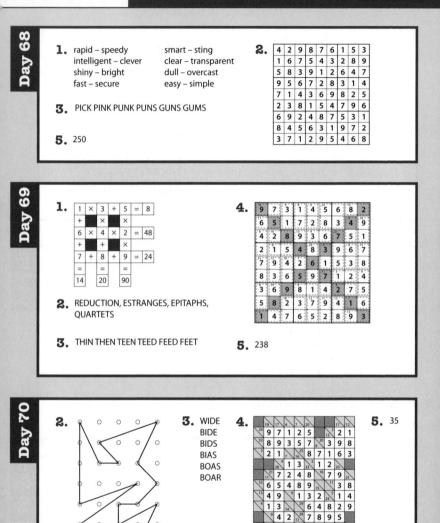

Day 68

1. rapid – speedy
intelligent – clever
shiny – bright
fast – secure

smart – sting
clear – transparent
dull – overcast
easy – simple

3. PICK PINK PUNK PUNS GUNS GUMS

5. 250

2.

4	2	9	8	7	6	1	5	3
1	6	7	5	4	3	2	8	9
5	8	3	9	1	2	6	4	7
9	5	6	7	2	8	3	1	4
7	1	4	3	6	9	8	2	5
2	3	8	1	5	4	7	9	6
6	9	2	4	8	7	5	3	1
8	4	5	6	3	1	9	7	2
3	7	1	2	9	5	4	6	8

Day 69

1.

1	×	3	+	5	=	8
+		×		×		
6	×	4	×	2	=	48
+		+		×		
7	+	8	+	9	=	24
=		=		=		
14		20		90		

2. REDUCTION, ESTRANGES, EPITAPHS, QUARTETS

3. THIN THEN TEEN TEED FEED FEET

4.

9	7	3	1	4	5	6	8	2
6	5	1	7	2	8	3	4	9
4	2	8	9	3	6	7	5	1
2	1	5	4	8	3	9	6	7
7	9	4	2	6	1	5	3	8
8	3	6	5	9	7	1	2	4
3	6	9	8	1	4	2	7	5
5	8	2	3	7	9	4	1	6
1	4	7	6	5	2	8	9	3

5. 238

Day 70

2.

3. WIDE
BIDE
BIDS
BIAS
BOAS
BOAR

4.

9	7	1	2	5			2	1
8	9	3	5	7		3	9	8
2	1		8	7	1	6	3	
		1	3		1	2		
	7	2	4	8		7	9	
6	5	4	8	9			3	8
4	9		1	3	2		1	4
1	3			6	4	8	2	9
	4	2		7	8	9	5	
		1	2		1	7		
1	3	4	9	6			2	9
4	9	7		4	7	3	1	8
2	7			8	9	1	4	7

5. 35

1.

2	5	8	6	3	9	1	4	7
4	7	5	9	8	2	3	6	1
8	2	3	5	4	7	6	1	9
3	9	6	2	5	1	4	7	8
9	1	7	3	6	8	2	5	4
7	3	4	1	9	5	8	2	6
1	4	2	8	7	6	9	3	5
6	8	1	7	2	4	5	9	3
5	6	9	4	1	3	7	8	2

2. HOST POST
PEST PEAT
NEAT NEAR

4. FINALE
CLIMAX
CULMINATE

5. 26

3. There are 14 triangles:

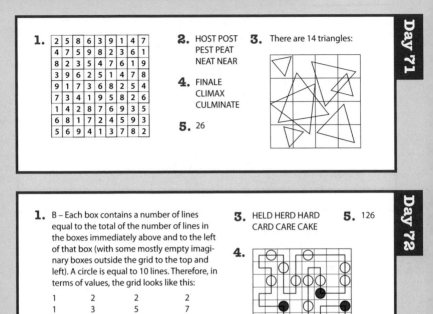

---

1. B – Each box contains a number of lines equal to the total of the number of lines in the boxes immediately above and to the left of that box (with some mostly empty imaginary boxes outside the grid to the top and left). A circle is equal to 10 lines. Therefore, in terms of values, the grid looks like this:

1	2	2	2
1	3	5	7
1	4	9	16
3	7	16	32

3. HELD HERD HARD
CARD CARE CAKE

5. 126

4.

1.
Dog & Bucket	4:00pm	Steak
TexyMexy	5:30pm	Chicken
Les Français	7:00pm	Fish

2.

4	7	1	3	9	8	6	2	5
3	8	5	6	1	2	9	4	7
9	6	2	5	4	7	8	3	1
7	9	3	1	2	5	4	8	6
1	2	8	7	6	4	5	9	3
6	5	4	8	3	9	7	1	2
8	1	6	4	7	3	2	5	9
2	4	7	9	5	1	3	6	8
5	3	9	2	8	6	1	7	4

3. SUNK
SANK
SANE
SAVE
NAVE
NAVY

5. 87

4.

G	O	D		L	E	A		R	U	N	I	C
L		I			B	U		O		R	
O	U	S	T		G	L	A	D	I	O	L	I
W		M	O		A	E		N		N	
S	T	A	R	G	A	Z	E	R	S		K	
		L		L	E			Q		L	
J	O	L	T	E	D		L	U	X	U	R	Y
U		Y		R		N		A		
S			E	M	B	I	T	T	E	R	E	D
T		S	O		V		O		R		R	
I	M	P	R	O	V	E	D		P	E	S	O
F		A	R		R			L		N	
Y	A	R	D	S		S	O	W		S	H	E

V	P	D	G	W	U	B	E	C	T	I	J	Z
L	F	Q	O	H	Y	A	S	M	K	N	R	X

SOLUTIONS

Day 74

1. 1. A
2. B
3. C

3. HARD
CARD
CORD
CORK
COOK
BOOK

4.

						15	3	21		
				19	8	1	9	27		
			12	7	6	2	8	9	16	
		10	6	3	1		19	6	8	5	5
	12	3	8	1		35		21	3	1	2
	20	5	9	8	7	30	6	7	8	9
		1	2	12	9	1	2	10	2	8
					5	3	1			
	2	13		13	8	6	9	11	27	8	2
	13	4	1	2	6	13	3	2	7	1
	13	2	3	8	11		18	5	9	4
	17	7	9	1	8	4	1	3		
		17	4	2	1	7	3			
			23	8	6	9				

5. 155

Day 75

1. S – Planets from the sun out: Mercury, Venus, Earth, Mars, Jupiter, Saturn; S – Ordinals: first, second, third, fourth, fifth, sixth; O – uppercase letters with curved sections; C – The periodic table: Hydrogen, Helium, Lithium, Beryllium, Boron, Carbon; O – months with 31 days: January, March, May, July, August, October

2.

```
                817
            462     355
        260     202     153
    146     114     88      65
  83    63    51    37    28
44    39    24    27    10    18
 9    35    4     20    7     3    15
```

3. LAST
PAST
POST
POUT
POUR
FOUR

4.

1	9	5	3	4	2	7	8	6
3	4	7	6	8	5	2	9	1
8	6	2	9	7	1	5	3	4
6	7	3	5	1	4	9	2	8
2	8	9	7	3	6	1	4	5
4	5	1	2	9	8	3	6	7
9	3	8	4	5	7	6	1	2
5	1	6	8	2	9	4	7	3
7	2	4	1	6	3	8	5	9

5. 44

Day 76

1.

1 < 3	7	6	4	5	2
4	2 > 1	7	3 < 6	5
2	5 > 4	1	6	3	7
7	6	2	3 < 5	1	4
3	4	5 > 2	1	7 > 6
5	1	6	4	7	2	3
6 < 7	3	5	2 < 4	1

2. WRONG
PRONG
PRONE
PROSE
PRISE
POISE

3. Pink T-shirt + red shorts
Yellow socks + orange trousers
Purple shoes + green jacket

5. 27

1.

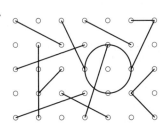

4.

3	7	2	8	B	C	6	A	5	1	9	4
C	9	5	6	7	4	8	1	3	2	B	A
A	4	B	1	5	2	9	3	8	7	C	6
B	6	3	9	2	8	7	C	A	4	1	5
1	8	7	A	3	5	4	6	C	B	2	9
5	2	C	4	A	9	1	B	7	8	6	3
8	1	4	B	C	3	5	7	6	9	A	2
9	3	A	2	1	6	B	8	4	5	7	C
7	5	6	C	4	A	2	9	1	3	8	B
6	B	8	3	9	7	A	5	2	C	4	1
2	A	1	5	8	B	C	4	9	6	3	7
4	C	9	7	6	1	3	2	B	A	5	8

3. READY
REEDY
REEDS
SEEDS
SEEPS
STEPS

5. 108

---

1. Glory is fleeting, but obscurity is forever.
Napoleon Bonaparte

(Replace B with A, C with B, D with C and so on, right through to replacing Z with Y and A with Z.)

2.

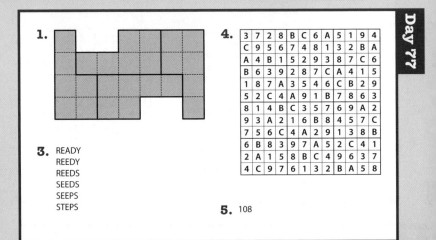

4.

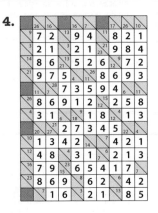

5. 37

3. ROVER ROWER RAWER RARER BARER BARES BARKS

SOLUTIONS

Day 79

1. air, airs, anise, are, arise, bait, baits, ban, bar, bare, bares, barest, bars, bier, biers, bin, bit, bits, bra, brain, brainiest, braise, bran, era, ire, its, nab, nib, nit, nits, rabies, rain, rainiest, raise, raisin, ran, rein, resin, rest, rib, rise, sin, sir, sire, sit, stir, tie, tier, tiers, ties, tin, tinier, tire, tires

2. baedc (1,000,000; 929,575; 1,515,000; 1,465,794; 1,040,094)
abdce (2178; 2505; 4127; 3737; 5037)
abedc (30,975; 39,975; 159,975; 120,475; 116,525)

3. MOUSE ROUSE ROUTE ROUTS POUTS POSTS PESTS

4.

5	1	4	6	8	9	3	7	2
8	7	9	3	5	2	6	4	1
3	6	2	7	1	4	9	5	8
1	3	7	9	6	8	4	2	5
9	2	8	4	7	5	1	6	3
6	4	5	2	3	1	7	8	9
7	8	3	1	2	6	5	9	4
2	9	1	5	4	7	8	3	6
4	5	6	8	9	3	2	1	7

5. 226

Day 80

2. B – the circle stays fixed at the top-left, and the square outside the box at the top toggles on and off at each step. The triangle at the bottom-right rotates 90 degrees anti-clockwise and the other shape moving clockwise around the square increases its number of sides by 1 at each stage.

3. STICK STACK SLACK CLACK CLANK CRANK CRANE

4.

7	9	8	3	5	2	4	1	6
4	2	5	1	6	8	9	7	3
6	1	3	7	9	4	5	8	2
1	5	7	4	8	3	6	2	9
8	6	2	5	1	9	3	4	7
3	4	9	2	7	6	1	5	8
5	3	4	9	2	7	8	6	1
2	8	1	6	3	5	7	9	4
9	7	6	8	4	1	2	3	5

5. 216

Day 81

1.

2. GREEN GREED CREED CREEK CHEEK CHECK CHICK

3. mileage
artistic
retake
aerodynamic

5. 456

Day 82

1.

		29	16	20			16	17	8
	24	8	7	9		17 23	7	9	1
	19 16	7	9	3	29 6	5	9	8	7
14	9	5	22 18	8	5	9		30 17	
24	7	9	8	9 24	1	8	17 16	8	9
	16 28	7	9	18 16	1	7	2	8
29	2	7	3	8	9	20 16	9	7	10
17	8	9	11 16	7	1	3	16 16	9	7
	8 13	1	7	30 20	6	9	8	4	3
27	7	8	9	3 16	9	8	1	27 17	
11	8	3	8 16	1	7	24 20	7	9	8
	4 10		19 16	7	9	3	16 16	7	9
19	1	2	7	9		24	9	7	8
20	3	8	9		20	8	9	3	

2. 2 – the sequence is +2, -3, +4, -5, +6, -7; 51 – add the preceding two numbers; 328 – add the preceding two numbers and multiply by two.

4.

5. 199

3. BROWN BLOWN BLOWS BLOTS BOOTS BOATS MOATS

Day 83

2. THICK
CHICK
CHECK
CHEEK
CREEK
CREAK
CREAM

3.

B	2	7	9	8	5	A	1	6	3	4	C
6	3	8	5	7	C	9	4	2	B	1	A
4	1	A	C	6	2	B	3	5	8	7	9
1	9	6	A	B	7	C	8	3	5	2	4
7	C	3	4	5	1	2	9	B	6	A	8
5	8	2	B	3	6	4	A	C	7	9	1
C	7	9	6	2	4	1	5	8	A	3	B
8	5	1	3	A	9	7	B	4	C	6	2
A	4	B	2	C	3	8	6	1	9	5	7
3	A	C	7	1	8	6	2	9	4	B	5
2	6	4	8	9	B	5	7	A	1	C	3
9	B	5	1	4	A	3	C	7	2	8	6

5. 428

Day 84

1.

3	×	7	−	5	=	16
×		×		×		
4	÷	1	×	2	=	8
×		+		+		
6	×	9	+	8	=	62
=		=		=		
72		16		18		

2. 1. A   2. B   3. C

3. SUPER SURER CURER CURES CURDS CORDS WORDS

4.

		5				
2			3		6	4
	3	6				
2					8	
			2			
	8		6			2
						2
3				2		

5. 192

SOLUTIONS

2. A – each row consists of the following two sequences overlaid, with each sequence starting at an offset one greater than on the previous row. Each of these sequences loops around continuously. Due to their different lengths a range of patterns result, particularly on the lower rows of the grid.

△ ▢ ○ ▽

▽ ▷ △ ◁ ▢

3. SHINY SHINS SHIPS SHOPS SLOPS SLOBS BLOBS

4.

7	5	6	>	3	2	1	4
4	6	1	7	5	2	<	3
1	3	<	5	2	7	>	4	6
6	>	4	7	5	>	1	<	3	2
3	1	<	2	<	6	4	5	7
2	7	4	>	1	3	6	>	5
5	2	3	<	4	<	6	7	1

5. 552

1.

2	9	4	8	7	3	1	6	5
6	3	1	2	4	5	9	8	7
5	8	7	6	9	1	4	2	3
1	4	9	5	8	7	6	3	2
8	6	5	1	3	2	7	9	4
3	7	2	9	6	4	8	5	1
4	1	6	3	5	9	2	7	8
7	5	8	4	2	6	3	1	9
9	2	3	7	1	8	5	4	6

2. PHONY PHONE SHONE STONE STOLE STILE SMILE

3. $635 = (10 \times (75 - 9)) - (5 \times (2 + 3))$

4. 5 pairs of anagrams: REBATING and BERATING; PREMISED and SIMPERED; CREDITED and DIRECTED; CLOBBERS and COBBLERS; CHARMING and MARCHING

5. 123

1.

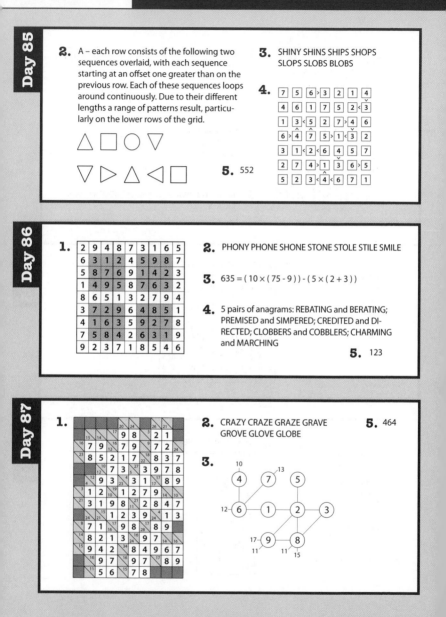

2. CRAZY CRAZE GRAZE GRAVE GROVE GLOVE GLOBE

3.

5. 464

1.

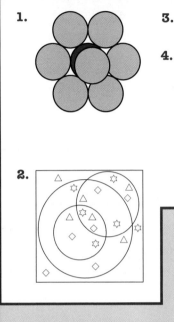

3. NOISY NOISE POISE PRISE PROSE PRONE DRONE

4.

8	5	9	3	6	2	1	4	7
3	2	4	8	1	7	5	9	6
1	6	7	5	4	9	8	3	2
9	7	6	2	5	3	4	1	8
2	1	3	7	8	4	6	5	9
4	8	5	1	9	6	7	2	3
7	9	8	4	2	5	3	6	1
6	4	1	9	3	8	2	7	5
5	3	2	6	7	1	9	8	4

5. 365

2.

4. 4m: I can reach 1.5m above the ground, so the rope has a vertical distance of 3m (4.5m - 1.5m) to travel. We can imagine the rope as the hypotenuse of a right-angled triangle formed along with the ground and the post. We want to find the length of the ground section, given the other two, which are 3m and 5m. Using Pythagoras's theorem (the length of the hypotenuse of a triangle is equal to the square root of the squares of the other two sides), we take the square root of ($5^2 - 3^2 = 25 - 9 = 16$), which is 4. This is the well-known 3, 4, 5 right-angled triangle.

4 in 17: It doesn't matter what the first card I take is, but the second must be one of the 12 remaining cards of the same suit out of the 51 left in the pack. The likelihood is therefore 12/51, which can be simplified by dividing the top and bottom by 3.

2. SHARK STARK STARS SOARS SOAKS SOCKS ROCKS

3.

3	C	5	B	2	9	4	1	6	A	7	8
4	7	1	8	A	C	B	6	3	2	5	9
2	6	A	9	7	8	3	5	C	4	B	1
9	A	B	6	8	5	C	4	1	7	3	2
C	1	8	7	3	2	9	A	5	B	6	4
5	3	4	2	6	B	1	7	9	C	8	A
B	5	C	A	1	7	2	9	8	3	4	6
8	9	2	3	4	A	6	B	7	1	C	5
6	4	7	1	C	3	5	8	A	9	2	B
1	B	9	4	5	6	7	C	2	8	A	3
7	8	3	5	9	4	A	2	B	6	1	C
A	2	6	C	B	1	8	3	4	5	9	7

5. 174

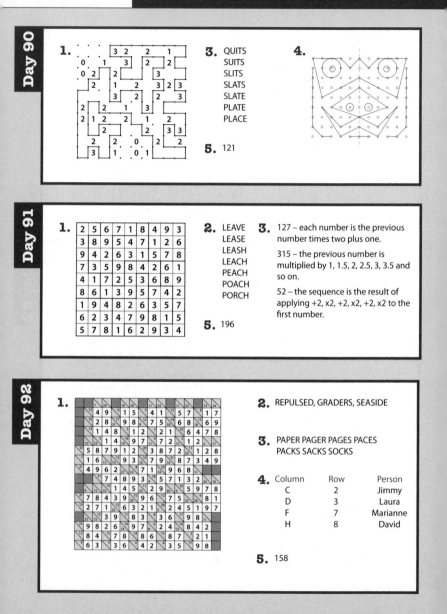

Day 90

1. (solution grid)

3. QUITS
SUITS
SLITS
SLATS
SLATE
PLATE
PLACE

4. (diagram)

5. 121

Day 91

1.

2	5	6	7	1	8	4	9	3
3	8	9	5	4	7	1	2	6
9	4	2	6	3	1	5	7	8
7	3	5	9	8	4	2	6	1
4	1	7	2	5	3	6	8	9
8	6	1	3	9	5	7	4	2
1	9	4	8	2	6	3	5	7
6	2	3	4	7	9	8	1	5
5	7	8	1	6	2	9	3	4

2. LEAVE
LEASE
LEASH
LEACH
PEACH
POACH
PORCH

5. 196

3. 127 – each number is the previous number times two plus one.

315 – the previous number is multiplied by 1, 1.5, 2, 2.5, 3, 3.5 and so on.

52 – the sequence is the result of applying +2, x2, +2, x2, +2, x2 to the first number.

Day 92

1. (solution grid)

2. REPULSED, GRADERS, SEASIDE

3. PAPER PAGER PAGES PACES PACKS SACKS SOCKS

4.

Column	Row	Person
C	2	Jimmy
D	3	Laura
F	7	Marianne
H	8	David

5. 158

SOLUTIONS

1. anion, anions, anoint, anoints, anon, anons, clan, clot, con, cons, constitution, constitutional, cost, cot, cots, inn, inns, ins, into, ion, ions, its, lain, loan, loin, loins, lot, nit, nits, not, notion, notional, notions, onion, onions, onto, son, sot, stint, tin, tins, tint, tints, tit, ton, tonal, tons, tuition, ulna, unconstitutional, union, unions, unit, units

2. A – the grey squares stay fixed, but on each row the white square moves either left or right at each step, wrapping around from one side to the other: on the top row it moves right; on the middle row it moves left; on the bottom row it moves right.

3. WINDY WINDS WINES WIVES WAVES EAVES ELVES

4.

2	1	C	6	9	5	8	4	3	B	A	7
B	3	4	7	2	6	A	1	9	8	C	5
A	9	5	8	B	7	3	C	1	6	2	4
4	7	8	C	1	9	5	A	B	3	6	2
6	B	2	A	C	3	4	7	5	1	9	8
9	5	3	1	6	2	B	8	A	4	7	C
7	4	9	5	A	8	6	3	C	2	1	B
8	C	6	3	5	B	1	2	7	9	4	A
1	A	B	2	7	4	C	9	6	5	8	3
3	2	1	B	4	A	7	6	8	C	5	9
5	6	7	9	8	C	2	B	4	A	3	1
C	8	A	4	3	1	9	5	2	7	B	6

5. 269

1. D – the right-most triangle of the shape net is pointing the opposite way compared with all of the other cubes.

2. LOVES DOVES DOLES DOLLS DOLLY JOLLY JELLY

3.

5. 105

1.

8	2	4	1	9	6	5	3	7
3	5	6	7	2	8	9	1	4
1	9	7	5	3	4	2	8	6
4	6	5	2	1	9	3	7	8
2	1	3	8	6	7	4	9	5
7	8	9	4	5	3	6	2	1
9	7	8	6	4	2	1	5	3
6	3	1	9	7	5	8	4	2
5	4	2	3	8	1	7	6	9

2. 35 + 66 + 40 = 141; 70 + 61 + 40 = 171

3. CALLS MALLS MALES MILES MIRES SIRES SIREN

5. 140

SOLUTIONS

Day 96

1.

3	7	8	1	9	4	2	5	6
6	4	5	3	2	8	7	1	9
1	2	9	6	7	5	3	4	8
4	8	1	7	3	2	9	6	5
5	3	2	9	4	6	8	7	1
7	9	6	8	5	1	4	2	3
8	1	7	4	6	3	5	9	2
9	5	3	2	1	7	6	8	4
2	6	4	5	8	9	1	3	7

2. abcde (14,999,940;
55,608,480; 57,563,020;
306,653,710; 1,631,466,696)
abcde (4783; 5329; 42,875;
331,776; 759,375)
bdeca (4312.35; 739.26;
3942.72; 1108.89; 1478.52)

3. MAYOR MANOR MINOR
MINER MINED MIRED FIRED

5. 228

Day 97

1.

2. STOPS SLOPS SLAPS CLAPS
CLASS CRASS CRASH

3.

4. 22cm^2: The cubes must be arranged with three across the top of the "T" with a stem of two cubes. On the top and bottom sides, looking down or up at the "T", we therefore can see 5 cube faces, and from each of the 4 other possible perpendicular perspectives we see 3 more cube faces, giving a total of 22 faces (5 + 5 + 3 + 3 + 3 + 3). Each face is 1cm x 1cm in size, giving an area of 1cm^2. Therefore the total surface area is 22cm^2.

36 seconds: The front of the train travels 2km through the tunnel, and then the length of the train requires another 250m (50 x 5) to clear the tunnel. Therefore the question is: how long does it take to travel 2250m? Speed is given in kilometres per hour, which means "kilometres divided by hours". If speed = kilometres divided by hours then rearranging gives hours = kilometres divided by speed, or in other words the train takes 2.25/2250 hours to travel this distance. This might be easier to read expressed using metres and metres per hour, which makes it 2250/225,000. Either way, the fraction is equal to 1/100, so the train takes 1/100 hour. Each hour has 3600 seconds (60 x 60), giving us a total of 36 seconds (1/100 x 3600).

5. 555

Day 98

1.
clear – open
tolerant – patient
aware – enlightened
green – naïve
blue – sad
alive – extant
ready – done
prone – liable

3.
CRIES
TRIES
TRIMS
TRAMS
TEAMS
TEARS
TEARY

4.

4	9	5	2	8	6	3	1	7
7	6	1	9	3	5	4	2	8
8	2	3	7	4	1	9	6	5
1	3	7	6	5	8	2	9	4
9	4	8	3	2	7	6	5	1
2	5	6	4	1	9	8	7	3
3	7	4	5	6	2	1	8	9
5	1	2	8	9	4	7	3	6
6	8	9	1	7	3	5	4	2

5. 136

Day 99

1.

8	7	C	3	5	6	A	4	2	9	1	B
A	1	6	B	8	3	2	9	7	C	5	4
9	5	2	4	1	B	C	7	A	8	3	6
6	3	4	5	C	9	1	A	8	B	2	7
1	8	7	2	4	5	B	6	3	A	C	9
C	9	B	A	7	8	3	2	4	5	6	1
7	4	5	6	A	C	8	1	B	3	9	2
2	B	1	8	9	4	7	3	C	6	A	5
3	C	A	9	B	2	6	5	1	4	7	8
B	A	8	1	6	7	9	C	5	2	4	3
4	6	3	7	2	A	5	B	9	1	8	C
5	2	9	C	3	1	4	8	6	7	B	A

2. NEARS HEARS HEIRS HAIRS HAIRY DAIRY DAILY

3. There are 23 rectangles. The image can be broken down into the 8 rectangles required to draw it, which form an additional 10 rectangles without any lines passing through them plus an additional 5 in the centre formed from multiple smaller areas.

5. 716

Day 100

1.

1	4	2	8	7	9	3	5	6
5	2	7	1	6	3	8	4	9
7	1	4	9	8	2	5	6	3
8	6	3	2	5	1	7	9	4
6	9	8	7	1	4	2	3	5
3	8	5	4	9	6	1	2	7
9	7	1	6	3	5	4	8	2
4	5	6	3	2	7	9	1	8
2	3	9	5	4	8	6	7	1

5. 390

2.

3. SUPER SURER SURES SIRES FIRES FINES FINIS

4.

Person	Inst.	Seat	Composer
Eliza	Violin 1	D	Mozart
Kevin	Cello	A	Bach
Lindsay	Viola	B	Liszt
Simon	Violin 2	C	Beethoven

Test 1

1.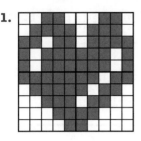

3.

91 − 19 = **72**	2 × 12 = **24**	4 × 4 = **16**
9 × 5 = **45**	20 + 36 = **56**	87 − 27 = **60**
70 − 22 = **48**	198 ÷ 2 = **99**	99 + 27 = **126**
9:30a.m. to 10:40p.m. = **13:10**		10:30a.m. to 4:35p.m. = **6:05**
4:25a.m. to 11:00p.m. = **18:35**		4:45a.m. to 7:25p.m. = **14:40**
4:20a.m. to 9:10p.m. = **16:50**		6:35a.m. to 6:50p.m. = **12:15**
£3210 + £4440 = **£7650**		£46.30 − £40.50 = **£5.80**
55p + £4720 = **£4720.55**		£3090 + £27700 = **£30790**
£89 − £2.89 = **£86.11**		£15 − £4.13 = **£10.87**

2. ace, aced, aces, acne, acre, acres, act, acted, acts, arc, arced, arcs, ascend, ascent, cad, cadet, cadets, cads, can, cane, caned, canes, canned, cans, cant, canted, canter, canters, car, card, cards, care, cared, cares, caret, carets, cars, cart, carted, carts, case, cased, cast, caste, casted, caster, cat, cater, caters, cats, cedar, cedars, cent, cents, crane, craned, cranes, crate, crated, crates, crest, dance, dancer, dancers, dances, decant, decants, descant, enact, enacts, nacre, nascent, nectar, race, raced, races, react, reacts, recant, recants, recast, sac, sacred, scan, scanned, scanner, scant, scar, scare, scared, scent, sect, stance, trace, traced, traces, trance, trances, transcend

Test 2

1.

3.

13 + 73 = **86**	94 + 11 = **105**	3 × 10 = **30**
152 ÷ 4 = **38**	48 ÷ 2 = **24**	16 ÷ 8 = **2**
28 + 97 = **125**	47 − 20 = **27**	10 + 18 = **28**
8:50a.m. to 10:00a.m. = **1:10**		3:55a.m. to 6:35p.m. = **14:40**
1:55a.m. to 3:05p.m. = **13:10**		12:30a.m. to 5:30a.m. = **5:00**
5:35a.m. to 1:05p.m. = **7:30**		1:00a.m. to 2:30p.m. = **13:30**
£5700 − £22.30 = **£5677.70**		£1560 − £345 = **£1215**
£44 − £4.01 = **£39.99**		£361 − £22.10 = **£338.90**
£4 + £3.46 = **£7.46**		£20400 − £3.57 = **£20396.43**

2. ail, ails, aisle, ale, ales, elf, equal, equals, fail, fails, false, file, files, flea, fleas, flies, flu, flue, flues, fuel, fuels, isle, lea, leaf, leafs, leas, lei, leis, lie, lies, lieu, life, quail, quails, qualifies, sail, sale, seal, self, squeal

1.

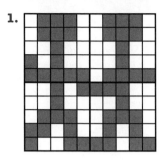

3.

34 ÷ 2 = **17**	19 + 68 = **87**	14 × 11 = **154**
40 − 12 = **28**	78 ÷ 3 = **26**	14 × 5 = **70**
56 − 8 = **48**	24 + 29 = **53**	6 × 5 = **30**

4:15a.m. to 5:55a.m. = **1:40**	5:10a.m. to 4:55p.m. = **11:45**
7:50a.m. to 2:15p.m. = **6:25**	3:10a.m. to 6:50p.m. = **15:40**
5:00a.m. to 11:55a.m. = **6:55**	1:00a.m. to 3:15a.m. = **2:15**

£49100 − £1.20 = **£49098.80**	£28800 − 65p = **£28799.35**
£4330 − £29.90 = **£4300.10**	£43.50 + £1.51 = **£45.01**
£320 + £204 = **£524**	£1510 − £2.39 = **£1507.61**

2. figs, fist, fits, fives, fugitives, fuse, gets, gifts, gist, gives, guest, guise, gust, guts, ifs, its, ivies (plural of ivy), set, sift, sit, site, sue, suet, suit, suite, ties, tugs, use, vest, vets, vies, visit

1.

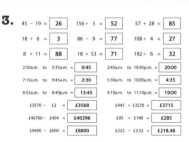

3.

45 − 19 = **26**	156 ÷ 3 = **52**	57 + 28 = **85**
18 ÷ 6 = **3**	86 − 9 = **77**	108 ÷ 4 = **27**
8 × 11 = **88**	18 + 53 = **71**	192 ÷ 6 = **32**

2:50a.m. to 3:35a.m. = **0:45**	2:45a.m. to 10:45p.m. = **20:00**
7:15a.m. to 9:45a.m. = **2:30**	5:30a.m. to 10:05a.m. = **4:35**
6:55a.m. to 8:40p.m. = **13:45**	4:10a.m. to 11:10p.m. = **19:00**

£3570 − £2 = **£3568**	£445 + £3270 = **£3715**
£40700 − £404 = **£40296**	£95 + £190 = **£285**
£9400 − £600 = **£8800**	£222 − £3.52 = **£218.48**

2. bend, bent, bond, bonded, bone, bound, bounded, bun, bunt, bunted, den, dent, don, done, dun, dune, end, eon, net, nod, node, not, note, noted, nub, nude, nut, one, ten, tend, ton, tone, toned, tun, tune, tuned, undo, undoubted, undue, unto

TEST SOLUTIONS

Test 5

1.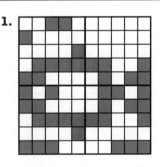

3.

88 − 7 = **81**	29 + 26 = **55**	156 ÷ 12 = **13**
49 − 20 = **29**	24 − 21 = **3**	8 ÷ 2 = **4**
24 + 83 = **107**	8 × 11 = **88**	93 − 20 = **73**
10:30a.m. to 8:00p.m. = **9:30**	1:40a.m. to 12:05p.m. = **10:25**	
10:05a.m. to 4:30p.m. = **6:25**	7:35a.m. to 2:20p.m. = **6:45**	
7:00a.m. to 10:20a.m. = **3:20**	9:10a.m. to 9:40p.m. = **12:30**	
£41.80 + £43600 = **£43641.80**	£42 + £1200 = **£1242**	
£800 − £630 = **£170**	£37800 + £319 = **£38119**	
£1750 + £3.42 = **£1753.42**	£3340 + £29 = **£3369**	

2. ago, agony, ahoy, along, alto, ant, anthology, any, gal, gaol, gay, gloat, gnat, goal, goat, hag, halo, halon, halt, hang, hat, hay, lag, lagoon, lay, loan, loath, nag, oath, tag, talon, tan, tang, tango, than, toga, tonal, yahoo, yoga

Day 6

1.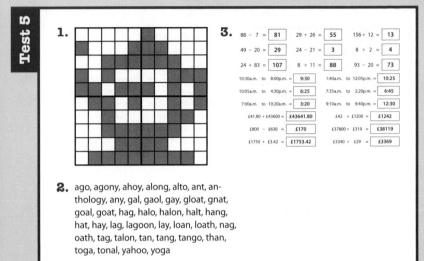

3.

13 × 8 = **104**	85 − 15 = **70**	64 + 8 = **72**
11 × 12 = **132**	12 × 7 = **84**	24 + 37 = **61**
57 ÷ 3 = **19**	54 + 8 = **62**	94 − 10 = **84**
1:15a.m. to 10:10p.m. = **20:55**	2:35a.m. to 5:15p.m. = **14:40**	
6:10a.m. to 6:30p.m. = **12:20**	12:15a.m. to 2:05p.m. = **13:50**	
7:00a.m. to 3:55p.m. = **8:55**	5:05a.m. to 11:20a.m. = **6:15**	
£7 + £160 = **£167**	£3360 − £3.68 = **£3356.32**	
£49 − £11.20 = **£37.80**	£177 − £2.35 = **£174.65**	
£42600 + 20p = **£42600.20**	£9.40 − £2.87 = **£6.53**	

2. cede, cedes, cent, cents, decent, den, dens, dense, dent, dents, descent, end, ends, nee, need, needs, nest, nested, net, nets, scene, scent, scented, secede, sect, see, seed, seen, send, sent, sentence, sentenced, set, steed, tee, teed, teen, teens, tees, ten, tend, tends, tens, tense, tensed

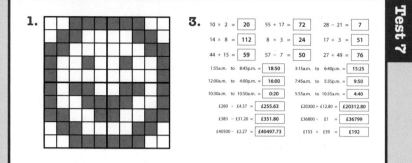

1. [grid puzzle]

3.

10 × 2 = **20**	55 + 17 = **72**	28 − 21 = **7**
14 × 8 = **112**	8 × 3 = **24**	17 × 3 = **51**
44 + 15 = **59**	57 − 7 = **50**	27 + 49 = **76**

1:55a.m. to 8:45p.m. = **18:50**	3:15a.m. to 6:40p.m. = **15:25**
12:00a.m. to 4:00p.m. = **16:00**	7:45a.m. to 5:35p.m. = **9:50**
10:30a.m. to 10:50a.m. = **0:20**	5:55a.m. to 10:35a.m. = **4:40**

£260 − £4.37 = **£255.63**	£20300 + £12.80 = **£20312.80**
£383 − £31.20 = **£351.80**	£36800 − £1 = **£36799**
£40500 − £2.27 = **£40497.73**	£153 + £39 = **£192**

2. deities, devise, die, diet, diets, digest, digestive, dive, dives, divest, edge, edges, edgiest, edit, edits, eve, eves, gee, geed, gees, get, gets, give, gives, ides, ivies, sedge, see, seed, set, side, siege, sieve, sieved, site, sit-ed, steed, tee, teed, tees, tide, tides, tidies, tie, tied, ties, vest, vested, vestige, vet, vets, vie, vied, vies, visited

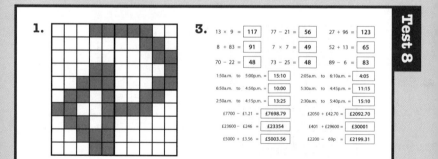

1. [grid puzzle]

3.

13 × 9 = **117**	77 − 21 = **56**	27 + 96 = **123**
8 + 83 = **91**	7 × 7 = **49**	52 + 13 = **65**
70 − 22 = **48**	73 − 25 = **48**	89 − 6 = **83**

1:50a.m. to 5:00p.m. = **15:10**	2:05a.m. to 6:10a.m. = **4:05**
6:50a.m. to 4:50p.m. = **10:00**	5:30a.m. to 4:45p.m. = **11:15**
2:50a.m. to 4:15p.m. = **13:25**	2:30a.m. to 5:40p.m. = **15:10**

£7700 − £1.21 = **£7698.79**	£2050 + £42.70 = **£2092.70**
£23600 − £246 = **£23354**	£401 + £29600 = **£30001**
£5000 + £3.56 = **£5003.56**	£2200 − 69p = **£2199.31**

2. deep, deeps, despise, despises, dip, dips, dispense, dispenses, espied, espies, nip, nips, pen, pends, pens, pie, pied, pies, pin, pine, pined, pines, pins, pis, seep, seeps, sip, sips, snip, snipe, sniped, snipes, snips, sped, speed, speeds, spend, spends, spied, spies, spin, spine, spines, spins

TEST SOLUTIONS

Test 9

1.

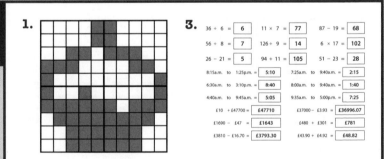

3.

2 × 6 = **12**	46 − 22 = **24**	25 − 10 = **15**
10 × 7 = **70**	37 − 21 = **16**	2 × 11 = **22**
57 + 10 = **67**	40 + 22 = **62**	34 − 16 = **18**
5:05a.m. to 9:45a.m. = **4:40**		5:40a.m. to 4:50p.m. = **11:10**
1:05a.m. to 10:40p.m. = **21:35**		12:10a.m. to 10:40a.m. = **10:30**
10:50a.m. to 11:05p.m. = **12:15**		12:30a.m. to 8:35a.m. = **8:05**
£125 − £1.67 = **£123.33**		£8.40 + £286 = **£294.40**
£3180 + £3290 = **£6470**		£22300 − £3270 = **£19030**
£80 + £433 = **£513**		£3440 − £14 = **£3426**

2. bid, bids, big, bin, bind, binds, bingo, bins, bird, birds, bison, boding, bog, bogs, bond, bonds, bong, bongs, boring, born, boss, bossing, brig, brigs, bring, brings, gob, gobs, nib, nibs, orb, orbs, rib, ribs, rob, robin, robing, robins, robs, snob, snobs, sob, sobs, songbird, songbirds

Test 10

1.

3.

36 ÷ 6 = **6**	11 × 7 = **77**	87 − 19 = **68**
56 ÷ 8 = **7**	126 ÷ 9 = **14**	6 × 17 = **102**
26 − 21 = **5**	94 + 11 = **105**	51 − 23 = **28**
8:15a.m. to 1:25p.m. = **5:10**		7:25a.m. to 9:40a.m. = **2:15**
6:30a.m. to 3:10p.m. = **8:40**		8:00a.m. to 9:40a.m. = **1:40**
4:40a.m. to 9:45a.m. = **5:05**		9:35a.m. to 5:00p.m. = **7:25**
£10 + £47700 = **£47710**		£37000 − £3.93 = **£36996.07**
£1690 − £47 = **£1643**		£480 + £301 = **£781**
£3810 − £16.70 = **£3793.30**		£43.90 + £4.92 = **£48.82**

2. ace, ache, acre, act, actor, arc, arch, cache, car, care, caret, cart, cat, catch, catcher, catchy, cater, char, chart, chat, cheat, chore, coach, coat, core, cot, cote, coy, coyer, crate, crochet, cry, each, echo, etch, hector, ochre, race, racy, reach, react, roach, taco, teach, theocracy, torch, trace, yacht

Resources

Books

Books about the brain

Your Memory: A User's Guide *Alan Baddeley* (Carlton Books, 2004)

An enjoyably thorough guide to our memories by a leading memory scientist.

Neuroscience: Exploring the Brain *Mark F. Bear, Barry W. Connors & Michael A. Paradiso* (Lippincott Williams & Wilkins, 2006)

If you really want to learn a lot about the brain, this quite literally heavyweight textbook is extremely comprehensive. With over 900 large pages and in full colour throughout, you'll be an expert if you make it all the way through.

Use Your Head *Tony Buzan* (BBC Books, 2000)

The classic book by the inventor of mind maps: an excellent introduction to many powerful learning and studying techniques.

The Brain That Changes Itself: Stories of Personal Triumph from the Frontiers of Brain Science *Norman Doidge* (Penguin, 2008)

Neuropsychologist and psychoanalyst Norman Doidge tells stories about the remarkable flexibility of the human brain.

The Rough Guide to the Brain *Barry Gibb* (Rough Guides, 2007)

An accessible introduction to the science of how your brain works, from the story of its evolution up to our contemporary knowledge of it.

Outliers: The Story of Success *Malcolm Gladwell* (Penguin, 2009)

A superbly well-written investigation into how exceptional people become that way. Lots of practice and the right environment are two key factors the book explores.

Mind Performance Hacks: Tips & Tools for Overclocking Your Brain *Ron Hale-Evans* (O'Reilly, 2006)

Another book designed to be dipped in and out of, this one focuses on taking advantage of your brain's innate strengths to improve your real-world performance. The tips and tricks offer help with your memory, mental arithmetic and a range of other faculties.

Your Brain: The Missing Manual *Matthew MacDonald* (Pogue Press, 2008)

A very easy to read and well-illustrated full-colour introduction to your brain, its curiosities and its triumphs. It has some great visual illusions in it too, providing a powerful demonstration of the brain's automatic processing which you just can't overrule.

Keep Your Brain Fit: 101 Ways to Tone Your Mind *Gareth Moore* (Duncan Baird Publishers, 2009)

A practical introduction to your brain and how it works, packed with advice on taking advantage of your brain's natural abilities. Chapters alternate with brain workout sections that practise a wide range of skills.

The Brain: A Very Short Introduction *Michael O'Shea* (Oxford University Press, 2005)

A pocket-sized book that covers how the brain works in surprisingly intricate detail – not a light read, but if you prefer text with a more deliberately scientific bent then this might suit you well.

The Stuff of Thought: Language as a Window into Human Nature *Steven Pinker* (Penguin, 2007)

A book which approaches how the brain works from a different angle – through an exploration of how we use words and language, and what this tells us about how we think.

Mind Hacks: Tips & Tricks for Using Your Brain *Tom Stafford & Matt Webb* (O'Reilly, 2004)

This book is full of revealing mental tricks you can try, which demonstrate various features of how your brain works, broken down into bite-sized sections which can be read pretty much independently of one another.

The Student's Guide to Cognitive Neuroscience *Jamie Ward* (Psychology Press, 2006)

A good introductory textbook about the basis of mental functions. As the title suggests, this is one for the seriously studious.

Brain workout and puzzle books

Beyond Sudoku: Kakuro, Hanjie and Other Japanese Puzzles *(Chambers, 2006)*

A great collection of logic puzzles at a range of difficulties, featuring not only the regular contenders but also some of the more unusual types.

The Times Japanese Logic Puzzles: Hitori, Hashi, Slitherlink and Mosaic (Times Books, 2006)

Not as varied as Chambers' *Beyond Sudoku*, but a reasonable selection of the titular Japanese puzzles – albeit printed on paper that's far too thin.

The Riddles of the Sphinx *David J. Bodycombe* (Penguin, 2007)

A fantastic collection of an enormously wide and varied range of puzzles, from ancient times to the modern day. The book follows a written narrative, covering the history of puzzles in some detail, and has a particularly good set of both word and logic puzzles.

Kids' 10-Minute Brain Workout *Gareth Moore* (Buster Books, 2006, UK) / **Sudoku Makes You Smarter** *Gareth Moore* (Simon Scribbles, 2007, US)

Aimed at a younger audience this features a very wide range of puzzles, from picture puzzles through to word puzzles and even including a mix of Japanese puzzles – suitable for children from eight upwards.

The Mammoth Book of Brain Workouts *Gareth Moore* (Robinson, 2008, UK; Running Press, 2008, US)

Nearly six hundred pages of brain workouts – essentially a daily exercise book designed to test all areas of your brain.

Train the Brain: Use It or Lose It *Gareth Moore* (Michael O'Mara, 2008, UK; Tarcher, 2009 US)

A range of types of brain workout, focusing more on core visual, word and number skills than on traditional puzzle types.

The Big Book of Brain Games: 1000 Play-Thinks of Art, Mathematics and Science *Ivan Moscovich* (Workman Publishing, 2007)

A reprint of an earlier book with a revised title, this huge tome is full of colourful and esoteric content with a phenomenal amount of variety that will certainly make you think. The only downside is that some of the puzzles have "trick" solutions – so when you get stuck on some of the tasks, it's best to get someone else to check the answers at the back and let you know if you're unlikely to find a solution.

The Logic of Sudoku *Andrew C. Stuart* (Michael Mepham Publishing, 2007)

If you have ever wanted a comprehensive encyclopaedia covering every Sudoku-solving technique you could ever think of – and many that it's incredible anyone ever did – then this book is for you. Exhausting even the hardest logic requirements of most published puzzles by page 34, it runs on to nearly 250 pages of ever more esoteric techniques. You'll never think of Sudoku the same way again.

Magazines

UK magazines

Beyond Sudoku *6 issues per year* Puzzler Media (www.puzzler.com)

Similar to *Sudoku Pro* but with much more of an emphasis on picture-revealing logic puzzles than Sudoku and its many variants.

Brain Trainer *13 issues per year* Puzzler Media (www.puzzler.com)

Full-colour and with a range of different brain training exercises, but much of the content is somewhat easy – such as 4x4 Sudoku.

Sudoku Pro *13 issues per year* Accolade Publishing (www.accoladepublishing.co.uk)

If you enjoyed the Japanese puzzles in this book then *Sudoku Pro* will bring you a monthly supply of more of them, covering a wide range of different types including many different Sudoku variants.

US magazines

Brain Boosters *6 issues per year* Dell Magazines (www.pennydellpuzzles.com)

An excellent mix of brain training puzzles, including some that are unique to the magazine, as well as a full-colour centre section.

Games *10 issues per year* Kappa Publishing (www.gamesmagazine-online.com)

Each issue features a selection of unusual and novel puzzles, including a wide variety of word and logic content. Also features a small set of quirky full-colour problems.

World of Puzzles *6 issues per year* Kappa Publishing (www.gamesmagazine-online.com)

A sister publication to *Games* magazine, it features slightly more traditional puzzles but still maintains an excellent level of variety.

Newspapers

If you need a daily puzzle fix in printed form, then the puzzle pages in the *Daily Mail* provide the largest range in a national UK paper. The occasional weekend supplements in the *Daily Telegraph* and *Sunday Telegraph*, and *The Independent* and *The Independent on Sunday*, are also well worth looking out for.

Websites

Griddlers.net

If you enjoyed the Hanjie puzzles in the test spreads, then griddlers.net is for you – it features a huge range of different types of Hanjie puzzle, including variants such as triangular grids, diagonal shapes, patterns and colours.

Nikoli.com

Nikoli are the Japanese puzzle company that gave Sudoku its name. Their online puzzle subscription site features a range of their content for about the same cost as a monthly magazine. The site attracts puzzle aficionados so some of the average solve-times can be intimidating for a beginner, but the puzzles are top quality.

PuzzleMix.com

Features daily logic puzzles, including a range of Sudoku variants and other Japanese puzzle types, all of which can be played online.

PuzzlePicnic.com

PuzzlePicnic attracts a varied set of online players and encourages its users to write and upload their own content for everyone else to play. It includes a wide range of logic puzzles that can be hard to find elsewhere.

Puzzles.com

Puzzles.com is a repository collecting content from a wide range of sources. As a result it has a diverse and varied selection of puzzles, with something for everyone.

Games

Videogames

Big Brain Academy for the Nintendo DS is similar to *Dr Kawashima's Brain Training*, but with more of a random element. It may be good for your brain but makes it harder to track your progress.

Big Brain Academy for Wii is a completely different game to the Nintendo DS version, featuring a huge range of excellent and challenging brain-training activities, as well as some extremely entertaining head-to-head games for multi-player brain fun. (Known as **Big Brain Academy Wii Degree** in the US.)

Brain Challenge is the most comprehensive brain-training program available

for the iPhone and iPod Touch, as well as a huge range of other mobile phone handsets and games consoles. With a wide selection of brain tasks to try, the software follows your progress and offers challenges at your current ability level each day, rather than starting from scratch each time you play.

Dr. Kawashima's Brain Training: How Old Is Your Brain? and **More Brain Training from Dr Kawashima: How Old Is Your Brain?** for the Nintendo DS were two of the first of the recent wave of brain-training games to be released. Providing a daily programme of a few minutes of training every day, they feature a relatively small range of tasks with a fixed set of difficulty levels. (Known as **Brain Age: Train Your Brain in Minutes a Day!** and **Brain Age 2: More Training in Minutes a Day!** in the US.)

Who Has the Biggest Brain? is one of the most popular *Facebook* applications, and features sixteen different brain-training games that are very similar to many of those in *Big Brain Academy* on the Nintendo Wii. It's also available for the iPhone and iPod Touch.

Board games

Big Brain Academy is also available in a board game format, featuring static versions of many of the games featured in the Nintendo DS version, providing brain-training for the family to try together.

Cranium is a board game with a wide range of activities to be performed in a group setting – as such it's a good workout for your brain, just as its title suggests.